DATE DUE

MAR 2 5 1996	
NOV 1 7 1998	

BRODART   Cat. No. 23-221

WHEN STRANGERS COOPERATE

WHEN STRANGERS COOPERATE

*Using Social Conventions
to Govern Ourselves*

DAVID W. BROWN

THE FREE PRESS

New York   London   Toronto   Sydney   Tokyo   Singapore

The Free Press
A Division of Simon & Schuster Inc.
1230 Avenue of the Americas, New York, N.Y. 10020

Printed in the United States of America

printing number

1 2 3 4 5 6 7 8 9 10

Library of Congress Cataloging-in-Publication Data

Brown, David W.
    When strangers cooperate : using social conventions to govern ourselves / David W. Brown.
        p.   cm.
    Includes bibliographical references (p.   ) and index.
    ISBN 0-02-904875-3
    1. Community.   2. Cooperativeness.   3. Interpersonal relations.   4. Individualism.
    I. Title
    HM131.B7158   1995
    302'.14—dc20   95-13620
                                                                             CIP

TO PETER AND SARAH

CONTENTS

ACKNOWLEDGMENTS

I will always be grateful to the Kettering Foundation and its president, David Mathews, for their timely support of my work on conventions. In the summer of 1991 when my wife's prolonged illness foreshortened my term as a college president, David graciously offered me the opportunity to pursue a project of mine begun at Yale in the late eighties when I was still teaching. I became a visiting scholar at the Foundation during 1991–92, making it possible to produce a monograph on conventions that became the basis for this book. Kettering and its staff also provided generous assistance while I expanded the work even when it was obvious early on that their priorities for renewing public life and my own are sometimes dissimilar.

As my work progressed, I received many helpful comments from innumerable friends and colleagues for which I am grateful, and I remain indebted to Charles Lindblom and Thomas Schelling for their conceptual work on social problem solving and strategic thinking, which I consider part of the scaffolding for my examination of conventions.

The initial enthusiasm of Adam Bellow, my editor, for my work-in-progress and his sure hand in bringing it to publication have been, of course, indispensable. The manuscript also profited from the editing assistance of Adam's colleague, Alice Greenwood.

Finally, I should acknowledge my wife Alice, whose support along the way has been invaluable and whose health, ironically, made this project possible in the first place. We would both have preferred it to be otherwise, but we have shared, nonetheless, a remarkable three years of love and learning.

Introduction

"SWEET LAND OF LIBERTY"

So Many Strangers

CONTRADICTIONS

This book had its genesis on the winter sidewalk of the block where I used to live. I was shoveling snow up and down Huntting Lane—not just in front of my house, but all the way past the five houses of my neighbors, and I was getting very tired.

During the previous winter, the village snowplow had ripped up a foot of sod all along the edge of our narrow sidewalk when clearing the snow. It seemed the blade was too wide for the sidewalk but it was the only one available. The seasonal damage was evident after snowmelts and in the early spring. But the village public works department was not about to purchase a smaller plow and blade just for our block; and the plow in question, with its damaging blade, was bound to return whenever it snowed because, I was told, if the sidewalks were not promptly cleared, the village might be sued by someone falling on the "damn ice." I thought that the best solution was to have each home-owner shovel his or her own sidewalk.

I realized, however, that two of my neighbors were not full-time residents and were not around after each snowfall. Another was an elderly woman who was not likely to volunteer. Another couple was in the

1

midst of a separation and not available. One house was vacant. Nonetheless, as the resolute homeowner of #38, I set off to do the job all by myself. The first snowfall of two inches was good exercise. The second snowfall of four inches was a distinct challenge. By the third snowfall in two weeks, I was talking to myself as I cleared a path to the corner. Without some cooperation from my neighbors, there was no way I could keep shoveling the snow on Huntting Lane. My back, if not my will, would soon give out.

Robert Kennedy said, "One person can make a difference and each of us should try." But I have to report that unless enough of us try, one person can't make a difference for very long. I went home and let it snow. Under certain circumstances, some things worth doing are just not worth doing. This contradiction intrigued me then, and it still does. How strange that, like Kennedy, I believe that what I do can make a difference and that I should try. Yet I also know that, for most public problems, what really counts is what others do or don't do.

Most of us would like to improve various situations that touch our everyday lives, but we usually conclude that our individual effort would be minuscule and futile. How long was I willing to shovel the sidewalk on Huntting Lane? Not for very long. How long will you pick up litter in your neighborhood if you don't see anyone else doing it and your solitary effort has no visible impact? Normally, we don't see enough others doing something about these problems to reassure us that our contribution is worth making. When you and I just mind our own business, we certainly don't improve the situation, but then neither did our public-spiritedness. The fact that each of us goes his own way or does her own thing does not mean, however, that we are happy with the result.

It seems that the more you and I do as we like, the less you and I get what we want. We are avid consumers and we don't know what to do with the waste stream that our consumption produces. We go where we please and find highways congested and our favorite recreational areas crowded with strangers. We seek professional attention for our manifold physical complaints and then complain when health costs make professional attention almost prohibitive. We celebrate sexual freedom and mourn the loss of friends to AIDS or deplore the cost of supporting unwed teenage mothers. We walk out of marriages that aren't working and are confronted by a generation of sullen and angry children. Our bittersweet predicament is loving liberty and having to live with its consequences. Worse yet, the blessings of liberty may prove to be a curse if we are incapable of addressing our social problems without the heavy hand of costly and inefficient government.

Although we live in an increasingly interdependent world, both socially and economically, the animating force of our short and spectacular history has been to seek, maintain, and even flaunt individual freedom. "Liberty" remains our watchword and it sends us off in all directions.

We establish competitive, rather than cooperative, learning environments where students are tested on their individual abilities to be self-sufficient. Our education system values individual development and is oblivious to our need to learn how to solve problems together. Our experience in organizations and communities, where little gets accomplished without collaboration with others, makes clear how few lessons of the "real world" are included in the classroom.

Our social mobility lets us move up, move out, and move on—leaving old neighborhoods, relocating businesses, or looking for places where we can start over. We have always glorified cowboys for their rugged independence, and although few of us ride on horseback, we do get in our automobiles and take off. Some of us just go to the edge of our hometown and back. But many of us leave town and never turn back, and we often go alone—"Cowboys don't ride buses."[1]

There have been times in our history when we have organized ourselves collectively. They have been episodes ignited by events and moral issues—abolition, temperance, segregation, war, abortion—like forest fires fueled by a lot of dry timber. And, like forest fires, they eventually burn themselves out. Although the great majority of Americans have felt the heat of these social movements, most of us have preferred to stay at home and look after business.

Our involvement in politics has been devoted essentially to parochial matters close to home. We have never taken kindly to government, preferring that economic self-interest and individual liberty be unfettered. In the New World our early public life was pregovernmental, and we constructed formal governments to referee the clash of interests and to secure individual liberties. In the United States, government was not meant to "administer the affairs of men." It was meant to administer "justice among men who conduct their own affairs."[2]

Paradoxically, our healthy and long-standing desire for both individual autonomy and equality has made us more dependent on government—not less. "We have our rights," and we have come to depend on what government can do for us, sensing little help from any other quarter. We have become clients, litigants, and petitioners, looking for remedies that lie outside of the immediate communities where we live. "Rights" are trump cards that we use to make demands on one another through judicial or legislative relief. We still prefer that government would leave us alone, but "the problem now is that citizens won't leave government alone."[3]

As a consequence, the cost of government has mounted to pay for our demands. The right to be left alone or to be included and not suffer discrimination would appear, at first blush, to be a matter of government forbearance or enforcement, not of government spending. But many rights are considered vacuous without compensatory programs, entitlements, and mandates. So we spend billions in an attempt to undo damage already done or forestall further damage to aggrieved individuals and groups.

It is impossible, however, to think of the increase in government spending as a cost borne by the majority of taxpayers for the sake of "minorities." We have all piled on with claims, if not rights, to the public purse. As we say, "It's a free country," and we press our case for being old or young, a veteran or a student, a small businessperson or a large failing industry, a steward of the environment or a family farmer. The list is endless and so is the cost.

At the same time, our libertarian history and disposition prompt us to resist higher taxes to pay for the aggregate demand of "special interests," forgetting that each of our respective claims on the public purse is "special" too. And so we have become the world's largest debtor; we attempt to finance budget deficits of ugly proportions, which expose the difference between what we want and what we are willing to pay for.

Liberty's contradictions add up, or rather contradictions never add up. We liberate ourselves and find ourselves overwhelmed by the problems that individual liberty creates. Since we don't count on one another for help, we look instead to government, whose intrusion we resent and whose costs we consider excessive. Even more befuddling is our reliance on government to solve problems that cannot be solved unless enough of us alter our individual behavior.

Hard-pressed governments—local, state, or federal—do not have the resources, financial or otherwise, to compensate for our individual failures to protect the environment, to conserve energy, to deter crime, to maintain racially integrated schools, to practice "safe sex," to keep marriages going, or to do more for the care and development of children. Our reflex is to put the onus on government in the vain hope that we will be left alone to do as each of us pleases. It is one thing to run up the costs of government if there is a likelihood that public problems can be fixed with tax dollars alone. But it seems ludicrous to spend so much of our public treasury when those problems are insoluble without changes in our private behavior. Talk about government waste!

The truth is that many of the solutions to public problems depend more on what each of us does in our everyday lives than what government tries to do on our behalf. For example, at an inner-city junior high school in Oakland, California, it is estimated that over 50 percent of the 750 students "live with neither a mother [nor] a father." The school's principal says, "The person who's supposed to have taken care of them didn't."[4] A youth agency official, who works with upper-middle-class young people on Long Island, New York, estimated that the divorce rate in their families is about 50 percent, that about 60 percent of their parents remarry and that 70 percent of those marriages fail.[5] As a consequence, should it be so surprising that the major problems in public schools are drug abuse, alcohol abuse, pregnancy, suicide, rape, robbery, and assault? Fifty years ago, public schools worried about children talking out of turn, chewing gum, making noise, running in halls, cutting in line, violating dress codes, and littering.[6] Do we really think government can now repair the damage for us?

Very few of us, however, want to abandon our traditional preference for putting individual interest ahead of social interest. So those who devise government macropolicies and programs rarely acknowledge the impact of private behavior on public problems. When I asked one of President Clinton's assistants why there was not more use of the "bully pulpit" to make such a connection and ask Americans for their help, I was told that political leaders "rarely know what to ask for." I thought it a rather lame answer.

By way of contrast, we don't hesitate to acknowledge the influence of private consumer and producer behavior on our economy. We believe in markets and the "invisible hand" explanation that the profit motive is not inconsistent with the general economic welfare. But motives in social and political life are more complicated than economic behavior and thus outcomes are less predictable.

If we do get around to exploring the private roots of our public problems, we entertain partisan distortions, conspiracy theories, religious jeremiads, and scapegoating, whether it is the media, or Wall Street, or Japan, or a particular minority group, or politicians in general.[7] Someone else is always to blame. Someone else got us into this mess. Someone else has to get us out of it. Much of the finger pointing is honest confusion. Some of it is simply evasion; we would like to be free of one another.[8]

COMMUNITARIANS

Some observers are alarmed that Americans have become preoccupied with their rights and have shunned their responsibilities. There has been a wave of social criticism in the last decade from what I think of as reform liberals. They deplore the excesses of individual liberty or what they call "individualism."[9] They do not fault liberty, only what individuals make of it. They are often called or call themselves "communitarians."

The communitarian platform, as patched together by the highly regarded sociologist Amitai Etzioni, seeks the reconfiguration of communities with developed moral values which balance individual rights with a sense of "personal and collective responsibility."[10] Etzioni is better organized than many of his colleagues in academia, but the published work of Alasdair MacIntyre, Michael Sandel, Robert Bellah, Charles Taylor, and Philip Selznick, among others, has also brought public notice to the criticisms and ideas that are loosely described as "communitarian." Unlike Etzioni, most scholars are not so much interested in a new social movement as in a public dialogue about the possibilities of renewing or creating "community."[11] Communitarians remain, however, thoroughly liberal in their assumption that each of us can, more or less, choose to go it alone or join others in a social world where "individualism" and "community" vie for our loyalties. But both concepts are very abstract and do not begin to explain how we now live together.

Interdependence, not community, is a more reliable way of understanding how American public life works and what its possibilities are. Interdependence is less a choice than a situation that confronts us in our modern circumstance. Interdependence is implicit in the division of labor and professional specialties of our organizational lives, in the ways we do business with other firms and in distant markets, in the communication and transportation systems we rely on, and in the range of social services on which we have come to depend. It is not our community ties but our interdependence that keeps us entangled. "We start from here," and not, as the communitarians would have, "from someplace else."[12]

A friend wrote me:

I was probably never more deeply involved in "community" than I was as a young boy and man in West Virginia, but I am delighted that I got out. I have nowhere near the sense of community here in Chicago, but I find living here to be immensely rewarding. Economic and cultural opportunity and freedom to move in and out of city and of neighborhoods are a part of what I find rewarding here.[13]

The sense of community is elusive or short-lived when 17 percent of us move at least once each year, 50 percent of us change jobs every two or three years, and 50 percent of our marriages end in divorce. We are now, more than ever, strangers to one another even as we depend, more than ever, on one another to cope with the complexity of every-day life—its elaborate physical infrastructure, wealth of information, innumerable consumer options, and public problems.

Our social ties are governed, for the most part, by expediency. We need one another to do business, to get to work, to care for our children, to learn new skills, and so on. Our ties are not multifaceted as in closely bound communities of religious faith, ethnic choice, or rural circumstance, which surely exist but hardly predominate. For the middle class, especially, social ties have become more far-flung—professional networks, commercial and workplace contacts, support groups, sports leagues, electronic mail cohorts—and rarely intersect in more than one discrete part of a daily routine. We often know little about one another and, if we do, there is no expectation or obligation to look out for each other's welfare except in the most superficial ways. In the vernacular of professional sports, each of us is a "free agent."[14]

Where we are able to experience some kind of community life at all, it arises for the most part because of our interdependence. Many of us live in neighborhoods where we look out for each other's property or children, and we share gossip, opinion, garden tools, and baby sitters. Our daily contacts also provide a reliable basis for the small-scale cooperation of blockwatches, car pooling, or local protests, which naturally arise from living in close proximity. When our neighborhoods do organize, more often than not, we assert our rights rather than dwell on "collective responsibility." This has been called the NIMBY phenomenon, "not in my backyard," where, as neighbors, we come together to resist other people's solutions, not to solve a public problem. We oppose siting a homeless shelter too close to home, or a drug rehabilitation center, or a trash-burning incinerator. It usually takes a crisis of major proportions for us to put aside our differences and solve a problem, such as fortifying levees against the great floods in the summer of 1993. As the waters recede, however, so does our enthusiasm for working together.

Some "communities" are in reality simply homeowners' associations whose overriding goal is maintaining the value of individual properties. Such groups are not formed by those who know and trust each other, but, on the contrary, come into existence precisely because neighbors come and go and often neither know nor trust one another. One out of eight Americans lives in such residential communities and there are an estimated 150,000 of these "community associations" nationwide.[15] They levy taxes in the form of assessments to pay for upkeep and improvements; they elect governing boards, which in turn devise and adopt community rules about children, pets, parking, noise, landscaping, and architectural details.

When you look at individual ties to the larger jurisdictions that we often call "communities"—towns, counties, and small cities—the evidence is that such ties are unraveling: There is resistance to paying taxes for things that don't provide corresponding benefits; there is physical and capital flight from our cities; there are self-help and education strategies that promise individual empowerment without regard to a community context; and there are "special interest" groups with perfectly legitimate but narrow concerns that do not include the community-at-large. Much of this social stress is occasioned by old racial wounds, new immigration, and the quickening of more voices to be heard, more claims to be honored, and more differences to be sorted out.

Under such conditions, Stephen Macedo poses the obvious question: "Once we recognize that our pluralism makes us multi-communal and not simply 'communitarian' . . . which communal standards should we apply?"[16] How do places like San Jose, California or Hoboken, New Jersey or Aurora, Illinois or Miami, Florida develop a set of community moral values that the communitarian platform calls for? Who decides and how is that done? When people in such places don't take the trouble to reach some consensus, they don't necessarily deny the possible existence of a central core of truths that might order and direct their mutual affairs. It is only that they may want to settle for something less in order to coexist in multicultural communities. Diversity is what they have in common, so they continue to live without any consensus on moral values. Their tolerance and forbearance is more of an achievement than the communitarians give them credit for.[17]

What many communitarians overlook is that consensus, finding a "common good" through public dialogue, is not a precondition but only one possible outcome, among many, of politics as actually practiced in any community. Consensus sometimes emerges, but it is not pursued in the abstract. And if consensus is reached, it may be no more than temporary and expedient so as to deal with the problem at hand. Still, communitarians are disappointed with those who would settle for the thin gruel of pluralist politics. They are ashamed or angry with its unjust outcomes, and the more our communities unravel, the more insistent is the rhetoric about community.[18] As that currency is debased so is its value inflated.

Moreover, the talk about common good is more than incongruous during a time of social stress; it may even be dangerous. The disease metaphor for the body politic, so often used by communitarians and others, misrepresents the legitimate conflict going on in communities as more voices are heard and more claims are pressed. Those who seek a disinterested common good to moderate conflict pursue, intentionally or unintentionally, a very conservative strategy that favors existing power holders over those who seek to secure power for themselves and "the redistribution of pain."[19]

It is no wonder then that professionals and government officials become agents to adjust relations among us on the assumption that as contentious strangers we are likely to harm each other. They do not mend our community ties. Their role, more often than not, is to intervene on behalf of the individual, as victim. Like it or not, it is the way our system is supposed to work when the object is to protect or enhance individual liberties. The focus is on particular individuals or families or groups who are in trouble or who have grievances—even when such professional and governmental attention comes under the rubric of "community action." Even nonprofit agencies, churches, foundations, and other established associations, which traditionally have done much of a community's work, have become tied up by federal purse strings and told what they can or cannot do. Moreover, many of these local institutions have become ossified and ineffective as strong currents of change sweep by them or cut new channels, leaving some of them high and dry.[20]

As our community relations become more legalistic, the social distance among us lengthens even further. We invite court cases and regulations that define and police our relationships. They tutor us in our rights and obligations as spouses, parents, neighbors, consumers, producers, co-workers, and employers; or government and professional services assert such rights or assume such obligations for us through shelters for battered women, child welfare departments, youth programs, mental health halfway houses, vocational rehabilitation centers, drug abuse clinics.

Nothing commands more attention or promotes more disruption in local affairs than the oversight of federal judges and members of Congress, who construct national standards, often grounded in constitutional guarantees, for the benefit of aggrieved minorities or the protection of endangered species. Each jurisdiction or community finds that it must measure its actions against these national standards as local officials become agents for the enforcement of federal policy or the delivery of mandated services. Some of us welcome such federal oversight and intervention as a check on local initiatives, which such standards frustrate or often preempt. But as we become more dependent on outside help just to monitor or stabilize everyday relations, the possibilities for community action, free of government supervision or intervention, become more remote. Our communities are "less eradicated . . . than compartmentalized . . . and no longer able to organize much of public life."[21]

If interdependence, not community, is the more reliable concept for explaining how we now live together, what can we make of it?[22] Does interdependence give us a reason for large-scale cooperation in response to problems that no amount of government spending will solve? Is voluntary cooperation possible among strangers beyond the boundaries of identifiable neighborhoods and the larger jurisdictions that we loosely call "communities"? I think the possibilities should be explored for those problems that have proved intractable for any one community to solve.

The commonly held view of social scientists is that voluntary cooperation is possible only in small groups among people who know each other, and even small-scale cooperation may be problematic. The anthropologist Mary Douglas is quite blunt. "In practice, small scale societies do not exemplify the idealized vision of community. Some do, some do not, foster trust. Has no one writing on this subject ever lived in a village?"[23] Douglas's point is well taken for small groups or large groups—cooperation is not a stable or permanent state of affairs. Conflict is just as likely to exist. Just think of any family that you know. There is a constant modulation between conflict and cooperation. Some things never quite get settled; there are quarrels, reconciliations, betrayals, sacrifices, understandings, misunderstandings, and so on.

The objective of large-scale cooperation is simple enough: to provide something beneficial for a large number of people which might not otherwise exist without their individual involvement. What is not simple is how to get a large number of people involved in order to bring that beneficial something into existence. Most economists and political scientists assume that large-scale cooperation is very unlikely without the profit incentive of private markets or the coercion of government. They rely on milestones of philosophy, economics, and game theory that mark the way for them.

AN EXCURSUS ON COOPERATION

I want to discuss the milestones by linking them in a story of my own invention centered on "the citizen from Hoxton" and his descendants. I am indebted to L. Ivor Jennings for the idea of this ordinary Englishman, which Jennings used to good effect in his popular study, *The Law and the Constitution*.[24] I have recreated Jennings's "citizen" for my own purposes in order to draw Hume, Rousseau, and other commentators into a circle—and I hope, without distortion, to dramatize their rather dismal account of human cooperation. And so my story . . .

The citizen from Hoxton gained lasting notoriety when his neighbor, the young philosopher David Hume, conceived his *Treatise on Human Nature*. In his *Treatise*, Hume used the example of the citizen from Hoxton's working cooperation with another neighbor named Partridge. Before planting, in the spring of each year, the two neighbors drained the small bog in the south meadow if it was necessary. Hume observed it was "easy for them to know each others mind; and each must perceive, that the immediate consequence of his failing in his part, is, the abandoning the whole project."[25]

It seems that Hume queried his neighbors about what they would do if such a project, assuming a much larger bog in a much larger meadow, were to require the cooperation of "a thousand persons." The citizen from Hoxton apparently told young Hume that he would not be so ready to do his part under such circumstances. Partridge also chimed in with the same opinion. When Hume asked why, they thought it quite obvious but indulged the young man, who seemed to particularly enjoy such neighborly conversations about large subjects—and, in this case, about a very large bog indeed.

"For one thing," Partridge said, "it would be difficult to conceive of and execute such a complicated design."

As reported by Hume, the citizen from Hoxton added that he "wou'd lay the whole burden on others."[26] "Mr. Hume, if the meadow can be drained without me, all the better." Then the citizen from Hoxton paused and added with a smile, "It doesn't much matter what I do, does it, when so many other blokes are involved?"

The three neighbors agreed that such a large project would require some form of government to coordinate the undertaking and to compel Partridge and the citizen from Hoxton to do their share of labor, or to pay taxes so that others could do it for them. Hume concluded in his *Treatise* that "by the care of government" are "bridges . . . built; harbors open'd; ramparts rais'd; canals form'd; fleets equip'd; and armies disciplin'd. . . ."[27]

After Hume's *Treatise* was published in 1739–40, the citizen from Hoxton, although he did not read "the weighty tome," still took pleasure in learning that the meadow-draining matter had been mentioned. His descendants refer to the citizen from Hoxton as the family's illustrious "free rider," a person who counts on others to produce a desired outcome without his help, but who stands to benefit just as much as anyone else.

Two hundred years later Mancur Olson, an economist, reworked Hume's meadow-draining example in his discussion of large voluntary organizations.[28] Olson disputed "the logic of collective action" (collective action is another way of talking about large-scale cooperation), arguing that it is illogical that self-interested individuals will contribute to the welfare of a large group if they can "free-ride" on the contributions of others. Olson concluded that it is difficult to secure any benefits for a large group unless incentives are offered that directly benefit each person—such as a tote bag for contributing forty dollars or more to public television; group tours to the Dead Sea for joining an alumni association; or a 5 percent discount on car rentals for anyone joining a bar association, lobbying organization, consumer alliance, or frequent flyer club.

Hume's "draining the meadow" example is also used to support the common assumption that there is little likelihood of voluntary large-scale cooperation to create or maintain "public goods" (Hume's bridges, harbors, ramparts, or clean air, water, public space) since they are beneficial things that you and I cannot be excluded from enjoying. Conversely, "public bads" can result if we abuse or overuse public goods and diminish their common value; air and water become polluted, our parks become congested, beaches littered, and so forth. The "goods" we find hard to create or maintain on our own, without government intervention, become "bads" because no one gains anything for him or herself by exercising caution and restraint. As the citizen of Hoxton observed to Hume, "It doesn't much matter what I do, does it, when so many other blokes are involved?"

One branch of the Hoxton line emigrated to the New World with much the same attitude. There in New England, where each family was free to graze its cows on a pasture known as "the commons," each family looked after its own welfare and added a few cows each year until the commons was overgrazed and rendered worthless. Without a philosopher-neighbor to tell their story, it took almost 200 years before it was told by Garrett Hardin, a biologist, who called it "the tragedy of the commons."[29]

Now more distant heirs no longer graze cows on a New England common, but they have ranged across the continent looking for investment opportunities, grazing where the green is, as one of my former neighbors might have put it. In the beautiful and historic New Mexico valley where I lived while writing this book, there is an ongoing struggle over how much development—second homes, golf courses, airports—makes sense for the long-term future of those who live there. My neighbor didn't see any harm in one more subdevelopment or one more fast food stand. I didn't ask him, but he just might be distantly related to the citizen from Hoxton. For that matter, probably most of us are.

By coincidence, the citizen from Hoxton was drawn into another conversation about cooperation when, several years later, his neighbor Hume entertained the philosopher Jean Jacques Rousseau. As the story goes, one afternoon the citizen from Hoxton told the two gentlemen about an annual stag hunt with Partridge and several others. It usually required the entire hunting party to corner a stag, but on these hunts the citizen from Hoxton was often tempted to catch a rabbit on his own; he did so on occasion when the opportunity presented itself, even though he knew full well that the others could not succeed in catching the stag without him.

When Rousseau questioned the citizen from Hoxton about why he preferred to catch the rabbit and lose the stag, the citizen acknowledged that the rabbit was an inferior meal, but at least it was a sure dinner while the stag, well, it might take the better part of a week to catch, if at all. Rousseau persisted. "But why can't you all agree to stick to your preferred quarry, forgo the rabbit and have your stag for sure?" The citizen from Hoxton agreed that such a pact would be desirable, and indeed some in his party were insisting on it if there were to be another stag hunt, at least if it were to include the citizen from Hoxton again.[30]

More recently, Thomas Schelling, a political economist, reworked the stag hunt problem in game theoretic terms. Game theory is not really about games as we know them, but about how to make choices in circumstances of potential conflict. Game theory originated in the mathematical work of John von Neumann and Oskar Morgenstern, and it has become an influential analytical framework throughout the social sciences. Schelling has explored the possibility of cooperation among a large number of people (far more than in the citizen from Hoxton's hunting party) in what he calls a "multi-person prisoner's dilemma" ("MPD").[31] In an MPD, you and I have something to gain by not cooperating, very much like the defection of the citizen from Hoxton when he left the stag-hunting party to catch his own rabbit. The dilemma is that you and I gain more if everyone cooperates—getting part of a stag for the winter's larder. If too many hunt for rabbits, there will be no stag. Just like the citizen from Hoxton, our individual preference to catch a rabbit is not the choice we prefer others to make.

Schelling sees no correct choice for you and me in such a dilemma. It all depends on what others do. If enough others agree to pursue the stag so that their numbers ensure a successful hunt, then you and I are better off joining them. But if there is not a sufficient number of cooperators, then, like the citizen from Hoxton, you and I might as well look for our own rabbits.

Since you and I have no way of knowing what so many others will do in an MPD (there are just too many of us to keep track of), Schelling thinks that we have no alternative but to seek the enactment of government statutes and ordinances that more or less compel us to cooperate. Traffic signals tell us to take turns at an intersection; game wardens make sure that we don't take more than our fair share of stags; and taxes make us pay for police officers and firefighters and traffic signals and game wardens, etc.

So the assumption persists that voluntary cooperation among strangers is very unlikely without the profit incentive of private markets, in which self-interest is served, or the coercion of government, with which self-interest is subdued. The conventional wisdom is: (1) there are just too many individual conditions that must be satisfied; (2) there is little chance to communicate when so many strangers are involved; (3) with no chance for effective monitoring, too many individuals avoid doing their fair share; and (4) even well-meaning individuals are discouraged because of their inability to influence the behavior of so many strangers.

Are we stuck with the contradiction that I started with: that some things worth doing are just not worth doing? Are markets and governments the only forms of social organization that we have for large-scale cooperation? Milestones are important. They mark the way we've come. But they don't tell the whole story. We do have other ways of dealing with social order and innovation. Given the limitations of markets and the failures of government to solve many of our problems, it makes sense to explore another option that is readily available.

CONVENTIONS

We know that there are circumstances when large numbers of us do, in fact, voluntarily cooperate. What accounts for our voting in national elections, or participating in mass demonstrations, or serving on juries, or donating blood, or obeying the "rules of the road," or recycling bottles, cans, and paper, or "buying American"?

The British economist Fred Hirsch helped me to see what is perfectly obvious but strangely invisible. Hirsch concluded that there is a need to guide "certain motives of behavior into social rather than individual orientation, though still on the basis of privately directed preferences. This requires not a change in human nature, 'merely' a change in human convention. . . ."[32] When I stumbled across the mention of convention, I realized that there are many unnamed ways that we cooperate, and we can imagine, as Hume or Rousseau could not, opportunities for large-scale cooperation, especially given the revolution in telecommunications.

In fact, we have a varied repertoire of conventions, neither market-driven nor codified in law, that we take for granted in living together and governing ourselves—forming a line, joining a self-help group, bidding at an auction, returning books to a library, chaperoning a dance, adopting a child, boycotting a grocery chain, passing a collection plate, using a litter barrel, offering travel directions, sending an RSVP, keeping a secret, and on and on. Conventions are "regularities of behavior, sustained by an interest in coordination and an expectation that others will do their part."[33] David Lewis's definition is usefully limited, otherwise practically everything we think of as manners, habits, norms, and customs is brought into the "convention" tent, making further discussion wearisome, or worse, incomprehensible.[34]

The Lewis definition addresses coordination problems between two or more people, not individual behavior in general. For example, a particular dance step is a convention. The fox-trot solves a coordination problem of how two people keep from stepping on each other's feet and move together across a dance floor. A dance step does not, however, dictate how close my wife and I are to each other when we do the fox-trot. The dance step solves our coordination problem, but it does not determine how we choose to express our romantic inclinations. Or there is the convention of a "lost and found," which involves strangers, not dance partners. We use it to deposit and recover lost items, but it does not mean that if you or I find something of value we will necessarily choose to follow the convention. Depending on what is found, we may decide to keep the lost item, relying on an equally accepted, but less cooperative, standard of conduct: finders keepers, losers weepers.

In seeking a change in human convention, Fred Hirsch called for a new orientation where individuals act *as if* they put the social interest first, even if they do not.[35] Such a change in behavior seems very remote in the United States because the trajectory of our libertarian history does not put the social interest before the personal. Nonetheless, everyday conventions do help solve many coordination problems; despite weak community ties, our interdependence necessitates a modicum of cooperation. Cooperation, after all, can be expedient, much like our everyday social ties. Our social conventions promote regularities of conduct that are consistent with self-interest while at the same time producing, for the most part, desirable outcomes. And cooperation does not necessarily mean an absence of conflict. In some cases our cooperative goal is to compete, so we use conventions that coordinate our competition like "choosing up sides," which seeks to balance the talent of opposing teams, or agreeing that a majority of votes for one candidate determines the winner.

Most conventions are born of necessity and sustained by common sense. They establish a working trust among strangers, arising from the expectation that strangers will behave in a predictable way, rather than a personal trust based on steady acquaintance. Consider our "rules of the road" which help us overcome our fear of strangers hurtling toward us at sixty miles an hour. Driving on the right side is the law, but we don't do it because we are afraid of getting a ticket. The convention is that each of us will stay on the right side of the road so that we don't get killed. Can you imagine our state of mind when driving if we did not have such a rule or could not trust oncoming drivers to adhere to it?[36] Drunk drivers are such a menace because we often have no way of knowing that they are untrustworthy until it's too late. Experience has taught us that predictable behavior, rather than unpredictable behavior, is in everyone's favor. Even when the actors change, the convention does not.

The mistake that some commentators make in writing about cooperation is to assume that it is only through frequent and repeated interactions among the same individuals that cooperation is possible.

Robert Axelrod, a political scientist, has used game theory to argue that cooperation can evolve based on reciprocity between "players" who learn to trust each other over a period of time.[37] This is similar, in effect, to what communitarians advocate—that people can somehow come to know and trust one another. But strangers, by definition, do not have such opportunities or they would no longer be strangers. The evidence of conventions, which indeed promotes large-scale cooperation, is centered not on relationships, but on regularities of behavior.

Regularities of behavior, however, are not easily organized in a patchwork society where there is little ground for mutual trust and where Montesquieu's "bourgeois virtues" of self-restraint, self-reliance, frugality, and moderation are ignored or challenged. Most people think of conventions as inherently conservative practices, and conventions do, in fact, establish and maintain a status quo. It is like having an old suit of clothes that fits well, although the wearing has made it threadbare. I am always reluctant to chuck it out until I have no other choice. We rarely claim that the status quo, like an old suit of clothes, is better than something newer—only that we prefer the familiar.

New practices, however, that eventually become conventions are often considered radical at their outset—like new ways of dancing that initially shock, then settle down into predictable routines.[38] The process of change that secures the existence of new practices is more creative and disruptive than the regularity of behavior to which we ultimately give the name convention.

The study of conventions has been largely neglected in the current social science literature because, I suspect, conventions are considered "no brainers" among those who are concerned with critical thinking. For those who prize rationality as an essential condition for exercising informed choice, a convention is usually seen as the opposite of reason. Since the Enlightenment, "convention" has acquired a pejorative meaning associated with traditions and customs that have ruled arbitrarily and thus unreasonably. John Stuart Mill, the author of *On Liberty*, said, "He who does anything because it is the custom makes no choice. He gains no practice either in discerning or in desiring what is best."[39] For sure, conventions do not require much thinking, unless, of course, you are writing a book about them. Alfred North Whitehead said, however, that "civilization advances by extending the number of important operations which can be performed without thinking about them."[40] Conventions work because we can note the fact of a line forming to buy tickets at a movie theater rather than having to imagine how to solve the problem of congestion caused by too many of us arriving at the same time for the 9:00 P.M. showing.

There has been some thinking about conventions within the analytical framework of game theory, which presupposes rational "players" of narrow self-interest. Unfortunately, most of those using the game theory framework define conventions as simple coordination games where players' interests coincide from the outset and the object is to choose the same coordination point. Such thinking neglects the large question of how conventions originate and why some prevail and others do not. The life cycle of a convention is far more complicated than a pure coordination game. The development of conventions more nearly resembles an "assurance game": players prefer the same outcome but have other attractive alternatives so it is by no means certain that enough people will coordinate their behavior to produce the desired outcome.

My scaffolding for the examination of conventions is a settled assumption that problem solving in public life is more social than cognitive—an enterprise in which we learn that cooperation is necessary to produce a satisfactory outcome—not optimal from the perspective of narrow self-interest, but satisfactory in that a problem can't otherwise be solved. This assumption corresponds with my experience in government and with what I learned from problem simulations that I conducted for ten years as part of my teaching.

In public life, individual motivations are not singular or fixed. Our preferences are shaped, in part, by our social relations. We adapt. We do not think deductively from abstract principles about "the individual." Rather we harvest what we can from everyday experience where we find ourselves socially located among other unique individuals. Think of a street performer trying to drum up a crowd. He wants an audience, but people are reluctant to stop until they see enough others stopping. If you and I conclude that we like a performance regardless, a few others may join us and the performer is encouraged. He knows that others now passing by will say, "Something must be interesting over

there, or there wouldn't be so many people," and soon he has his audience. Or think of an empty restaurant that you and I pass by. Do we
want to eat there? Probably not. The absence of patrons tells us that
others already know that the food is not so good there. We move on to
find a place they patronize. We're not so much looking for a crowd as
for what a crowd tells us about a restaurant.[41] Have you noticed that a
beggar's cup always rattles? Beggars leave money in the cup to remind
us that others have already given—and it works. We are influenced by
what other people do.

When we deal with public problems in everyday life, our preferences
are also influenced by what others do. In public life you and I are powerless to solve a problem alone. "The solutions depend on some kind of
social organization, whether that organization is contrived or spontaneous, permanent or ad hoc, voluntary or disciplined."[42] If there is to
be a satisfactory outcome, it is when we arrive together at a different
place from where each of us started. Self-interest does not always
search for advantage—far from it. Our political rationality is essentially
empirical and pragmatic—that is, what I observe works for me also, to
some degree, has to work for others too. Political rationality does not
proceed from a fixed view of human nature or expect a self-transforma-
tion through the experience of community. Our public behavior should
not, therefore, be characterized as either self-serving or public-spirited;
it all depends, to a great extent, on what others do.

Social conventions, as one model for dealing with public problems,
navigate between those who assume that narrow self-interest, pinched
and cramped, rules public life, and those who believe that "communitarian" values should. I don't think the possibility of cooperation
among strangers can be dismissed any more than it can be invoked. It
all depends, and that is why I want to examine conventions. I hope to
make visible what, for the most part, is invisible to us because it is so
commonplace in everyday life, to explore how conventions originate
and change, to clarify some of the obstacles that impede their development in a "free country," and to explain why the potential of new
telecommunication networks makes large-scale cooperation look more
promising.

My examination of conventions is only a "thick description" of a social phenomenon accessible to all of us.[43] My examination does not presuppose how we should act or that new conventions can be a panacea for all our mutual problems. Liberty's sway gives us many options other than cooperation. But I hope that our stubborn streak of independence, which accounts for so many of the contradictions that we live with, also helps us find new ways to cooperate, given our unavoidable interdependence, instead of inviting new costs and the intrusions of government. Using social conventions to govern ourselves could make governance, rather than more government, our major preoccupation. Perhaps if we better understand conventions, we can better govern ourselves.

Chapter One

WHEN STRANGERS COOPERATE

Everyday Conventions

You and I participate in conventions every day. They ease our passage through the day's activities and make it possible for us to cooperate, even as strangers. Conventions organize and simplify many instances of potential confusion or chaos, yet most of the time we are not particularly aware that they exist. Conventions are like the air we breathe—unexamined but indispensable. I want to start with ordinary, even trivial, examples of everyday conventions in order to explain how they work for us.

Consider the convention of a line at a bank. A line forms when there are too many of us at one time for a teller to accommodate. I accept the convention of a line when I arrive at the bank and wait my turn. If I arrive at the bank before it opens, most of us waiting will note who was there first, second, and so on, and more than likely adjust accordingly when the doors are opened. If there is a revolving door, it starts to sort us out in an order that much resembles a line. Once inside the bank, there may be a few among us who either don't know, or pretend they don't know, who was there first and rush to the head of the line, but there will be a line, not something else, once we get inside the bank.

Standing there waiting our turn, we don't think of ourselves as altruistic. More likely we would describe ourselves as law-abiding or good sports. We are willing "to go along to get along" on the condition that enough others do the same. There was little calculation on our parts in getting in line. We don't have to think through what we should do. That is why conventions make sense. There is an established regularity of behavior that works more often than not. The convention of a line endures because it works for everyone . . . eventually.

A convention is like a well-worn path that I choose to follow in the woods. I know that many hikers in the past have used it to get from point A to point B. If I do not know the woods and follow the path for the first time, I may not even know of the existence of point B. I assume, however, that the path will take me somewhere—to the other side of the woods or to a place worth visiting. A convention is like that. We assume that it makes sense because other people have used it. Like the origin of a path, a convention may seem an arbitrary or random choice. There are, after all, a number of possible paths from point A to point B. Still we take the well-worn path because it offers advantages. We don't have to clear a way; we assume the path has some purpose; and well-worn paths, more often than not, get us where we want to go.

As strangers, we join a line not because we like lines or because we like those who stand in line with us, but because the line produces a satisfactory outcome for what would otherwise be a time-consuming and contentious situation caused by too many of us being in one place at one time. We create a problem of congestion for each other, and we need each other to solve it.

When we talk about solving problems, such as congestion, what we usually mean is improving a situation. Coordinating a response to a problem is not the same thing as solving the problem itself. When we form a line at the bank, we are not solving the problem of congestion. The line is a convention that helps us cope with the congestion. It solves a coordination problem and the solution depends on a regularity of behavior. If each of us accepts the convention of a line, we produce a satisfactory outcome. I might, however, urge a bank officer to hire more tellers or install more automatic teller machines to reduce the congestion. Existing conventions, like a line, often divert attention from the underlying problem that necessitates coordination in the first place.

Our line at the bank is not necessarily the best solution or outcome, but it is the one that we somehow have settled on. Imagine my problem at the bank of convincing those in line that there are other ways to solve the problem of congestion. Those in line undoubtedly have become more attached to the convention as they wait. They are already heavily invested in this particular solution and are not likely to be dissuaded.

If no line had yet formed, we might have decided among ourselves who had the better reason for going first, second, and so on. We could have used the criterion of who deserves to be waited on first, rather than who was there first. If you had a pressing appointment or I had a sick child waiting in the car, perhaps we could have prevailed on the others. But everyday coordination problems among strangers usually don't afford us the time to talk over such matters, and, in the case of a line, it would probably take more time to sort out our differences as to who deserves to be waited on first than just waiting our turn to be served. We settled on the line, not because it satisfies everyone (it certainly doesn't suit me with a sick child in the car), but because it generally satisfies almost everyone else under the circumstances. Some coordination is better than none—especially with a sick child in the car. It reassures me that there is a predictable outcome to what would otherwise be a confused situation. The success of a convention depends on whether enough of us go along with the outcome, not whether each of us prefers that particular outcome.

With many conventions we, in effect, tacitly agree on a precept that governs our behavior, or what I call a metaconvention. A metaconvention is a precept of behavior that clarifies the basis for our cooperation with strangers and consequently makes coordination problems easier to solve. In the case of a line, the metaconvention that promotes coordination and sustains the convention is first come, first served. This particular metaconvention is embedded in other conventions: rights of seniority in employee relations, waiting lists for public housing, air traffic control protocols, allotting seats to opera season subscribers or spaces in overenrolled university courses. When demand exceeds supply, if only temporarily, a choice has to be made about how to coordinate the demand, how to deal with the congestion.[1]

If anyone tries to crash our line, to undermine the convention, we will think that person is "out of line." A convention is immeasurably strengthened when we enforce it ourselves. When we yield to a convention, we become invested in its continuing success so that we can experience the benefit that comes with solving a coordination problem and not just the cost of establishing a solution.

The enforcement of a convention, however, has its own complications. Few of us will think of taking responsibility for the entire line. There is always the chance that if you or I were to leave the line to enforce the convention against a line crasher, our places would not be saved for us. We may trust that the convention of a line will work for us, but we may not altogether trust each and every stranger standing in the line with us. In Australia where "queue" behavior is more predictable, overnight queues for football tickets allow for a "queuer to take brief leaves of absence while retaining undisputed rights of reentry."[2]

When each of us is left to police our respective part of the line, there is no convention that tells us how to handle a line crasher directly in front of us. If a burly, gruff fellow steps in front of me out of nowhere, I may choose not to object. After all, if I am unsuccessful in stopping his intrusion, I will have to be in close proximity to him for the remainder of our time together in the line—not a pleasant prospect. On the other hand, if a line crasher appears less threatening, I may object, knowing that others near me in the line will be more ready to support my policing. I have noticed, however, that a person who crashes a line will often talk to those he joins, hoping, perhaps, that others of us will think that he is part of a group already in line. And if we hesitate and there is no immediate challenge from some quarter, the suspected crasher gets his way.

My desire to enforce a convention may also depend on where I am in the line. If I am near the front, I am more likely to be assertive because I may have waited some time and I would resent someone not having to do the same. Of course, if it is that burly, surly fellow again, I may desist from complaining, knowing that I will be served shortly anyway. From the back of the line, I may be less assertive, feeling that one more person won't make that much of a difference. It also depends on what I'm standing in line for. If there are just so many seats available in the movie theater, then any line crasher diminishes slightly my chance of getting in before that showing is sold out. But if the commodity is not limited and there is only temporary congestion that makes me wait for my money deposited in a personal account, then line crashing poses no threat of depriving me of what I am standing in line for.

Sometimes the convention of a line may be temporarily overthrown. A teller at the bank will open his window and say, "I can help someone over here," and people behind me rush over ahead of me. Many businesses try to combat such turmoil by asking us to form a "snake" or single line for all work stations serving us. It is not more efficient, but it does seem more fair. Many conventions satisfy our desire to be treated fairly because everyone is treated equally.

Although each of us may be required to enforce a convention at some time, no doubt we rely on the monitoring of other strangers in close proximity to help make the coordination work. In situations where we are isolated from one another, for example, when we are ensconced in our automobiles, our "line" behavior can be atrocious. I've noticed that many drivers will try to butt into a slow-moving line of cars where two lanes merge into one, as in the case of highway construction. All the other drivers can do is honk their horns or glare. But a driver who doesn't want to cooperate by waiting his turn usually avoids making eye contact, as if he is not really aware of other drivers waiting their turn. If most drivers cooperate by staying in line when traffic is stalled, the line crashers have an advantage. If, however, too many of them converge, they defeat themselves, and we all suffer from the resulting chaos.

The convention of a line is also vulnerable when we prepare to board an airplane. An airline employee tries to regulate entry onto the plane by dividing the passengers into categories: first, those with small children, the elderly, and first class passengers; then, those with coach seats in the rear of the plane, and so on. The coordination can break down, however, when passengers, like me, anticipate a shortage of space for their luggage in the overhead racks on the plane and try to pass through the gate out of turn. If the employee doesn't turn us away, enough others may sense the overthrow of the convention and the boarding becomes more anxious and less orderly. When a convention is temporarily defeated, there is no readily available alternative that coordinates our public behavior. Once again we are uncertain of what to do.

WHEN THERE IS UNCERTAINTY

Conventions are established to solve the problem of uncertainty as to how we should coordinate our response to any number of problematic situations in everyday life. Coordination does not work if people are uncertain what to do in a given situation. To prepare for emergency routines, we rehearse simple exits, sometimes with sirens, bells, or whistles, that coordinate what would otherwise be dangerous disorder. "Walk, don't run" and "women and children first" are simple declarative statements that tell us how to exit and in what order. In medieval Europe the white flag of truce was a convention to allay uncertainty when warring sides could afford no misunderstanding. Similarly, we now use the time-out sign in sports contests to bring the action to a halt.

When we are uncertain about what to wear, the invitation to a banquet will say "black tie," telling us what others will be wearing so we don't have to guess. Since it is impractical to bring different outfits to the banquet and then change on the scene, the invitation tells us what to do in advance. When the host is uncertain as to how many of us will attend the banquet, we are asked to RSVP.

If novice spectators are uncertain about how to behave at athletic events, they follow the crowd: keep absolutely quiet when someone putts in a golf match, take a seventh-inning stretch at a baseball game, boo the referee in basketball, but hiss the linesman at a tennis match. The "wave" is a new spectator convention that is performed in large, outdoor stadiums. Section after section of spectators rise and fall. With very little effort on anyone's part—a spectator just stands up and sits down in the exercise—the crowd creates a show for itself. On the field, athletes have their own conventions to reduce uncertainty: a quarterback calls out a particular sequence of numbers to start a play, a catcher gives the pitcher a sign for throwing a curve ball, and the third-base coach tells a batter when to bunt by signaling with ear pulls, belly slaps, elbow touchings, and cap tugs.

Like following the wave or reading a bunt sign, most conventions are relatively simple to understand. Since one of the primary functions of a convention is to reduce uncertainty, it makes no sense if the regularity of behavior prescribed is too complicated to follow. A convention is like a handshake: it tells us what to do with our thumbs. We would be "all thumbs" if I offered my left hand when you offered your right, or if I grasped your elbow while you tried to squeeze my wrist. Handshakes don't work unless we can assume that both of us will do the same thing.[3] In the case of a potluck supper, we don't all do the same thing, but our parts are not complicated, assuming someone, with a checklist of salads, casseroles, and desserts, asks each of us to bring a different dish. Conventions are elementary. Once we understand what is expected of us, usually everyone has the capacity, if not the willingness, to go along.

There are many ways that conventions help us to negotiate uncertainty and unfamiliar situations. The convention of a line at the bank tells us, as strangers to each other, what to do when we find that there are too many of us in one place. Other conventions help us, as strangers, to simply find each other, whether it is on a bulletin board, in the classified ads of a newspaper, at a bus stop, an annual meeting, a class reunion, in a receiving line, a hiring hall, or during store hours. The same uncertainty of where to find something is why we have dictionaries, maps, user guides, road signs, and the yellow pages in a telephone directory. Imagine that you found my eyeglasses on the bench in the lobby of an office building and were told by the guard that there was no "lost and found" where you could leave them and that he would not take custody or responsibility. Imagine my dismay when told the same thing by a different guard the next morning when I returned to look for my glasses, not knowing exactly where I misplaced them. What is the likelihood that I will ever meet you or discover the ledge you put them on before leaving the building? A "lost and found" is a convention for eliminating your uncertainty and mine about how two strangers, who will never meet, can, nonetheless, find each other, so to speak.

When we are uncertain about the background and talents of strangers, we use the convention of seeking references—a three-cornered arrangement among strangers just like the convention of a lost and found. Instead of a finder, a loser, and a custodian of a lost item, who manage to coordinate their actions, references usually involve an employer, a job applicant, and a third party who is knowledgeable about the applicant. The employer asks one or more "references" for an opinion of the applicant. One stranger relies on other strangers about the employability of yet another stranger.[4]

When we are uncertain about the value of new goods, we resort to the convention of certification, whether it is the grading of eggs, a Good Housekeeping Seal of Approval, an Underwriters Laboratories marker, or an American Kennel Club pedigree. Certification is similar to the coordination of references, as are "credentials" which make the references of strangers even more credible. There are many occasions when we seek a kind of certification from those whose credentials allay our uncertainties and reassure us that someone better qualified than ourselves can help us. As strangers to us, they preface their testimony as expert witnesses in litigation by reciting their credentials; they list their credentials on letterheads when soliciting our business; and their credentials are conspicuous on book jackets that promise great wealth, good health, or just a greener lawn.

Instead of relying on an expert's credentials and the convention of certification, some of us resort to the convention of a self-help group. When we are uncertain about ourselves or our ability to cope with stressful situations, we seek out those with similar problems and complaints. They are often strangers who help us with self-understanding. Much of this exploration is coordinated through a self-governing group that pools its collective knowledge and experience to help individual members. There are self-help groups for someone who is an alcoholic, or a compulsive gambler, or overweight, or recently divorced, or a parent of a handicapped child, or who is unable to manage his or her money, or is stricken with cancer, or is caring for a spouse or parent with Alzheimer's disease, or is mourning the loss of a loved one.[5]

When we are uncertain about the value of used goods—collectibles, antiques, and art objects—we may collectively determine their value through the convention of an auction or, in the case of valuing stocks, bonds, and other investment instruments, through secondary market "exchanges" that resemble an auction. The convention of an auction departs from the more familiar two-party transaction of an offered price by a seller and an acceptance of that price by a buyer or their haggling over the price. An auction establishes a price for a particular item through the competition of bidding among a potentially large number of buyers. Although there may be an "upset price" that the seller requires as a minimum bid for the item to be sold at all, the competition among bidders to own the item creates a value for it. The auctioneer does not shout, "What is this vase worth?" but rather, "What am I bid for this vase?" An auction, like the conventions of a lost and found or references, is three-cornered—the seller, the auctioneer or broker, and the potential buyers. As strangers, they determine a value and coordinate a sale relying on a convention that works for all of them, even though the highest bid may be less than the seller or auctioneer wanted or more than the successful bidder wanted to pay. Starting with a minimum offering price and seeking higher bids is commonly known as an "English auction." When an auctioneer starts with a high offering price and then reduces it until a bid represents an acceptance, the competition is known as a "Dutch auction." In a "Japanese auction" bids are made simultaneously in public allowing potential buyers to react and adjust their bids.[6]

WHEN THERE ARE ENOUGH OTHERS

Unlike the congestion at the bank, we confront many coordination problems on a daily basis that are not of our own making. Consider our experience as pedestrians uncertain as to how we can get across a busy intersection. As pedestrians, your behavior and mine did not cause the problem, but we do need each other to solve it. We have to coordinate our behavior by entering the intersection in sufficient numbers to make drivers halt for our crossing. As strangers, there is a kind of unspoken communication among us. We watch each other, waiting for a leader, or perhaps leading ourselves, willing to venture into the intersection with enough followers to stop the oncoming traffic and for a moment shift the advantage to ourselves—or rather to enough other pedestrians—so that we can pass safely to the other side. A coordination solution, a temporary convention of sorts, arises spontaneously simply because there are enough people to make it so.[7]

Our coordination at a street corner is fleeting and we will probably never see each other again, although at the next busy intersection, you or I may seek to organize a solution among another group of strangers in which it is in everyone's interest to cross together. Our leadership of fellow pedestrians off the curb is timely but of only passing significance. If enough others follow, those of us who led the excursion are no longer needed.

Sometimes, of course, the attempt to establish a coordination solution fails. Not enough of us venture out together, and whoever miscalculates the others' willingness to follow has to fall back to the curb and wait for a break in the traffic, or a new temporary leader, or a new effort of strangers massing to cross. There is no precept of behavior, or metaconvention, for crossing the street as there is for the line at the bank. If enough of us cross, we will get our way. We might even defy the established convention of a stoplight if we succeed in crossing on the red.

"Enough others" is a simple way to express what is not so simple a proposition—the idea of critical mass. Critical mass is a threshold. It does not relate to sheer numbers of people, but to how many are needed to make coordination successful and, in the case of conventions, to make a practice more or less self-sustaining.[8] In any particular social context, there is no predetermined number of people who constitute a critical mass. It all depends. If there are enough of us to cross the street successfully, that number is determined by whether cars stop, not by counting noses. The same is true for getting a public utility to respond to a power outage or city hall to repair a pothole. The evidence of a convention is unmistakable when there are enough people, for example, to keep a chain letter going, produce a standing ovation at the opera house, or loot a store during civil unrest.

Sometimes coordination by enough others is achieved without a leader at the street corner. Successful coordination can turn out to be nothing more than a sequence of actions and reactions by strangers without any acknowledgment of each other's influence. How does the conventional speed get established on a highway? Unlike the person who first ventures into a busy intersection, it is hard to know on the highway whether we are leading or following. Nobody is in charge, but somehow one or more drivers' speed influences the speed of other drivers. It certainly doesn't mean that everyone prefers that speed. Conventions are established because we seek to coordinate our behavior with that of others, and one or more of us driving sixty-five miles per hour sets the speed temporarily for almost everyone else. A few drivers, of course, go at their own speed, even though that speed is too slow compared to what the majority of drivers are doing. But most of us know that it is safer to keep up. Differences in speed, more than the speed itself, put us at risk when driving.[9]

If events put the underlying reason for a particular conventional speed in doubt, then the conventional speed changes. For example, most of us accepted the fifty-five miles per hour speed limit during the energy shortage in the 1970s. The crisis made us more conservation-minded, and with the help of law enforcement, the new speed limit worked because we saw a reason for it. As the energy crisis dissipated, so, too, did our driving at fifty-five miles per hour. With or without law enforcement, speeds picked up.

You may not think of a speed limit as a convention, since the law would seem to have preempted our choice of how fast to drive. But whatever speed the great majority of drivers establish is the conventional speed limit. On the Long Island Expressway in New York, which I used to travel frequently, virtually no one observes the posted speed limit of 55 miles per hour. "I've clocked funeral processions at over 70," said one highway patrol officer. The same officer admitted that no one is ticketed for going 60 miles per hour when the traffic flow averages 65 miles per hour.[10] Of course, the conventional limit is influenced by visible law enforcement, just as law enforcement is influenced by the speed that most drivers consider suitable for any particular stretch of highway. We watch what others are doing and adjust our speed, to keep up and stay within the pack. Police call this "caravaning." Just like crossing the street, we think that there is safety in numbers, although the highway patrol, like a good sheep dog, can pull a whole herd of us over at one time.

DISCRETE, ORGANIZATION, AND COMMUNITY CONVENTIONS

The following discussion begins to sort out a sample of voluntary, cooperative practices which we take for granted in everyday life and which are largely independent of government and market forces, although in some cases influenced by them.

Discrete Conventions

There are conventions which I think of as "discrete" because they are practices that don't require a large number of people to make them work. "Enough others" may mean only two or three of us. The threshhold for effective coordination is not arduous to reach or complicated. This is not the case if a few foolhardy pedestrians venture into traffic by themselves. Most of us will find our opportunity to cross only when there seem to be enough others to make the crossing safe and successful. What is the point of forming a line of two or three passengers, if others rush the airline gate? Twenty people can start a wave at Dodgers Stadium, but they cannot sustain it without the cooperation of thousands more.

An example of a discrete convention is when we agree to use a "designated driver." If two of us in our party plan to drink and drive, it is in everyone's interest that a third companion not drink and keep the car keys. Of course, if other people in our driving area also observe this convention, our ride home will be even safer. Such coordination, however, has obvious benefits for those who cooperate, regardless of how many others do likewise.

The "designated driver" practice was initially promoted by Mothers Against Drunk Driving (MADD).[11] Discrete conventions often become commonly known and practiced as they are amplified by national organizations, as in the case of "designated driver." Other examples are "living wills," explained through the literature of the American Association of Retired Persons, or the "I Have a Dream" model, started by the New York industrialist Eugene Lang, that puts a benefactor together with a group of minority children to help them prepare and pay for college. Such a model is now promoted by the I Have a Dream Foundation. Sometimes a local organization accounts for a discrete convention being practiced citywide. Such is the case of Medic II, a Seattle program for citizens to learn cardiopulmonary resuscitation ("CPR"). Fifty percent of those who live in Seattle have learned CPR where the survival rate for cardiac arrest victims is much higher than in other American cities.[12]

Like CPR, discrete conventions are possible among strangers—for example, hitchhiking, prostitution, tipping, and appointments. We also practice discrete conventions with those we know well—for example, dinner hours, contraception, promises, and secrets. Patronage is a discrete convention practiced among both strangers and friends. Patronage involves using one's position and power to do favors for others. Those favored usually have already done something, or they become obligated to do something in the future, that merits the favor. The coordination in patronage rests on a tacit understanding that if the convention is to be sustained, each party, not simultaneously but at different times, will reward the other. The metaconvention that makes such coordination work is the simple expectation of reciprocity.

Here is how political patronage worked in one New York county that we investigated when I served as chairman of the State Investigation Commission. Both political parties observed a discrete convention when they controlled the county executive's office. The patronage extended to a small number of local insurance agents, who were rewarded for having made contributions to the party. The party leader, either Republican or Democrat depending on which party was in power, would dictate to the newly elected county executive which agent was to handle the county's insurance needs. The designated agent would then take the standard commission for services rendered but share his commission with the other local agents who had been regular contributors to the party. The patronage scheme was called "commission sharing." It not only involved very few people, it was known only to those who needed to know. It was a very discrete convention indeed.

Organization Conventions

One of the most common settings where many different conventions, discrete or otherwise, are observed is the American workplace, the corporate organization. Like a path whose direction we trust but whose origin we know little or nothing about, a convention in a particular organization often becomes firmly established when no one can remember how it got started.

Think of hard-won changes in an organization where you have worked. Perhaps the change involved increasing productivity levels, or promoting more minority members to executive positions, or consulting across departments before any major decision was made. At one time these practices, or others that come to mind, were unheard of or thought to be unattainable. Nonetheless, they were eventually put in place after some disruption and turmoil in the organization. At the outset, the practices were fragile and not expected to survive. There was confusion and resistance. As time went on, however, older employees accepted them or retired, and new employees assumed such practices were routine and expected. The status quo shifted, and eventually fewer people recalled or even knew how tenuous such practices once were. When someone now says, "That's just the way we do things around here," you can be sure that an organization convention is secure.[13]

At a small college where I worked there were too many rules and not enough conventions. Instead of shared understandings among 35 faculty members, 40 staff members, and 500 students, everything was committed to writing, and the enforcement of so many rules was impossible. There were rules about where you could park, how to justify your absence from class, what constituted a "dorm party," how many committees you were required to serve on or cultural events to attend, what the duties of freshmen advisors were, how jobs were assigned in the student work program, and even how the mail was to be distributed and coffee breaks allocated. It seems that there had never been a period in which practices were experienced before rules were developed. This small college organization had somehow bypassed that evolutionary phase and the rules had sprung full-blown from the head of a well-meaning provost, a student committee long disbanded, an imperious department chairman, or a president now retired. As a consequence, innovation was stifled because rules could not be changed easily. Administrators and faculty members were forced to perform as bureaucrats toward students, instead of mentors. In a small college, a maze of rules gets in the way of informal collaboration that makes genuine learning possible.

In the business world, the variety of organization conventions is prompted, in part, by the competition for market share and profits, which leads a company to produce a product, render a service, or do business in a manner different from its competitors. Most companies set organization goals and try to define a particular way of doing business with their employees and customers. Business managers are educated or trained to control, or try to control, their corporate environments through various rituals, hierarchies, and forms of specialization and standardization. Such executives engage in subtle, and not so subtle, forms of goal reinforcement to foster employee cooperation and customer loyalty.

So much of what goes on in all organizations, public, private, and nonprofit, are routines of memoranda and meetings—conventions, if you will—that coordinate the work of any firm. But such coordination may be lifeless without goals that inform it and new forms of cooperation that enliven the workplace, such as employee development workshops, quality circles, employee evaluations of managers, and reward programs. One of the central insights for such innovation is that people, by and large, want to identify with the goals of the organization they work for and are prepared to coordinate their behavior in support of those goals. They gain a measure of satisfaction from doing so, whether or not organizational survival and their jobs are at stake.

The literature of organizational behavior and management is an unending search for ways to gain some advantage through the use of new or borrowed organization conventions. The peripatetic Tom Peters is the best-known guru and chronicler of such conventions, old and new. He describes "chunking" where teams, task forces, and other forms of "adhocracy" keep an organization project-oriented. Small-group initiatives focus on specific tasks, and neither the groups nor the tasks are permanent. There are the "town meetings" and "hell week" of Dana Corporation where everyone makes it his or her business to listen to complaints, suggestions, and productivity stories. There is the "open lab stock" policy of Hewlett-Packard where electrical and mechanical components are never locked up and engineers take them home with the expectation that such constant access will lead to constant innovation. There is the 800 toll-free number, instituted by Proctor and Gamble in 1979, which produced 200,000 calls from customers, led to new product ideas, and has now become a widespread convention of manufacturing and service businesses.[14]

Community Conventions

Public life, in general, prompts many different "community" conventions that pool or recycle private resources and protect and conserve public space. And we often manage such coordination without government intervention. Many such conventions are a product of the voluntary spirit of those living in communities where, until recently, problems were addressed without the prod or involvement of government at all.

We still pool private resources in the communities where we live to create different forms of surplus through the conventions of a library, a blood bank, a museum, or a thrift shop. More recently, we have made greater use of local food banks and "harvest" agencies, which coordinate the collection and distribution of perishable food. It is like the convention of a potluck supper writ large, but instead of coordinating an evening's menu for our own eating pleasure, we provide a variety of foods for those who might otherwise go hungry. Churches, workplaces, schools, and firehouses facilitate the collection of food from members, employees, families, and neighborhoods. Donations also come from hotels, restaurants, and grocery chains, offering perishables to a harvest agency that in turn distributes what has been collected and donated to food pantries and soup kitchens. For example, on the day of the World Trade Center blast in 1993 when its two towers in New York City's lower Manhattan were shut to the public, one hotel and one restaurant in the Center contributed 10,000 pounds of perishable eggs, cheese, strawberries, and watermelon.[15]

The city of Berkeley, California, has a community convention to feed the homeless. Those who want to help can buy food vouchers at local stores which entitle the bearer to an equivalent value in foodstuffs. Residents then give the vouchers instead of cash to those who are soliciting money on Berkeley's streets. The convention works, assuming that the street people don't barter their vouchers for less useful things like liquor and drugs. The cities of Chicago, Boston, Seattle, Boulder, and New Haven have similar programs.[16]

There is also a widespread practice of distributing food and raising money for various social agencies at California highway rest areas. That is how I met "John" at a rest area off of Interstate 5 in Lakeland, California. He was offering food and seeking donations for Shascade Community Services, an agency for disabled adults. John had a small catering business and drove to such rest areas every Saturday. He told me that some people took food without leaving a donation, but he assumed that many of them were "just down and out" as he once was before a local food bank helped him get on his feet.

We pool community manpower by using the convention of deputizing citizens when government is shorthanded or short of funds. There are highway signs now in forty-five states that tell us that local associations, school groups, and businesses have adopted pieces of the local roadside, and their members periodically clean up the litter. "Adopt-a-Highway" is a new community convention to combat the pollution of those public spaces for which no one has taken active responsibility.[17] The same convention is used to coordinate the protection of parks, streams, and beaches. Community groups maintain paths, plant trees and shrubs to prevent bank erosion, and conduct annual beach cleanups when volunteer crews pick up millions of pounds of debris.

In East Hampton, New York, where I used to live, the Ladies Village Improvement Society (LVIS), a private group, now in existence for 100 years, maintains and preserves public landmarks, ponds, parks, greens, and trees. In 1895, twenty-one women banded together to have the streets sprinkled when dust was a problem; they arranged for the installation of streetlights; they exterminated tent caterpillars; and they put up a flagpole and displayed flags all along Main Street on holidays. In 1900, they started spraying elm trees, which to this day need constant care to resist Dutch elm disease and other plagues. The LVIS has been vigilant in campaigning against billboards, looking after the railroad station, planting "memorial" trees, and helping to care for a nature trail. There are more than 400 members of the Society and there seems to be no end to their projects.[18]

The organization of local land trusts is a relatively new conservation convention. Land trusts seek to protect private holdings from housing subdivisions and commercial development. Property owners and other concerned citizens have learned to devise their own strategies when local officials seek to broaden their tax base in conjunction with ambitious developers. In such a case, governments and markets are the source of a problem, not an answer.

There are now 900 such trusts in the United States. Their numbers have doubled in just a decade. They hold about three million acres in trusts nationwide. Some trusts actually buy land to keep it off the development market. Other trusts, with fewer resources, oversee conservation easements that let an owner keep the property, sell it, or leave it to heirs, but with restrictions on how the land will be used. Owners are restricted from subdevelopment, removing groves of trees, altering hillsides, damming creeks, allowing billboards, and so forth. The local land trust becomes the trustee for the perpetual enforcement of conservation restrictions. In the New Mexico valley where we lived for a time, a local land trust helped to facilitate a "neighborhood conservation easement." Landowners retained separate ownership of their respective properties but preserved a large tract of farmland that no one owner could manage alone.[19]

THE VAGARIES OF CONVENTIONS

Although most conventions are within the range of our everyday experience, some are used at one time but not another, others make sense in one place but not another. Most practices that become conventions evolve slowly, many conventions remain fragile, and some die. The vagaries of conventions enrich our understanding but confound any easy generalizations about them.

1. Some conventions are used at one time but not another. Suppose there are four of us who are going out to dinner but we can't agree on where to eat.[20] We have several conventions to choose from in solving

this coordination problem. After discussing possible restaurants, we can take a vote to determine where to go. Or if it comes down to two choices, we can flip a coin or let a passerby settle the problem for us. Another way to resolve the matter is to delegate the choice to one of our party, saying that this time Sarah can choose. Or one of our foursome may refuse to go with us unless we choose his favorite Chinese restaurant. By his preemptive behavior, we may agree to go along with him so as not to spoil the evening. We can coordinate an acceptable outcome by using any one of these procedural conventions: voting, chance, arbitration, delegation, or bargaining.

On this occasion we agree to let Sarah decide where we will eat, but nothing binds us to use the same convention the next time we dine out together. We often delegate choice at one time but not another. We delegate when we give a proxy in the case of our absence from a shareholder meeting. We delegate when we give a general power-of-attorney to someone we trust to manage our personal affairs during an illness or because of advanced age. We delegate when we elect representatives to conduct the public's business in city and county councils, state legislatures, and the halls of Congress. At other times we choose not to delegate, reserving decisions for ourselves through voter referenda, recall petitions, and bond issues. At one time but not another, we let negotiators represent us at a bargaining table, travel agents plan our trips, investment counselors manage our assets, and interior designers decorate our homes. Delegation works as a convention, not because everyone always uses it, but because when it is used it settles, for the time being, any number of coordination problems.

Many conventions, like delegation, have permanent features which we easily recognize but only occasionally employ. For example, a boycott is not an everyday routine like a line. A boycott is a convention used sparingly but often with great effect. The term *boycott* comes from a dispute in 1880 between peasant tenants and a British land agent, Charles Boycott, in County Mayo. Captain Boycott would not yield to their demands that he lower tenant rents by 25 percent on the large land holdings that he managed for absentee British landowners. The tenants refused to work for Boycott and he responded by hiring workers from Ulster and stationing several military regiments to protect these workers from the tenants. The convention of a boycott, however, predates its name. For example, our own colonist refusal in 1765 to buy British goods was a protest against new levies of the Stamp Act, which Parliament quickly repealed.[21]

More recently, the threat of a boycott forced the state of Alaska to rescind its plans to kill wolves after environmentalists ran newspaper ads asking people not to spend "a dime in a state that doesn't give a damn about wolves." It is reported that 7,500 people wrote the governor of Alaska and he backed down because of the state's one billion dollar tourist industry employing 20,000 people. A more publicized travel boycott was directed at the state of Colorado when its voters approved a constitutional amendment in 1992 that prohibited special civil rights protection for homosexuals. Before the amendment was successfully challenged in the courts, Colorado lost more than twenty million dollars in convention business. When Arizona voters rejected a state holiday to honor Martin Luther King, Jr., large membership organizations across the country canceled 166 trade shows and conventions scheduled for Arizona. The state lost $190 million in anticipated revenues.[22] By coincidence, it was a bus boycott in 1955 that launched the twenty-six-year-old Martin Luther King as a civil rights leader. The boycott in Montgomery, Alabama, was a watershed victory in the desegregation movement of that era; Rosa Parks was arrested for refusing to move to the back of a city bus, and in response 15,000–20,000 black Montgomerians refused to ride their buses for a year. Perhaps the best-remembered boycott was the refusal of seventeen million Americans, in the late 1960s, to buy California table grapes produced in the San Joaquin valley, in support of Cesar Chavez's efforts to unionize farm workers.

Sometimes boycotts go by other names. In the 1950s the film industry denied employment to those who were labeled Communist sympathizers, and that boycott was called "blacklisting." More recently, banks have refused to finance mortgages in certain inner-city areas by "redlining" them. "Buying American" has consumers spurning foreign-made goods by looking at labels, interrogating salespersons, and deciphering vehicle identification numbers that tell where a car was manufactured.

2. Some conventions make sense in one place but not another. Think of the games of childhood, which were perhaps our first intense experience with conventions, when we learned to coordinate our behavior with others for the pure pleasure of it. In some of our games, we created sacred places and asylums, where we were free from being tagged or captured. Do you remember the game of "hide and seek" and yelling, "Ole, ole oats on freedom" as you made a mad dash from behind a tree to that place where you were free? It was much like the long-standing convention of a sanctuary, which exists for one place but not another.

A sanctuary is a sacred place where strangers, who may be "offenders," are safe. Churches offer sanctuary to those who seek refuge from secular punishment. Embassies offer sanctuary to fugitives from political repression, and embassy diplomats make the entire country their sanctuary in which they cannot be prosecuted, only deported. We provide sanctuaries for birds and animals where they cannot be trapped or hunted. Outside the boundaries of our sanctuaries, the treatment of fugitives or wildlife is very different.

Conventions, by definition, belong in one place but not another. Every society or culture or tribe has conventions that would not necessarily make sense or be acceptable outside of certain boundaries. For example, in some parts of the world giving gifts to civil servants is considered appropriate, while in the United States we call it bribery. In addition, the array of conventions in American life varies from place to place.

Consider the roadside farmstand where fruits, vegetables, and flowers are sold. An unattended cigar box is the depository for purchases and making change. The exchange is made without the seller being present, trusting the purchaser will leave the proper amount and take no more change than he or she is entitled to. The convention works well in a place where there is a modicum of trust among strangers. It would not work in the downtown of a large city where such trust does not exist. There you find newspaper vending machines that don't make change. They do offer the opportunity of taking more papers than you have paid for. But except for those who occasionally set up their own temporary business of selling such purloined newspapers, the normal purchaser has no need for ten morning newspapers and, like the farmstand customer, knows that the convention will not last long if one takes unfair advantage.

This reminds me of the local convention that I observed in a seaside village where the key to a public bathroom hung on the outside door of the Chamber of Commerce. People apparently come and go using the key and returning it to the doorhook. I couldn't imagine such a convention in most gas stations, city parks, or office buildings. I asked a woman working inside the chamber office if the local practice worked. "Oh yes," she said. "No one bothers me anymore for the key and everyone seems to appreciate the service, especially the tourists." I asked her if the key disappeared frequently. "No," she said. "People seem to understand that, if that happened, we would just stop accommodating them." The cigar box at the farmstand, the downtown newspaper vending machine, and the unsupervised use of a bathroom key each worked in its respective setting.

A convention may work perfectly well in more than one setting, but we will try to limit its influence nonetheless. For example, we think that the convention of organized gambling belongs at bingo parlors, casinos, and racetracks. We do not acknowledge its existence on the trading floors of stock and commodity exchanges. We think of those as places for investors, not gamblers. It is much like a beach fashion where we strip down in public to very little clothing, but arrest people if they walk our downtown streets in the same flimsy apparel.

The convention of a sabbatical every seven years makes perfect sense for professors who need some time for research and writing without the competing demand of teaching. A sabbatical, however, for professional baseball players would disrupt the competitive balance among teams; for politicians, it would defeat the representative function of elected officials. The convention of tenure for full professors is a guarantee of employment that supposedly promotes academic freedom to inquire into any question and speculate about any answer. We would never think of such a convention for professional baseball players or for elected officials. Journalists are free to write or say what they want under the First Amendment, but unlike tenured professors, they get no guarantee of employment.

3. Most social practices require some period of time in order to become established as conventions. As a smoker, I can trace the gradual impact of enough others' disapproval of my smoking habit for me to eventually all but give it up. It took a considerable period of time, however, for them to marshal their forces and to overcome my resistance.

Before the Surgeon General's Report in 1964, which took most of the fun out of smoking, we could smoke "nearly everywhere except in an oxygen tent." This was before smoking around kids was likened to "child abuse."[23] First my children chastised me at home after learning at school about smoking's pernicious effects. Then students expressed their disapproval in my university office while I tried to educate them in other matters. Then restaurants segregated me and airlines denied me the pleasure. As the 1980s wore on, there were very few places where the "no smoking" convention was not put in place. Although local government in many jurisdictions responded to the vocal majority of nonsmokers and threatened me with fines, it was the private policing of my children, my students, and the ever-offended strangers whom I encountered that made the difference. A visitor from abroad, an unrepentant smoker, observed that "'I feel like a mosquito,' . . . flailing his arms in imitation of the way Americans bat away his offensive tobacco fumes."[24]

Finally, the continued unpleasantness of social disapproval made me fall in line. Now that I can no longer smoke in public, I don't want anyone else to have that dubious pleasure. I may choose to endanger my own health by smoking in some secluded private place, but the new convention has persuaded me that no one should be so foolish as I am, at least not in public or in my presence. When you yield to a convention, you invest in its being a success.

Another public practice that is taking time to establish itself is the recycling of household waste. Prompted by the precept of conservation and the increasing problems of disposal, many of us have come grudgingly to accept recycling as part of daily life. We have even begun to change our consumer behavior as well. On a trip to the supermarket, you and I may now bring our own shopping basket rather than using the paper or plastic at the store. We look for cardboard, not Styrofoam egg cartons; some of us have started to buy in bulk and therefore use less packaging; we also look for "recycled" packaging, stationery, greeting cards, and paper towels; and we buy beverages in glass or aluminum containers that can be recycled. The inside flap of my raisin bran cereal box told me that we could save over 500,000 trees each week if we recycled our Sunday newspapers, so I have started to do that too.

Just as the convention of a line does not solve the problem of congestion, the convention of recycling is not likely to solve the problems of waste disposal and resource depletion. The cost of recycling is not paid for by the recovery value of cans, bottles, newspapers, and especially plastics. Recycling is gaining acceptance, but its costs may require us to consider other options, such as putting the onus on manufacturers, not consumers, to limit or dispose of the waste generated.[25]

Recently I asked my wife whether she would join me in refusing to go on daylight saving time. I have never liked the sudden change. I wanted to continue my daily walks at sunset, and daylight time left the sun too high in the sky. I suggested that we go for another month on standard time. But Alice would have none of it. "I want to be in step with the rest of the country," as she put it. If Alice had only known how long it has taken for Americans to agree on what time it is—daylight saving or otherwise.

For the past 100 years we have tried to regulate time in a uniform way. Until 1883, each community determined twelve o'clock noon when the sun reached its zenith. As a consequence, when it was noon in Washington, D.C., it was 12:24 P.M. in Boston and 11:43 A.M. in Savannah.[26] The ubiquity of railroads in various parts of the country prompted a change. In 1883 the railroads adopted their own convention of operating on standard railway time and designated four time zones, which we still use—eastern, central, mountain, and Pacific. The great majority of cities in the country adopted the new standard time within six months.

It took fifty years, however, to get most of the country on daylight saving time, which "saves" daylight by making it more available in the waking hours. Daylight saving time postpones the sunrise, so to speak. Except for a short period from 1918 to 1919 when daylight saving time was federally mandated, the practice of turning the clocks ahead one hour in the spring was left to states and localities to decide for themselves whether they wished to go along. After 1966, local option was greatly curtailed by Congress, but certain states could still except themselves from daylight saving time, which Arizona did in 1968.

In Indiana, individual counties still get to choose what time it is. In Richmond, Indiana, where our son attended college, everyday life is regulated by eastern standard time all year long because that part of Indiana chooses not to go on eastern daylight time. The effect is to put Richmond on central daylight time from April through October. It really gets confusing in Vevay, Indiana, seventy miles south of Richmond, where some businesses stay on eastern standard and others go on eastern daylight. As a news reporter noted, "It is possible to keep a 10 am appointment with the optometrist and then drive to the doctor's office for a 10 am check-up."[27] Now if only Alice and I lived in Vevay, I could set my walks by my time and my wife could go on with whatever time was in favor in our part of town. Whether she and I could settle on the same dinner hour is another matter.

4. Some social practices struggle to become conventions and don't quite make it. They remain fragile because there is no overwhelming interest in coordination and each of us has a number of alternatives. Consider the case of car pooling, a practice to reduce traffic congestion and curb pollution, organized by employers and municipalities in urban corridors. Their aim is to get more drivers to share their cars with other commuters going the same way to and from work.

In some places car pooling works without any prearrangement. Commuters form a line at bus or train stops, and drivers pick up these "perfect strangers" so they can take advantage of designated lanes on freeways and at toll booths. But prearranged car pools and van pools often don't work. Commuters find it hard to coordinate pickups, share costs, or manage the disruptions when "regulars" move or change jobs. People also want to maintain flexibility in their commuting schedules, to listen to their favorite radio programs, or to smoke. Some commuters are quick to give up car pooling when gasoline is plentiful and relatively cheap, or when they buy more fuel-efficient cars.

The practice of staggered work hours to relieve rush hour congestion, as an alternative to car pooling, has also failed to take hold. Employers and their employees often have conflicting interests over who works 7:00 A.M. to 3:00 P.M., 8:00 A.M. to 4:00 P.M., and so on, or truck delivery schedules can't be changed, or children's school hours interfere, or some people don't like to drive in the dark, and so on. With such problems, even when commuters want the same outcome—less traffic congestion—there has been no obvious regularity of behavior that they can agree on or coordinate.

No doubt there will always be some people who will car-pool regardless of what others do. They want to save money, or they enjoy the company and conversation, or their employer makes it a condition of their employment. But like the pedestrians who retreat to the curb, if enough others don't car-pool, the coordination problem cannot be solved. More cars are on the highways and rush hour delays mount. With little to show for the effort, fewer commuters have been willing to car-pool. Without a satisfactory outcome, less congestion, the personal adjustments required to car-pool do not seem worth the effort. For a convention to work the benefit of coordination should exceed the cost. Car pooling declined from 33 percent in 1980 to 22 percent in 1990, a year when Americans spent two billion hours stuck in traffic jams and used three billion gallons of gasoline doing it.[28] Certain jurisdictions, however, continue to grapple with the problem, if only because the Clean Air Act amendments in 1990 mandate employers of 100 or more in polluted regions (Philadelphia, New York, Chicago, Houston, Milwaukee, Baltimore, San Diego, Los Angeles) to keep trying to put their employees in car pools or mass transit. Special lanes for car poolers on interstate highways may become the dominant strategy in those jurisdictions. It is estimated that by 2000 there will be 950 miles of carpooling lanes.[29]

5. Conventions can falter or die of natural causes. Some conventions remain fragile and may be undone by the same critical mass that

secured them. Think of a failing convention like a "run" on a bank. Again a line is formed, but a very anxious one, of depositors seeking to withdraw their funds due to rumors that the bank's assets will soon be frozen. For example, a racially integrated neighborhood may "tip" and become predominantly black, not because whites or blacks living there want it that way, but because the "run" on the neighborhood, like a "run" on the bank's deposits, undoes the fragile convention of residential integration. A white family moves out and a black family moves in. Then a white neighbor decides that the previous racial balance of the neighborhood is threatened. Not wanting to wait for the "tipping" to happen, the white neighbor promotes the tipping by selling his house. Just as there was an accidental leader stepping off the curb whom we followed and crossed with en masse to the other side, so the neighborhood may have its accidental leader who undoes the precarious convention of a racial mix in housing. The equilibrium of an integrated neighborhood becomes unsettled and changed, which is perhaps to no one's liking.[30]

Some conventions die, not because they are fragile, but because circumstances change, attitudes shift. There are any number of conventions that you and I can think of—dueling, smoke signals, town criers, underground railroads, social registers, coats of arms, barn raising, circuit riders—that have come and gone from the scene. I came across a very old and discarded convention when talking with my son, a young actor in New York. Peter told me about "cue scripts," a theater convention during the Elizabethan era in England, where each actor had a truncated script that contained only his particular part in the play to be performed. Such a precaution was to keep an actor from pirating the entire play by taking the script to another acting company. This was before copyright laws rendered the convention of cue scripts superfluous.

Recently, I read that "less than one in eight of unmarried fathers provide even token support payments" for their children.[31] I can remember in the not too distant past when there was a convention that a man married a woman who became pregnant by him. The name for it was a "shotgun wedding" because the woman's family, or more precisely her father, insisted that the man make his daughter "an honest woman." More to the point, an unmarried woman could be forced to give up her baby for adoption. Few people now think of shotguns or weddings. More and more mothers have never been married and there is little condemnation of such women or the men who fathered their children. So it is with social taboos, or the military draft, or fallout shelters, or the Sears catalog—times change and with them, so do conventions.

HABITS, FASHIONS, AND NORMS

A convention is not the same thing as a habit. A habit is a regularity of behavior but, unlike a convention, it does not require coordination with others. Habits are rule-like regularities that we impose on ourselves. Conventions are rule-like regularities that we tacitly agree to impose on each other. Smoking is a habit. Not smoking in certain public places is a convention. Standing up and sitting down may be a habit. Doing it together in order to create a wave at Dodger Stadium is a convention.

A convention is not the same thing as the imitation inherent in fashions and fads. The banquet invitation, alerting us to how others will dress, is a convention. Wearing a tuxedo to a banquet is merely following fashion.[32] Imitation is not conditional on others' conforming their behavior.[33] A young man may like the fashion of wearing his baseball cap backwards, but he does so whether or not those he works with during the day do the same. His baseball cap may be in imitation of a rap group and have nothing to do with other fashions that he sees at work. The fad among college students of "streaking" across campus wearing nothing but a large grin imitates the behavior of others, but does not depend on their joining in. The solo streak on a balmy spring evening requires no coordination.

A convention is not the same thing as a norm. A norm is a model of correct behavior and, more than likely, an end in itself. Something is simply done or not done for its own sake or to avoid disapproval. Like a habit, a norm may have no evident consequences for others.[34] With a convention, we are usually focused on the satisfactory outcome that our cooperation can produce, not the behavior itself. We participate in mass demonstrations, offer directions to a confused motorist, check our hats and coats at a restaurant, return items to a lost and found, or look after someone's luggage while she does an errand. We depend on the predictability of regularized behavior. That is what makes it acceptable. There is no external warrant for it unless it works.

As a convention becomes established, however, a norm will in all likelihood emerge to support that particular regularity of behavior. The convention of a line is enforced by those in it against anyone whose behavior is "out of line." Consequently the distinction between a norm and a convention can become blurred.[35] Fragile conventions stand a better chance when there are norms that support them. Jury duty is a fragile convention because there is no overwhelming interest in coordination and, unlike our line at the bank, each of us has a number of alternatives. There are a variety of reasons that you and I can give in order to be excused from jury duty. The same is true of elections, litter barrels, and collection plates. But such conventions become less fragile when norms develop to support them—getting us to vote, or avoid being a "litterbug," or tithing to a church. Metaconventions, which are norm-like, also reinforce our conventional conduct, such as first come first served, in the case of lines. When we have norms or metaconventions that support otherwise fragile conventions, we may be acknowledging that coordination alone is not a good enough reason to make some conventions work.

Neighborhoods, just like organizations, conceive of and promote their own conventions, whether it is a curfew imposed on young people by their parents; the maintenance of church cemeteries; the branding of cattle; the staging of a local parade; the vigilance of volunteer school crossing guards; or the less attractive convention of real estate brokers unofficially segregating neighborhoods by race. Furthermore, when you or I move to a new neighborhood, there may be an unofficial spokesperson who will tell us about the norms that support the conventions of that particular place. The phrasing is familiar, "The way we do things around here," or "A little word to the wise." What the neighborhood takes for granted has to be made explicit to a stranger. In an organization the norm-like convention might be "We all cover for each other when someone is out sick or has to leave early." In a neighborhood the message might be "No one lets their kids do" such and such, or "I can't recall anyone from these parts renting to 'them.'" Norms in support of local conventions instruct strangers and convey to children what is expected of them and what they should avoid.

ROBUST CONVENTIONS AND LAWS

A convention becomes robust when almost everyone prefers the same outcome and no one seriously entertains alternatives to it anymore.[36] A dance step is a robust convention because otherwise partners would be helplessly stumbling over each other if each chose to perform a different step at the same time. Nodding your head to indicate "yes" and shaking your head to indicate "no" are robust conventions for the simple reason that we want to be understood.

Many robust conventions work simply because no one has any reason to change them, although surely there are alternatives to the fox trot, the parking lot, Labor Day, the typewriter keyboard, and driving on the right side of the road. One might conclude that such conventions are robust because their origins were purely arbitrary, that no one really cared which side of the road they drove on as long as everyone did the same thing. After all, the convention of driving on the right side of the road in the United States is just the opposite in England where people drive on the left side. No doubt such conventions are robust because they carry their own penalty. If we don't respect the "rules of the road," we are likely to be killed or seriously injured. No one needs to tell us that driving on the wrong side of the road is not in our best interest.

The convention of driving on the right side of the road in the United States became robust because it also made sense from the outset. It was not an arbitrary choice. The primary reason for the right-side convention in the United States was that freight wagons and prairie schooners had no front seat, and drivers controlled their horse or oxen teams while sitting on the left rear animal and using a whip in the right hand. When two such vehicles approached each other from opposite directions on a narrow road, the drivers could look left and have a decent view of the gap between the passing wagon's wheel hubs. British freight wagons, on the other hand, had a driver's seat in front on the right side, permitting them to use their whip without getting it entangled in the cargo. Consequently, driving on the left side of the road made sense to ascertain clearance with wagons coming from the opposite direction and passing by on the right.[37]

Conventions often become robust when we "institutionalize" them, so to speak. Institutionalizing a convention means that it is promoted by organizations that are created for that very purpose—emergency relief by the Red Cross, orphanages under church auspices, day-care centers, or insurance companies. More often conventions become robust when they are enacted into law, after which we cease to think of them as conventions at all—whether it is the "rules of the road," or rationing, or affirmative action. But enacting conventions into law does far more than just secure a social practice. Our standard of judgment shifts from everyday coordination to what is right or wrong. A convention wins our assent because it produces a useful outcome. A law commands our obedience whether we ever recognize its utility. Instead of a game involving many persons in the throes of cooperation or defection, our relation to law becomes a simpler two-party game, where rewards or penalties are more certain.

We are law-abiding, not just because we fear the consequences if we break the law. We are law-abiding, as we are convention-abiding, because we fear the disorder that otherwise will occur if we do not cooperate. In jurisprudence, "customary law" presupposes "a complex collaborative effort between state and citizens" and rests its legitimacy in practices that have evolved from conventions into law or in laws that rely more on a working consensus than coercion.[38] To coerce an unwilling majority is usually beyond the will or capacity of democratic government. What representative government often seeks to do by enacting laws—using the influence of regulations and fines—is to reassure the majority of us that no one will take advantage of our voluntary cooperation.

When conventions become law, enforcement shifts to government. Many of us don't have the time or inclination to police others' behavior. We often prefer that government do it for us. For example, it is easier for me to point to a public sign that prohibits parking, or smoking, than to instruct someone about his inappropriate conduct. Even better, let the police officer or the health inspector do it for me. With strangers, sometimes we prefer a buffer, an envoy—someone cut out for such things.

Laws also help to clarify what specific regularities of behavior we expect of each other. Most conventions depend on tacit agreements among strangers that are rarely discussed and debated, and that is why they remain so invisible to us in everyday life. Laws, on the other hand, are shaped by debate and, in our system of government, interpreted by written regulations of the executive branch and written opinions of the judicial branch. Legal clarification is especially important when a choice has to be made between two competing conventions, such as segregation versus integration in race relations, or rationing gas versus asking for voluntary conservation, or voluntary versus compulsory prayer in public schools. Every convention has its partisans. Some people want government to establish their practices as preeminent. Others resist government and seek to curb its influence.

Finally, there are laws and regulations that we require not for the purpose of anointing certain conventions, but to coordinate activities among strangers that few of us have an interest in doing ourselves: regulating hunting and fishing on public lands; operating lighthouses; maintaining a weather service, an infectious disease center, jury lists, or fingerprint files; issuing passports; collecting tariffs; circulating currency; or conducting a decennial census, among others. In such cases, we bear the costs of government and put up with its intrusions.

Although our frame of mind may be very different in the presence of government coercion as opposed to the everyday coordination of social conventions, laws lie along the same continuum as conventions. Both seek to regulate behavior using precedents that provide a measure of stability and predictability. Oliver Wendell Holmes wrote: "The life of the law has not been logic: it has been experience."[39] For Holmes the common law, like a convention, survives in all its bewildering manifestations, long after most people can recall its origins and rationale.

Chapter Two

HOW FOOTPATHS GET STARTED

The Origins of Conventions

In chapter one I used the analogy of a well-worn path to explain why conventions are easy to follow. We don't have to clear a way; we assume the path has some purpose; and well-worn paths, more often than not, get us where we want to go. But what accounts for a particular path? Why is the path here and not someplace else? How conventions originate and how they become well-worn paths are matters of history, observation, and, admittedly, considerable speculation.

I should say at the outset that we don't know much about the specific origins of many conventions, but we should understand why that is the case and, at least, identify the principal ways in which any convention originates. If we are to establish new conventions to address problems that markets and governments have no answer for, we need to know how those footpaths get started.

Just as we trust the directions of paths that we follow, we take part in conventions without a thought to their origins. I think of conventions as resembling "precedents" in British and American common law, which have survived although the original reasons for them have been forgotten.[1] Like children in their grandmother's attic, we examine artifacts of another person's life. These artifacts still have obvious purpose, but we have no way of knowing how a particular object came into our grandmother's possession or why it was preserved. Like children we delight in what we have found, but our play is centered on the moment; we know little of the history that explains the treasures in the attic.

Even if we wanted to know, it would be difficult to determine the specific circumstances that gave rise to a new form of cooperation that we now think of as a convention. The origins of any phenomenon are often elusive, as physicists, biologists, archaeologists, and historians well know. Perhaps some readers can locate the origins of specific conventions that have eluded me. There is no rich and authoritative compilation to turn to as a reference. We do much better with the etymology of words whose footprints are left in actual writings, whereas conventions arise with little or no comment. Conventions may be as common as everyday language, but their introduction is rarely chronicled. And if there are social histories that do account for them, they have yet to be gathered in one place.

Many conventions are demonstrably sensible. Others have little intrinsic merit except within the social context of the culture from which they emerged. Unless we know something about the particular social world in which conventions originate, we often can't understand why they originated. When guests come to your house and tell you how they cope with a problem you are having, for example, getting everyone to come to dinner on time, their suggestion may not be plausible for your family because of how you have raised your children. You might say to them, "Oh, that would never work here." Granted their suggestion makes sense for their household, but not for yours.

It would be stretching reason to say that a line is the only self-evident solution to a coordination problem of congestion. The first line, assuming it involved a number of people, probably was fraught with difficulties. Individual interests very likely did not coincide, just as your pressing appointment or my sick child waiting in the car makes us wish that some arrangement other than a line would favor our respective interests. Perhaps the convention of a line makes sense only in those societies where time is valued and meant to be efficiently used. Who knows the story of the first line? Did it arise spontaneously when a group of strangers sorted themselves out at a bakery shop, a bus stop, or the entrance of a theater? Or was it organized by the baker, the bus driver, or the ticket taker with the agreement of those seeking to be served? Or was some decree issued by a sovereign, church prelate, or other important person that, henceforth, a line will be formed by those subject to the very important person if they know what's good for them?

No doubt the first footprints of almost every convention exist somewhere. But where do we look for them? We have never assembled a search party to do that. The reports that come in are isolated sightings. As far as the origins of conventions are concerned, there is a need to coordinate the search so more footprints can be found.[2]

Whether or not there is a remedy for our ignorance, there is another reason why scant attention has been paid to the origins of conventions. It is more philosophical than empirical. Some commentators think the origin of a convention is of no consequence since a convention by definition becomes significant only when enough others subscribe to the same practice. In the beginning there is only an isolated event of successful coordination among strangers; there is no convention.

Think of two drivers who reach an intersection at the same time. One is heading west, the other north. Who gives way? We know from the convention of yielding the right of way that the driver heading north yields to the driver heading west. But imagine the first time such a coordination problem arose. What happened? We cannot account for what the two drivers did at the very first intersection. But Robert Sugden, who is one of the few who has looked at the question of origins, argues that if a preference for yielding to the right was more prevalent than yielding to the left, the initial tendency set in motion a process that magnified itself into the "right-of-way" convention. Sugden concludes that many conventions simply evolve out of anarchic situations. "[L]ike seedlings in a crowded plot of ground: whichever is the first to show vigorous growth can stifle the others."[3]

David Lewis's definition of conventions as "regularities of behavior, sustained by an interest in coordination and an expectation that others will do their part" does not address the question of origins. For Lewis, an expectation that others will do their part can exist only if there is evidence that certain behavior has already been regularized, giving rise to the expectation in the first place.[4]

The disassociation of conventions from their origins may make what histories they have seem unimportant. In chapter one I used the example of driving on the right or left, a convention not arbitrarily chosen, but dictated by the circumstance of where the driver sat on an animal or wagon while navigating a narrow road with oncoming vehicles. But once we moved on to other means of transportation, the original reasons for the right/left convention were no longer of any significance.

And it is true that some conventions become firmly established only when nobody can remember how they started. I also used the example of "organization conventions" in chapter one—increasing the productivity level, or promoting more minority members to executive positions, or consulting across departments before a major decision is made—where hard-won changes were secured only when few could recall or even know how tenuous the practices once had been. If those in an organization think about it at all, they can only guess at what alternatives were available. They don't know who prescribed the practice that survived to become a convention in their organization, or whether the practice arose by agreement or more or less spontaneously in response to an incident now long forgotten. Whatever its origins, the path is now well worn and enough others in the organization have made it so. The convention may eventually falter, but there will be a considerable hiatus until people change the way they do things in the organization. It may take time to clear a new path and have others follow it.[5]

A convention confirms the proposition that nothing succeeds like success even if its history should make us reconsider its present worth when better alternatives have been rejected. This is certainly the case of the QWERTY keyboard, which remains the standard on typewriters and computers. The "QWERTY" keyboard originated with Christopher Sholes, the inventor of the typewriter. In 1867, Sholes used the QWERTY arrangement of keys to reduce typing speed so the keys would not jam on the first primitive machines of his invention. If the keys had been alphabetically arranged, apparently the keys would have jammed. When the "DVORAK" keyboard was later introduced to improve typing speed, it never caught on despite the advantage of typing speed. The QWERTY keyboard, sensible in its origin, prevailed despite invention of a more sensible keyboard that sought to replace it. No doubt there is an arbitrariness about this outcome. Like our line at the bank, a convention is not necessarily the best solution, but having settled on it, those who are already heavily invested in its success are not likely to change. When enough others coordinate their behavior one way, it usually makes little sense for you and me to try to coordinate our behavior differently.[6] Once a convention becomes entrenched, it is hard to dislodge.

Without being able to know much about how specific conventions originated, it is still worth examining the principal ways in which any convention originates. Those who want to establish new conventions should know about the conditions for how that happens. If residents of a neighborhood want safe streets or a community wants a fair allocation of scarce water or seeks to avoid an epidemic of a communicable disease, then it helps to know how so many individual interests can be coordinated.

How does large-scale cooperation get organized? There are three ways which I think encompass most of the possibilities of how conventions originate: unplanned coordination; coordination by agreement; and coordination by central authority.

UNPLANNED COORDINATION

Montaigne wrote: "Whatever position you set men in, they pile up and arrange themselves by moving and crowding together, just as ill-matched objects, put in a bag without order, find of themselves a way to unite and fall into place together, often better than they could have been arranged by art."[7] Montaigne understood that the spontaneous coordination of behavior is as likely to succeed, assuming the circumstances persist that warrant its origination, as the coordination arising from voluntary agreements or enforced by some central authority.

Think of how pedestrians on a crowded sidewalk will sort themselves out. Hundreds, thousands of us can navigate our way, through what might seem an anarchic situation, maintaining a steady pace and usually without incident. It is unusual that any two strangers will even touch, much less run into each other. As pedestrians, we have no name for this everyday example of coordination, but like Montaigne's "ill-matched objects" put in a bag without order, we sort ourselves out spontaneously. Furthermore, the pedestrian journey is never the same from day to day. There are different strangers, different conditions, and yet we give little thought to our moment-to-moment coordination that makes the passage seem routine rather than unique.[8]

Unplanned coordination is sometimes rationalized as the work of an "invisible hand," suggesting that some organizing force is at work that we acknowledge, but cannot ultimately know. In fact, the "invisible hand," as originally conceived, was not otherworldly at all but simply "the result of human actions . . . not the execution of any human design."[9] Sometimes the path from point A to point B is seen as purposeful only in retrospect. A well-worn path is rarely the result of some conscious design. The path became well-worn because it served the interests of those who used it. No one gave any thought to how using the path made it easier for others who followed. Frederick von Hayek made the positive case for unplanned coordination in the social realm:

> It is because it was not dependent on [central] organization but grew up as a spontaneous order, that the structure of modern society has attained that degree of complexity which it possesses and which far exceeds any that could have been achieved by deliberate organization. . . . To maintain that we must deliberately plan modern society because it has become so complex is therefore paradoxical and the result of a complete misunderstanding of these circumstances.[10]

Existing conventions, however, may help to account for some instances of what appears to be spontaneous coordination. In February 1993, thousands of strangers organized their own exit from the Twin Towers of New York City's World Trade Center, when the on-site police command center, which was set up to coordinate evacuation, was knocked out by a terrorist blast. What happened that day? Had so many strangers already rehearsed such an emergency exit in their minds? The testimony of those interviewed indicates that it was simply a case of enough people looking out for each other and finding ways to cooperate to make the exit relatively efficient. In the absence of a coordinated effort by on-site police to evacuate everyone, there were "emergency" routines or conventions that the buildings' tenants were able to recall from schooldays, theater going, and airplane trips. In many seemingly anarchic situations, we bring some memory of prior conduct, some precedents, some conventions and supporting norms, that help us coordinate our behavior. The reasons for the successful evacuation of the Twin Towers probably did not originate in New York's World Trade Center, but somewhere else.

Just as there may be existing conventions that promote spontaneous coordination, there also may be the disproportionate influence of those who make early choices of how to behave in a particular situation that shapes the ultimate outcome. Random individual actions do not all fall into place simultaneously. Think of the influence of the first person who panics in an emergency evacuation, or the first pedestrian off the curb whom we follow and stop traffic, or the first opportunist who, seeing a broken store window, starts the looting of a row of stores.

I have observed that those who arrive early to a meeting room, without any intention whatsoever, influence the seating choices of those who come later. If the early arrivals set a boundary of a few rows back from the front, almost everyone will find a place somewhere behind them. If early arrivals sit near the back to watch others arrive, a curiosity that many of us enjoy while waiting for a meeting to get underway, then later arrivals may set the boundary, but again not too distant from where the early arrivals have established a base camp.[11]

For an individual's early behavior to be influential to others, it must be visible. The first cluster of applauding opera fans who get to their feet are more likely to trigger a standing ovation thoughout the house if they are seated in the orchestra than in the balcony. When the balcony fans start a standing ovation, they have to be vocal enough so people will turn to see them and follow their lead by standing too. If we don't look closely or in the right place in the opera house, we will not be able to account for how the standing ovation started. And we may forget that our own early conduct in an auditorium or on a street corner influences an ordering that we witness but find difficult to account for.[12]

It is not immediately apparent what specific conventions may arise from instances of unplanned coordination. It doesn't hurt, however, to try to figure out what social conditions are more favorable than others for producing new forms of cooperation. For example, when I was president of a small college, the lack of faculty interaction across departments troubled me. Faculty members had lost touch with one another even in that small place. How could I find a way to create new intersections where they would meet without feeling that some "administrator" was being manipulative? (Faculty members resist such conscious designs on their time or inclinations.) So I decided to put a coffeepot and the departmental mail in one spot, where faculty would be forced to interact despite themselves. I hoped that the new coffee/mail intersection would cause a spontaneous occasion for conversations; where projects across departments might hatch; where better acquaintance might lead to new academic practices that might be shared. The new intersection for daily exchange was not unplanned. It was pure calculation on my part. But any new conventions that might emerge, discrete or otherwise, would be of their making, not mine.

Unplanned coordination is a difficult concept to grasp. We cannot recall a voluntary agreement among ourselves that shapes or coerces our social conduct. We cannot attribute outcomes to some central authority issuing directives or enforcing a body of laws. Often we don't even have a name for the evidence of our everyday cooperation. When examining conventions, we naturally want to name them, pin them down, like a butterfly to its mounting board. A coordination solution, however, such as enough pedestrians stepping off a curb to stop traffic, may have no name. Regularities of behavior often help to solve a coordination problem whether or not they eventually acquire a name. Without deliberation or instruction, people somehow manage to cooperate.

Since I have already used several examples of spontaneous coordination among pedestrians, I want to extend that discussion but connect the unplanned coordination of street life to the issue of personal safety, which troubles so many of us. The shrewd observations of Jane Jacobs and William Whyte tell how the unplanned coordination of a myriad of daily activities can promote safe streets, even though those engaged in their routines rarely consult or agree on making that happen. In the 1950s, Jane Jacobs surveyed neighborhood street life primarily from her New York City home in Greenwich Village and produced a report of her observations in *The Death and Life of Great American Cities*. My wife and I lived for six years, in the late sixties and early seventies, only a block away from Jacobs's building on Hudson Street, and we came to appreciate how well she described what she called the "intricate ballet" of our neighborhood's street life.

For Jacobs, almost every street activity had significance and together they contributed to the overall safety of the street. Eyes and ears were everywhere. There were the daily routines of residents putting out garbage, children going to school, small stores opening, people going to work, housewives chatting here and there, the stolid storeowner keeping an eye on the street, people taking lunch at the local luncheonettes, blue-collar workers dropping into the bars on their day off, baby carriages being wheeled about, children's street games, teenagers hanging out, and delicatessens, pizza parlors, and drugstores staying open into the evening.

Only late at night did the streets become less predictable. But even in the wee hours, the eyes and ears of the street from bedrooms in brownstones, no more than five stories tall, responded to incidents and alerted the police, or people materialized at the street level to settle the matter. Jacobs's "intricate ballet" obviously did not involve just neighbors and friends. "The strangers on Hudson Street" also "helped to keep the peace of the street." And for Jacobs it did not matter that from day to day they were different strangers; they were nonetheless "allies."[13]

The West Village of Jane Jacobs's era was not a tight-knit community and was far from homogeneous. That did not matter. What mattered was the unplanned coordination that Jacobs observed which arose from the seemingly unrelated, yet overlapping, activities of residents and strangers. Jacobs's daily street dance was unchoreographed but nonetheless contributed to the overall safety of the neighborhood. Jacobs saw that "public peace—the sidewalk and street peace" was not maintained by the police, but "by an intricate almost unconscious network of voluntary controls and standards among the people themselves, and enforced by the people themselves."[14]

Twenty years later William H. Whyte stationed himself on the city's commercial streets where neighborhoods negotiated daily life with an abundance of strangers and in sections of Manhattan with little residential character where workplaces spilled onto the streets and behavior was monitored. Like Jacobs, Whyte observed many random street activities that nonetheless had some bearing on keeping the peace. For example, he observed the practice of "schmoozing" engaged in by office employees who went outside to fraternize and watch passersby. There were the small storeowners who stood in their doorways surveying the street scene. Often there was an unofficial "mayor" of a particular part of a block who knew his turf, was sought after by others for daily bulletins of what was going on, and who even felt accountable to no one in particular for what, in fact, did go on. He might be a building guard, newsstand operator, or food vendor at the curb. These "eyes" on the street—food vendors, storeowners, schmoozers, and the police on foot patrol—could easily spot potential trouble makers or street criminals, like "the guy who is moving around a lot but is not going anywhere. He keeps coming back, circling, like the predator he is."[15]

The unplanned coordination that Jacobs observed from her window thirty-five years ago and the street traffic of strangers that Whyte studied fifteen years ago have all but disappeared in some urban neighborhoods. In chapter five I take up the problem of our mean streets and explore the current possibilities of using new conventions to take them back.

COORDINATION BY AGREEMENT

There is little mystery about some well-worn paths. They are the shortest distance between two points or they follow a creek bed or go through a mountain pass. Conventions that originate by voluntary agreement are similarly simple and direct. They are not ideal constructions of how to solve a problem, but rather the inventions of enough like-minded individuals who know they need each other to solve the problem. For example, when one or more of us seeks out others like ourselves who are stricken by uncertainty or trying to cope with a stressful situation, a self-help group is in the making. But without some agreement as to what our group is for and how it should function, there is little chance that we will make it work. We may not know the particular circumstances that produced the very first self-help group, and that story may be worth telling, but we don't need to know about it to understand how to get self-help groups started.

Coordination by agreement also explains how dance steps originate, or land trusts, or designated drivers, or boycotts, or the practice of patronage, or the adopt-a-highway convention. In these instances coordination of behavior cannot arise spontaneously. Each person's contribution needs to be specified so that each person can reasonably expect others to do their part. You don't want to hand over your car keys to me as our group's designated driver unless you can be assured that I will refrain from drinking. Someone else doesn't want to work for a political candidate unless he or she can reasonably expect to be favored with a job or a government contract. Members of an organization have no desire to "adopt" one mile of the highway outside of town if other organizations in the community don't agree to do the same and cover enough roadside to keep the entire area relatively free of trash. In some cases, tacit agreement can produce coordination as effectively as explicit agreement. Certainly this would be true of the convention of political patronage. Another example would be the unilateral reduction in arms undertaken by President Bush in the late 1980s to which the USSR reciprocated, even though there was no treaty that compelled such a reduction. President Kennedy did much the same thing in 1963 when he unilaterally ended nuclear tests in the atmosphere. Nikita Khrushchev reciprocated and a treaty was subsequently signed.[16]

"Community conventions," in particular, often arise from the same process of deliberation and consent out of which communities come to be governed by the establishment of charters and the enactment of laws. There is nothing arbitrary or accidental about social compacts, and once made they may have a coercive authority much as any government would. Those who are party to them monitor and regulate each other's conduct. Eventually conventions that originate from a community-wide agreement may be codified into law. This is the case of acequia associations in New Mexico that have allocated scarce water resources and governed themselves for over 300 years but which now are, in turn, governed by over seventy-five state statutes and, since the 1960s, have become political subdivisions of the state. The story of acequias is worth looking into as an example of how people coordinate their own solutions to the complex problems that they share.

Water, like personal safety, is an obvious priority in everyday life. Neither is guaranteed and each requires some effort to secure and maintain. Where water is concerned there has always been a great deal of uncertainty. Such anxiety naturally promotes conventions to deal with the problem whether it is "water witching," using a divining rod to discover where to dig a well, or weather prediction, using data to divine what kind of day it will be tomorrow, or rain-making dances to induce ancestors to return with clouds.[17] The acequia is a water resource convention that has been notably successful.

Acequias are irrigation ditches. They are also associations of local landowners (*parciantes*) who maintain and govern the use of the ditches. Most of the *parciantes* depend on the irrigation ditches for their subsistence farming. Irrigation ditches are not nature-given, but are man-made. One *parciante* explained it this way: "Take away the man and you take away the ditch. Take away the ditch and you take away the water. Take away the water and you take away the man. You leave only the sound of the river."[18]

The acequia takes what water nature has to offer from one season or one year to the next, and the acequia association rations that water in some fair division to those who use it for cultivation. Ditch management requires allotting the amount of time that such water is available for irrigation, the size of the flow, its distance, and the maintenance of the entire ditch to reduce water loss and facilitate flow. In the New Mexico valley where we lived for a while, there are over fifty ditch associations. About 70 percent of the ditch flow comes from snow melt off the surrounding mountains. The rest comes from rainfall. Each acequia has its own headwaters and mother ditch. The secondary ditches depend on gravity to deliver this surface water by periodic flooding of the fields that need irrigation. Each *parciante* gets his portion of water by raising the wooden gate on his property which abuts the ditch. When his allotted time is up, he closes the gate, effectively blocking off any more water.

The origins of acequias go back, at least, to irrigation techniques brought westward with the Arab conquests of the Iberian Peninsula in the eighth century. The acequia convention is based on voluntary agreements that there be defined physical boundaries of each acequia; common-sense rules that tell each *parciante* how much water he is entitled to and what labor he must contribute to get the water; and mechanisms that facilitate the monitoring of each *parciante*'s use of the ditch and the conflicts that arise among them.[19] According to one scholar, local control was prevalent in medieval Valencia, but in other parts of Spain, a municipality, not the irrigators themselves, would control the distribution of water.[20] Later the self-governing acequia convention moved west again, this time to those lands settled by the Spanish in the New World. The history of irrigation in New Mexico combines both Pueblo Indian and Spanish traditions, but the acequia convention is primarily identified with the early Spanish settlers. When there were new settlements and the need to exploit existing water resources and to coordinate their use, the acequia convention arose among those *parciantes* who were often not neighbors or friends, but linked only by an irrigation system that they shared. By 1700 there were 62 acequias; by 1800 there were 100 more. In 1851, when New Mexico achieved territorial status, new laws governing water use faithfully reflected Spanish and Pueblo Indian customs. In fact, it would be thirty years before a case reflecting a local water dispute was brought to the territorial supreme court. Such was the strength of the established acequia convention.[21]

If the origins of acequias are only dimly perceived, the agreement that has sustained the convention is acknowledged daily through local practice: (1) a water user receives water in proportion to the amount of land requiring irrigation; (2) each water user is responsible for helping to maintain the entire ditch system; and (3) water users themselves try to govern the system without outside intervention. It is the reciprocity between the water user and the ditch system, and the enforcement of mutual expectations through a *mayordomo* and three *parciantes* (called commissioners), who rule on various matters, that sustains the common agreement.

The convention of acequias does not work without a "mayordomo." The mayordomo organizes and leads the annual spring cleaning of the ditch. This is usually a week-long project to clean out the natural debris of winter and other rubbish. Each *parciante* is expected to contribute labor or pay for those who do it for him. In addition, there is a levy on each *parciente* to pay the mayordomo's salary and other administrative expenses. The entire length of the ditch is cleaned at one time, avoiding the need to monitor each *parciante*'s work on his section of the ditch. The place and time are joined for everyone, and the job gets done.

The mayordomo also has to see to it that there is a rough equality of access to the water. Some *parciantes* live at the bottom of the ditch, others near the top. Some years there is abundant water, but when there is a drought, water diversion from the ditch is a more delicate matter. Arthur Mondragon, who helped care for the property and orchard that we leased, told me that you always take your share of water when the mayordomo says it is your turn, even though it may be from 3:00 A.M. to 5:00 A.M. (to be "on hours") or during a period when you might think you don't need any more water. "You can't be sure," said Arthur, "when your turn will come next." Arthur knew that water availability was never certain, and that those who do not use water regularly may not get it regularly. *Parciantes* who do not use water can lose their right to use the water at a later time. Ditches are delivery systems, not ownership systems. The acequia convention orders the common sense of neighbors much like a ditch channels the flow of water. For three centuries, such coordination by local agreement has solved the paramount problem of life on the high desert: how to share a precious and limited resource with your neighbors.[22]

COORDINATION BY CENTRAL AUTHORITY

Sometimes the exercise of central authority is a necessary precondition for the emergence of a particular convention. This is true when government is called upon to choose between conventions, as was the case in choosing between integration rather than segregation of public facilities, or when government must change conventions in an orderly manner, as was the case in Sweden, when motorists, in the 1960s, switched from driving on the left to driving on the right. Central authority is also the author or sponsor that originates practices that eventually become convention-like.

Coordination by central authority might at first glance seem contrary to the notion that conventions should be forms of cooperation that arise spontaneously or by voluntary agreement. But in many instances coordination has little chance of working unless central authority is involved. It need not be the authority of government, although it usually is. We also accept the authority of airline personnel in the emergency evacuation of airplanes; we credit railroads for the original standardization of time across the continental United States; and we do not question the authority of restaurants to divide smokers from nonsmokers.

One indispensable role of central authority is preventing the spread of communicable diseases. The public health measures of quarantine and immunization have long required the coercion of government to prescribe and coordinate certain kinds of private behavior for the sake of the public interest. Whether we think of quarantine and immunization as conventions or laws, they presuppose "a complex collaborative effort" between state and citizens, to use Lon Fuller's phrase.[23]

Communicable disease poses three threats to public health that require official intervention. The first threat is posed by those who are unaware that they are carriers of a communicable disease and thus unable to regulate their conduct for the benefit of others even if they were disposed to do so. The second threat is posed by those who know they are carriers of a communicable disease but prefer not to be restrained from pursuing a normal life. They will not restrict their public activities or voluntarily confine themselves. The third threat is posed by those who do not have a communicable disease but do not have the good sense to immunize themselves and so run the risk of contracting a disease; they enlarge the risk that they and others like themselves will spread the disease unnecessarily. Such persons think that if enough others get immunized, they themselves will be protected. This "herd immunity" excuse, as public health authorities call it, is a wager that if 80 to 90 percent of the population is resistant to disease because of vaccination, then the disease is sufficiently contained and will not seriously threaten the 10 to 20 percent who are not so protected. The

wager is based on the expectation that enough others will exercise better sense than those who don't want to be bothered.[24]

It is hard to imagine that these three public health threats could
ever be adequately contained by some unplanned coordination of private behavior or by voluntary agreement, since the potential and actual bearers of communicable disease are so invisible to us in the
interactions of social and commercial life. We can often coordinate a
response among ourselves to the conspicuous and visible problems that
we encounter daily without the intervention of government. But when
we don't even know that there is a problem until it is too late, as is the
case of a communicable disease which can quickly produce an epidemic, then the impulse for coordination must come from those who make
their living at being more alert to such threats than we are. That is one
reason why we entrust weather prediction to the National Weather
Service, or the weighing of truck vehicles over public bridges and roads
to a highway patrol, or the detection of counterfeit currency to the
Treasury Department.

The convention of quarantine once was the primary public health
measure available to contain outbreaks of infectious disease. The quarantine convention arose to help communities deal with their fear of
strangers who might be carriers of an invisible but potentially fatal disease. Disease often is introduced into a community by those coming
from somewhere else, and the suspicion of infected strangers posing
such a threat made quarantine a logical choice as a means of self-de-
fense. The frontier of any state has always been a place where quarantine has been employed. The other obvious source of disease was any
domestic residence or public facility where it was discovered. At such
places, quarantine was imposed by some central authority to confine
those identified as already ill or dying.[25]

In America, it wasn't until after the Civil War that local and state
boards of health were firmly established and the federal government
exercised quarantine jurisdiction over ships suspected of being the carriers of contagious disease.[26] In this century, with the great advances in
bacteriology and the subsequent development of the science of im-
munology, the role of government was greatly enlarged although it became less overtly coercive. Through a growing public health network,

governments sought to educate members of the public about the importance of immunization as a convention of first resort to protect both individual health and the health of the public.

Diphtheria antitoxin was introduced in the 1890s. Some success followed in the battles against typhoid, tetanus, and syphilis. As the discovery of new and effective vaccines accelerated, immunization became the most important public health measure in saving children's lives since the purification of public water.[27]

Nonetheless, in the United States much of the regulation of health care, left in the hands of state and local officials, did not produce accurate record-keeping systems or extensive education campaigns. By 1993 less than half of America's children between two months and two years of age were properly vaccinated, according to the Centers for Disease Control and Prevention. Ninety-five percent of children, however, entering school at the age of five, had the required shots because local laws and school regulations deny them entrance unless they are properly vaccinated.[28]

Although Congress had required the Department of Health and Human Services to develop a national plan to immunize children, it was not until 1993 that the Clinton administration sought to enlarge government's role. Many argued at the time that the cost of vaccines was preventing children from getting properly immunized. Many others argued that cost was not the issue, but the problems encountered in extending the reach of vaccinations through the private and public health care systems. A total of 168,000 Americans became ill during the 1980s with diseases for which there are effective vaccines.[29] Parents themselves were blamed for not taking advantage of free vaccine programs that would protect their children. A 1993 Gallup poll reported that 47 percent of the parents polled were unaware that polio is a contagious disease.[30] Even the cost of vaccines was not seen as prohibitive. "If they can pay for cable TV, they can pay for their children's immunization."[31]

Still, the Clinton administration preferred to fight its battle over finding the money to pay for comprehensive vaccinations throughout the country and secured a compromise program that covered children who were not the beneficiaries of health insurance or not enrolled in

Medicaid. The Clinton compromise, however, did authorize an annual expenditure of $200 million for public health outreach efforts that would educate parents to their responsibilities. A subsequent report of the General Accounting Office contended that educating parents to follow vaccination schedules and asking medical personnel to check immunization histories more carefully would be far more effective than dispensing free vaccine.[32]

Although immunization has long overshadowed quarantine as a preferred public health measure to combat contagious diseases, quarantine is still a conventional measure available to governments when confronted by outbreaks of tuberculosis, smallpox, scarlet fever, leprosy, cholera, bubonic plague, or venereal disease.[33]

In the case of sexually transmitted diseases, quarantine measures have had public support, certainly for prostitutes, who were periodically detained. An exception, however, was the much publicized, nascent effort in the mid-eighties to quarantine those carrying the HIV virus, which can develop into AIDS. Even the closing of bathhouses in San Francisco failed, as did the crackdown of sex clubs in New York City. A century ago all constitutionally guaranteed rights were to give way in the case of threats to the public health. Given the enormous advances in civil liberties, that doctrine was no longer acceptable.[34] The legitimate assertion of rights has made it more difficult to coordinate effective public health measures to fight AIDS. Furthermore, the particular populations primarily afflicted by AIDS, drug users and homosexual men, made the great majority of Americans less concerned about any health risk to themselves, which greatly mitigated any political pressure to confine those carrying the disease. The public came to understand that it was not so much sex itself that carried the disease from one person to another, but promiscuous behavior, having a large number of sexual partners, that put oneself and others at risk.[35]

Consequently, public health officials revised their strategies to combat AIDS in order to gain the support of the gay community through education campaigns and counseling, rather than making the problem an issue of civil liberties or promiscuous behavior in general. Public health conventions other than quarantine were proposed to combat the spread of AIDS. "Contact tracing" involves warning the sex partners of those identified as HIV-infected. Such a measure, usually voluntary, not mandatory, is used in venereal disease control. Even this convention was resisted by some on civil liberties grounds because contact tracing evolved from an earlier doctrine that legally prescribed a "duty to warn" others if you were the carrier of an infectious disease or a doctor whose patient was infected.[36]

The public health convention getting the most attention has been the campaign to educate young people and adults to practice "safe sex" by using condoms. When the convention of quarantine is out of the question and immunization is not yet available, the practice of "safe sex"—a discrete convention of the most private kind—seeks to promote cooperation among strangers—at least those with more than one sex partner. As one gay man in Manhattan told a reporter, "The health message is not stop having sex, but express yourself in a way that would keep you safe."[37]

The establishment of "needle exchanges" is another new convention to combat AIDS undertaken by private agencies with or without the sanction of public health departments. Needle exchanges replace the contaminated needles of drug addicts with clean needles. Volunteers also try to educate addicts about the health dangers of sharing needles with other addicts. In New York City, for example, there are an estimated 200,000 intravenous drug users, half of whom are believed to be infected with HIV.[38]

Some public health analysts think that the war on AIDS should be concentrated in specific neighborhoods of New York City, San Francisco, Los Angeles, Houston, Miami, and Newark, where drug use and paid sex are rampant. The premise of such a strategy is that the same street culture that threatens the public safety of such neighborhoods may also be threatening the public health. Whatever is done, the public health conventions that originate with government are not likely to be coercive. The new paths that officials will establish will probably try to accommodate the American penchant for freedom even if it is "the freedom to be a damned fool."[39]

Conventions get started either by unplanned coordination, by agreement, or by central authority. To determine which of these points of departure is most promising depends on where we want to go—that is, what regularity of behavior do we want others to adopt and what is the best way to gain their cooperation?

Chapter Three

"IT'S A FREE COUNTRY"

The Obstacles to Developing Conventions

The origins of specific conventions are elusive, even though general categories explaining their emergence can be contrived. The obstacles to the development of conventions are much easier to account for. The reason we have fragile and robust conventions is that some forms of co-ordination work better than others. Some regularities of behavior drive out any competing alternatives, while others do not. There is no prede-termined path, and not all of them become well-worn. If we intend to use new conventions, as well as market incentives or government coer-cion to address public problems, then we should know what obstacles may arise to thwart our intentions.

Those who rely on game theory as an analytical framework for ex-amining conventions assume that conventions solve coordination problems without much fuss because our individual interests coincide.[1] The assumption is warranted if you want to explain why robust con-ventions work so well. It is a mistake, however, to think that because such conventions work well, getting them to work well in the first place is easy. Some practices do seem relatively easy to coordinate—which side of the road to drive on, which direction, right or left, to yield to at an intersection. But these are hardly representative of our repertoire of conventions. It is not the nature of the solution, but the alternatives we have, that determine how difficult or easy it is to secure our cooperation.

For coordination to work it usually requires people agreeing to make use of a coordination solution—not just deciding how it will work. When you want to buy antiques, you may prefer some other convention than an auction so you can deal with a seller who knows less about the value of his goods than those who would compete with you to buy them at an auction. The lost and found is a simple way of coordinating the loser and finder of a particular item, but it may trouble the finder to use it if she would just as soon keep my lost briefcase as return it. When my wife and I try out a new dance step, we naturally want to coordinate our movements across the dance floor, otherwise we are likely to step on each other's toes, or even fall down. But working out the new dance step is not the only mutual accommodation we have to make. Both of us have to want to dance and neither of us has ever taken that for granted. Our dancing, like our marriage, takes a great deal more than just coordination. We have to want to work at it.

The problem of coordination, however, between dance couples or marriage partners doesn't begin to approximate the complications of getting a large number of strangers to try out a new dance step, so to speak, and work at it together. Let me introduce some of the obstacles with the following story. . . .

Imagine a large town or small city where you and I live which has an overwhelming litter problem. The problem is so bad that we have acquired the unofficial name of "Litterville." For years, as residents, we have let the problem mount as we went about our business. Now it is immense. Everywhere you look, at curbs, along roadways, in vacant lots, on lawns, and in bushes, downtown, uptown, across town, there is more and more litter. As more of it piles up and blows about, it is hard to know where it comes from and who is responsible for it. We do know that as more litter accumulates, people seem to be more careless, thinking that one more beer can or fast food bag won't make much of a difference. There is already so much on the ground and in the wind.

At one time, before we earned the name Litterville, there were those who littered, those who didn't, and some who picked up other people's litter. These divisions were not hard and fast. Many of us littered occasionally but tried not to do so most of the time, and once in a great while, some of us even policed other people's litter when we had the time and could find a trash can nearby. Now, however, the litter problem is out of control. Our town is a mess. Too many of us litter, too few of us don't, and hardly anyone picks up after others anymore. There is just too much of the stuff. Where would you start to address the problem and how long would you keep at it?

One day we read a news story in our weekly paper that a major service industry in town has decided to relocate its business elsewhere, which means the loss of 300 jobs. The CEO is fed up with the conditions in Litterville and finds it hard to attract new managers to live here. In another story, the paper reported that a Boy Scout troop discovered over a hundred birds strangled by discarded plastic six-pack rings. Finally, there was a story with details of an accident at Fourth and Main. It seems that swirling litter at that intersection so obscured the vision of one motorist and so distracted another that they crashed into a heating oil truck which was parked, setting it afire and destroying one home and the dry cleaners. Fortunately, no one was seriously injured, but a group of citizens has responded with a call to arms: "Litterville has to clean up its act."

Soon there was a meeting of concerned citizens who want to do something about the litter problem. You and I went, but we were disappointed by the turnout. "Why aren't there more people here?" the unofficial chairperson asked. Lots of opinions were offered—short notice, not enough publicity, too many don't care, and it was bowling league night at both alleys in town. The mayor of Litterville and city council members, however, did attend. They were bombarded with questions. They had very few answers. Nothing has worked. Antilitter posters have been torn down, litter barrels stolen, the town budget squeezed, a bond issue for more sanitation trucks defeated, and so forth.

"Let's face it," said one of our exasperated neighbors. "People who live here for the most part don't care. They're just slobs. Always have been, always will be." But those who had come out were not ready to give up so easily. "Whether or not folks who live here are slobs, we can't put up with the mess we've created anymore. Jobs are leaving, people won't settle here, half a block burned to the ground. Pretty soon there won't be any town to live in." A lot of heads nodded, as if to say, something just has to be done.

From the back of the room Miss Pickens, a small, wizened old woman, got to her feet, cleared her throat, and waited to be called on. When her turn came, she said, "If everyone in Litterville were to clean up their yard from back fence to front curb, each day and every day, the problem would eventually go away. Why can't we do that? As for downtown," Miss Pickens went on, "let each store owner do the same and the town sanitation department can take care of those places that are left over. That's the way our town is supposed to work, isn't it? I can remember way back when we did just that. It isn't impossible. We just have to get organized. Each of us pitches in, and before you know it, we're lookin' good again. Feelin' good, too." Miss Pickens sat down and everyone applauded her remarks. She made it seem so simple, and the sense of the meeting was: Let's give it a try.

Within a week, every homeowner, landlord, and storeowner received a letter from the Concerned Citizens detailing Miss Pickens's proposal. The reaction was not only disappointing but unsettling. Angry landlords accused tenants of being responsible for the mess around their buildings. Storeowners blamed their customers. Many homeowners considered the cleanup overwhelming and asked that City Hall do it instead. Many protested that the litter on their lots came from somewhere else, and it wasn't fair to be saddled with cleaning up what other people were responsible for. Some homeowners just ignored the hullabaloo. They still had their jobs and better things to do than spend their free time trying to clean up Litterville.

The Sanitation Department and the Boy Scouts did the best they could in numerous public places, but the litter from across the street or down the block would blow about and little improvement could be detected. Some homeowners did laboriously clean their properties but soon became discouraged when their neighbors didn't. When word got around that City Hall might raise taxes to pay for more sanitation workers if the voluntary cleanup didn't work, many homeowners organized and threatened to defeat anyone who voted for such a measure at the next election.

Two of our neighbors put their houses up for sale, deciding to move away from Litterville to other towns where the problem was less severe. One neighbor was just plain disgusted with the response to Miss Pickens's challenge. The other neighbor wanted to leave Litterville because he saw it turning into an anxious, unhappy place, where no one could agree on anything and everyone pointed the finger at someone else. "I don't want to spend the rest of my life picking up litter and worrying about whether my neighbors are doing the same. The aggravation isn't worth it."

So Litterville remained Litterville. The mayor and the City Council did not raise taxes, but were defeated anyway at the next election for even suggesting such a thing. Concerned Citizens disbanded, and Miss Pickens died a short time later.

The Litterville story may be exaggerated, but it does portray various attitudes that are obstacles to the development of new conventions. Clearly there was no convention in that town for picking up litter, although Miss Pickens seems to remember there once was. Small-scale cooperation obviously was not enough. The problem overwhelmed the Concerned Citizens, the Boy Scout troop, and conscientious home-owners who did their share, but who saw others unmoved and unhelpful. Some chose to leave Litterville, others passed the buck to City Hall, and some just couldn't be bothered, disregarding a littered future that might rob them of their jobs and the viability of their town. Others protested that their share of the cleanup was too much, or others were doing too little, and thus found a reason or excuse to give up or not even get started.

Even though we confront a range of social problems for which we would like to coordinate solutions, our individual interests usually do not coincide from the outset. The convention of not smoking in public did not happen overnight. There were just so many smokers whose interests were clearly not served by refraining from smoking in airplanes, restaurants, and workplaces. Recycling is ignored as much as it is observed. I think of my own daily defection when I put bottles or cans into the trash bag because I am in too much of a hurry to separate the stuff. Even when our interests do coincide theoretically, we don't seem to find coordination as natural as some think it should be. Some of us fail to get our children immunized, even when the government is willing to pay the cost. Others refuse to car-pool even though if enough of us did so, the practice would reduce our commuting time. Some drive drunk even with a sober friend who could take the wheel.[2]

Even robust conventions that regulate our behavior are not necessarily what we prefer to conform to on every occasion. They are robust because for whatever reason they have crowded out other alternatives. The convention of the line is surely one that I endure only because I usually have no alternative. The line is supposedly for everyone's benefit, but does not equally benefit everyone because each person's circumstances are not identical. Conventions restrain our preferences, but they do not necessarily change them.

What are our preferences, as illustrated in the Litterville story, that can frustrate the development of conventions? There are four that I want to examine: our preference to be free of social problems; our preference to have government solve our problems for us; our preference to put individual interest ahead of social interest; and our preference not to be put at a personal disadvantage.

I think of our preference to be free of social problems, which our mobility accommodates, as a preference for "exit." The problem doesn't go away, but we do.[3] I think of our preference to have government solve our problems for us as a preference for delegation. We have better things to do. I think of our preference to put individual interest ahead of social interest as a preference for private gain—one of the "better things" to do. And I think of our preference not to be put at a personal disadvantage as a preference for parity. For those of us willing to regulate our behavior with others, there is the expectation that others will also do their part.

These preferences do not represent the dark side but merely the very human side of our natures when living in a society where we value liberty and equality. Each of us goes about our daily business, guided by what we consider to be normal, healthy desires. Preferences in the context of a free society are what you and I are entitled to exercise, whether or not our preferences are desirable either for us or for society as a whole.

You and I know, however, that our individual preferences are often shaped by circumstances. They are desires that may or may not be exercised. Our preferences sometimes change as we are influenced by what others do. Assume for the moment that the four of us who were going out for dinner in chapter one finally settled on a restaurant. We agreed to let Sarah decide where we should eat and now we are at the restaurant of her choice and the menus are set before us. Each of us may have a preference for what to order, but we also listen to what the waiter recommends and ask what dish the others in our party are likely to choose. No one, of course, is going to insist that we have one dish or another, but we remain open to suggestion. We may put aside our original preferences and all order the same thing or eat family style with each of us ordering different dishes, which appeal to everyone, so we can share. There is no telling what we will do. The preferences that I want to examine, of course, run deeper in us than our tastes and appetites, but, just like the social occasions of choosing a restaurant or ordering a meal, our preferences are subject to change.

In discussing our preferences as obstacles to the development of new conventions, I do not assume that our preferences are fixed and unalterable. On the contrary. Despite our freely held preferences, we somehow manage to create and maintain conventions without legal coercion. If we were unyielding in our preferences, such regularities of behavior, in most cases, would not be possible.[4]

OUR PREFERENCE FOR "EXIT"

> They clutch everything but hold nothing fast. . . . An American will . . . settle in one place and soon go off elsewhere with his changing desires. [Tocqueville][5]

Liberty is our watchword and it literally sends us off in all directions. Our uncertainties about how to cope with social problems rarely lead to new conventions but rather to flight, which each of us has some control over. We don't try to solve the problems. Our personal solution is to extricate ourselves from circumstances where we have to confront or endure them.

"In a real sense, physical flight is the American substitute for the European experience of social revolution. And this of course has persisted throughout our national history."[6] Our nation was founded and has been reinvigorated by successive waves of newcomers. Emigration has been a principled option to staying in a homeland and having to fight or endure various forms of oppression and deprivation. Except for African-Americans, who were given no choice but to come to this country in chains, those who have immigrated to America have come willingly and with uncommon ambitions. And they still come. They take low-paying jobs with the expectation of better ones to come, renew old neighborhoods that others have given up on, start small businesses that find their niche, and provide an ethnic networking for others who follow.

Our preference for exit to America or in America implies moving to something better. (Totalitarian states usually don't permit free movement within their borders or across borders.) Exit is a choice made for private gain, family welfare, or whatever our heart's desire, even if compelled by circumstances that we think leave us no choice but to pick up and go. Our economic system offers little security, and throughout our history people have moved, uprooted by opportunities gone sour or attracted to new opportunities that promised more. We seek security for ourselves and our families when social upheavals threaten or overwhelm us. Mobility is an avenue away from trouble toward better prospects, whether driven by economic or social circumstance, and it is often a combination of both.

As a people we are liberty-centered, not problem-centered. Our vast continent and the relative freedom to roam and exploit it has always offered us a way out. We came to this country with the expectation of finding something better than we left. If we can't fix things quickly to our liking, our tendency is to move on. Someone else will move into the old neighborhood and try to make a go of it. They in turn will also probably move on as economic opportunities open up or as local problems become more severe. It is a cycle of entrance and exit that both renews and imperils the place of our birth, childhood, or where we once called home. Consequently, a quorum for dealing with social problems is never certain, always shifting, and many times nonexistent.

Like the Litterville neighbor who decided to move out, we may think that "things" are a mess in our part of town, and the solutions are taxing and don't seem to be working anyway. We often talk glibly about "fight or flight," but in fact if you or I stay put, we have a problem that has to be managed, whether it is working for better schools, safer neighborhoods, or a cleaner local environment. Such efforts take time and take their toll. Is it any wonder that so many of us choose to move elsewhere rather than become engaged? Like playing chess with a formidable opponent, we have no expectation that we can win, so we try to avoid being captured. Our game is defensive. Losing sight that checkmating our opponent should be the object, we move about the board with no plan except to survive. Heading for the exit can do a lot of good for each of us, although the problems that we leave behind don't go away. They, in fact, may get worse when we take whatever talents and resources that we have and move out of our Littervilles.[7]

We are rarely apologetic about exercising our preference for exit. We take for granted that individual interest deserves to be put ahead of social interest. When President Clinton enrolled his daughter, Chelsea, in a private school in the D.C. area, most people understood the Clintons' desire to do right by their talented daughter. If Chelsea had gone to a public school in the nation's capitol, it is possible that public education might have benefited from more attention by the White House, the media, and others attracted to the story. But in America, even the President of the United States, the most public of persons, is entitled to exercise his private preference for what schooling is most appropriate for his daughter. We know that if we were in his position, we might very well make the same choice.

It is quite natural for individuals and families, of whatever background, to look for better schools, safer streets, healthier climates, more chances for recreation—from whatever they don't have to wherever they think that they can do better. Many of us would say: "Isn't that the whole point of being here or going there? I can't solve the problems that I left behind, and if they pile up where I'm living now perhaps I'll move again. Life is short and my family is precious. What is wrong with that? Tell me, what is wrong with that?" But others might reply: "There is nothing wrong with making such choices, except that if social problems are not confronted, they may follow us. Perhaps finally we won't be able to outrun them."

Such a conversation, however, does not occur because most of us don't think that far ahead. We are too busy scrambling for position, or advantage, or peace of mind, hoping that the shadow of the past does not outrun us. We make choices, not rashly or with malice, but simply choosing an expedient to get out of harm's way, or what we have come to learn may be more of a problem than each of us can deal with alone.[8] It often does not occur to many of us that problems, other than recourse to government, can be confronted in any other way. We remain alone and unorganized, failing to consider how we might coordinate our behavior in the form of new social conventions.

Class and race are territories that we inhabit and often want to escape from. We are trying to do better than our fathers and mothers; we are trying to do better for our children. The largest divide is between blacks and whites, resulting from a tragic racial history and the persistence of poverty that sets apart not only black from white but white from white and black from black. Whites especially search for places where they do not have to confront differences in class and race. Look anywhere in American social life and you see blacks and whites separated, if not divided, in school and office cafeterias, dormitories and public plazas, on buses, and at shopping malls. Wherever there are encampments, the separation is evident.

I think of my own experience in higher education at a small college in Illinois where I served as president. Some local townspeople were suspicious and frightened to have young black men and women "bused" from Chicago and St. Louis to attend the college. (The students, white and black, actually came by car and train and at their own expense.) And some white students, as well as some black students, who attended the college did not feel comfortable with each other. Too many went home or transferred to find supposedly more comfortable settings in which to pursue their education. Later I read with dismay about a racial brawl at Olivet College in Michigan. I imagined that much the same thing could have happened at the college where I had been. After the brawl at Olivet, fifty-five black students picked up and went home with only two weeks left in the semester. Many white students also retreated to their home communities. And this took place at a college that had been integrated since the mid-nineteenth century—a pathsetter in race relations.[9]

Perhaps the most conspicuous example of our preference for exit is the flight from urban neighborhoods and schools, where poverty and racial problems often seem overwhelming. Banks withdraw available capital. Businesses relocate. Parents put their children in private and parochial schools. Even those who find it hard to escape pursue their own forms of evasion like dropping out of school, getting high on drugs, and so forth.

The migration from our cities during the past forty years has often been characterized as "white flight," and, of course, race is one major reason—the enduring problem of racial difference and prejudice. The black middle class has also exercised a preference for exit, on grounds of class, not race.[10] To be fair to both black and white parents who flee urban schools, the physical threat of crime in school and in the streets to and from school usually looms larger in their minds than whom their children sit next to in a classroom. The preference for exit comes naturally when the physical safety of their children is concerned—especially if they entertain little hope of solving the pathologies of city schools and streets through which their children must navigate safe passage.

It would be nice to believe, as some do, that the preference for exit alerts schools, neighborhoods, and local governments that they must do a better job if they are to retain productive residents. The argument certainly is made with respect to consumer behavior—that businesses try harder or perform better after seeing the loss of market share. But businesses are better organized to respond to consumer exit than neighborhoods in transition. Businesses do not have the quasi-monopolistic position of a public school system, which often ignores the correlation between its performance and the exodus of families. And businesses can adjust more quickly than local governments, whose agendas are broader, more troubled, and plagued by inadequate resources. Consumers often come back to the fold; former residents rarely do.

Given our preference for exit, the convention of school integration remains fragile. With existing school problems for all races and the special problem of achieving racial balance, no equilibrium has been established for putting black and white children in the same classroom, much less the same school.[11] Even in "integrated" schools, the practice of "tracking," separating children by aptitude in various subjects, often means that classrooms remain segregated by race. Black children, who represent 16 percent of all public school students, represent 40 percent of those who are classified as "mentally retarded, disabled, or otherwise deficient."[12] Tracking focuses on the scholastic achievement of each student rather than socialization for living in a multiracial society.

Eight states allow students to attend any school district in the state: Arkansas, Idaho, Iowa, Minnesota, Nebraska, Ohio, Utah, and Washington. Does this promote integration? It doesn't seem so. Minority families don't take advantage of the option nearly as much as white families do. For example, in Des Moines, Iowa, eleven minority students requested transfer in 1992 compared to 402 white students. (Minority children then composed 20 percent of the 30,000 students in the Des Moines school district.) When the Des Moines school board denied exit visas, so to speak, to white students, but granted the requests of minority students to transfer, white parents protested. One commentator remarked, "This is a democracy. You can't wall people in and tell them they can't get out. . . . They might as well let them go. They're going to lose these people anyhow."[13]

Commonly, racial segregation in schools has been linked with racial segregation in housing. The linkage, however, is rarely challenged any longer by court-ordered busing. Instead, specialized magnet schools, which use "specialized curriculums" to draw a racial mix of students, have been tried, as well as opening up some suburbs to new developments that offer an income mix in housing units. For the most part, however, segregated housing patterns prevail. As neighborhoods remain or become segregated, whether in major cities or in their suburbs, so do the schools that serve them. Andrew Hacker cites research showing that while 85 percent of blacks prefer an equal balance of black and white neighbors, whites prefer no more than 8 percent of blacks living near them.[14] That is an enormous difference in what people will settle for, and it is no wonder that whites, exercising a preference for exit, make it difficult for integration to succeed.

Sometimes residential integration may work when people remain strangers. In one neighborhood where integration endures, apparently there is little social mixing outside of one's own ethnic group. The Williamsbridge section of the Bronx, New York, is a neighborhood with a racial mix of homeowners on eighty-five blocks and approximately 20,000 people. (Neighborhoods tend to run on the large size in New York City.) One Williamsbridge resident commented, perhaps ruefully, "There is not much interaction . . . that may be one reason why we get along."[15]

In the case of racial housing patterns, I noted in chapter one that the phenomenon of "tipping" makes integration precarious in some neighborhoods. The preference for exit where racial balance is important means that those who, for whatever reason, first upset the balance can destabilize a neighborhood. If one white homeowner sells his house to a black buyer in an integrated neighborhood, it can prompt other white homeowners to sell. The first neighbor who sells his house probably has no reason or desire to undo the fragile convention of integration of his neighborhod. He may only want to move closer to his daughter, or to downsize to a smaller house. Conversely, the resegregation of a white neighborhood can happen if a black neighbor sells to a white buyer. Now the triggering sale leads black homeowners to feel more isolated and likely to sell.[16]

The preference for exit is as understandable as it is troublesome. Individual choice, seemingly so insignificant, influences subsequent choices and establishes patterns, as is evident in both residential and school segregation. It is like what happens when one newspaper decides to print a story about alleged private peccadilloes of a public figure that its competitors have held back on. The competing newspapers, not wanting to be scooped or fearing a loss of readership, decide to publish the story too, even if it violates their journalistic standards. So the newspapers let the least responsible among them dictate the outcome. I have already used examples in earlier chapters that show how one person's behavior can produce followers—stepping off the curb into traffic, setting the conventional speed on a stretch of highway, or starting a standing ovation in the opera house. If a few of us stand on tiptoe to see, does this force everyone else behind us to do likewise? Everyone standing on tiptoe—a ludicrous result, but done for what many consider a perfectly sensible reason.

If every time blacks want to get into the game whites pick up and leave, only to start the game somewhere else without them, then blacks don't just have a problem, whites have a problem too. It is a problem for blacks because it is harder for them to find jobs, raise kids, and educate them if their playing field is limited. It is a problem for whites because black unemployment and poorly educated black kids cost whites something too. But whites keep moving away, further out, fearing that blacks will somehow spoil their schools and neighborhoods if they move in. It is a fearful and vicious cycle.

Strangely enough, the preference for exit may become less an obstacle to the development of new conventions if we exhaust its possibilities. In seeking to be free of our social problems, we go away but our problems don't. The larger a problem becomes, such as race relations, and the more ubiquitous it is, the less likely that our preference for exit will make sense. But then what happens? Will we find new ways to get along, to cooperate despite our differences? What new social conventions will we need when our interdependence leaves no place to hide?

OUR PREFERENCE FOR DELEGATION

In times of democracy, private life is so active and agitated, so full of desires and labor, that each individual has scarcely leisure or energy left for political life. [Tocqueville][17]

Perhaps the largest contradiction in American life is how our penchant for living free leads us to government's doorstep—to have government solve our problems for us. Our resort to government compromises our libertarian instincts, but it also serves them. We really don't want to take the time to solve problems ourselves. We prefer to be free to pursue economic gain and private pleasures. And if we can't escape social problems by moving, we still resist having to get involved.

We look for other remedies that depend less on what you and I and others do to coordinate a solution and more on what those we pay to come up with answers do. In each of us there is a bit of Oscar Wilde, who is often remembered for his pithy statement about how socialism won't work because it takes up too many of our evenings.[18]

When we do take the time to attend a community meeting, there will always be those who prefer to take the government shortcut. And their argument can be persuasive. If there is reason enough to organize around any unsolved coordination problem, isn't that reason enough for government to intervene? Some of the residents of Litterville wanted City Hall to do the job for them. The prospect of a cleanup was overwhelming otherwise. Would we want to pursue the convention of yielding the right of way, when a stoplight settles the matter once and for all at a busy intersection?

Of course, the argument can be made that every coordination problem should be put at government's doorstep. If we don't have the time or don't want to take the time to try and solve a problem ourselves, what's wrong with asking government to do it for us? After all, that's one important reason why governments exist. We vote for representatives, we pay taxes so they can be problem solvers, and we can throw them out if they don't solve problems or we don't like their solutions.[19]

If there are conflicts among us at the meeting, some may want government to settle the matter; it has the authority we don't have. The resort to government is often supported or resisted on grounds other than the desire to be left alone or to pursue private gain and pleasure. Those at the meeting may also be politically divided. The difference between conservatives and liberals is often that one sees a problem where the other does not.

Unfortunately, at our community meetings we often forget to ask more probing questions. Can the government actually solve the coordination problem for us if government does intervene? What will it cost and how will it be paid for? If a new law is needed, will there be general compliance? Will we be able to get the law changed or scrapped once it is in place?

We do institutionalize some conventions by enacting them into law. Coordination by central authority is absolutely necessary, as is the case of community policing or public health measures to prevent the spread of communicable disease. But this is very different from turning to government to solve a problem, without acknowledging that we have to regulate our own behavior as part of the solution. The case for new conventions is not that they are easier for us to do than having government do it for us. The inconvenient fact is that many of the solutions to public problems depend more on what each of us does in our daily lives than what government tries to do in our behalf, whether it is the care and development of children, making neighborhood streets safe again, reducing the waste that each household disposes of, or improving race relations.

Getting enough others to coordinate their behavior on a regular basis is, no doubt, more trouble than producing a "public good," once and for all.[20] Getting enough others to practice Miss Pickens's convention is a greater imposition on everyone than getting enough others organized to prevail on the city council to install a recycling plant or build an incinerator or truck the stuff out of town. Putting Miss Pickens's convention in place poses an additional complication, which was captured by the comment of the Litterville neighbor: "I don't want to spend the rest of my life picking up litter and worrying about whether my neighbors are doing the same." Faced with regularizing his behavior over an indefinite period of time, the neighbor moved to the next town.[21]

Unlike a convention, a public good can sometimes be secured by only a few individuals whose interest and resources are equal to the task. For example, a major corporation headquartered in Litterville, which wanted to attract new managers from other parts of the country, might assume the expense of keeping the downtown clean without the help of storeowners, or a few large property owners might lend the labor of those who work for them to assist the Boy Scouts when they clean up vacant lots and other unsightly areas. More often than not we look to government to supply public goods. In Litterville it meant hiring more sanitation workers and buying more garbage trucks. If the Mayor and the City Council had such resources, their interest was undeniable to clean up the town and keep it clean with or without our help. Who can deny it would be easier letting City Hall do it for us than having to establish Miss Pickens's convention? Yet we object to paying the bill, which exposes the contradiction of wanting public goods that we don't want to pay for or can't afford.

If we accepted the cost and intrusion of government as the price that we pay for being free to pursue our private gain and pleasures, then we might have a version of Tocqueville's benign "despotism," perhaps deplorable to some, but workable for the great majority.[22] In many countries official intervention is far more intrusive than in the United States. But that is what most of us do not want and yet often act as if we did. We put difficult problems at government's doorstep, but refuse to pay the upkeep.

We do delegate problem solving to nonprofit enterprises with fewer reservations and less acrimony; many nonprofit firms, in fact, represent the institutionalization of conventions. As noted in chapter one, "harvest" agencies coordinate the collection and distribution of perishable food from those sources where there is an excess to food pantries and soup kitchens that feed the hungry. Of course you and I and others could do this ourselves, but it might easily become a full-time job. We much prefer that a social agency do it for us. For many of us, the extent of our participation is to help finance the coordinating activities of nonprofit enterprises through our tax-deductible contributions.

If we look closely at what is put on government's doorstep, it is possible to detect a good deal of self-interest. We are not just buck-passing; we often want something for ourselves when we exercise our preference for delegation.

> [E]ach one of them wants the state to help in the special matter with which he is preoccupied, and he wants to lead the government on to take action in his domain, though he would like to restrict it in every other direction. [Tocqueville][23]

There is nothing inconsistent, however, with this "rent-seeking" attitude. We use government not only to secure our liberties but to advance our respective interests as well—to referee or, even better, to take sides in the clash of interests.[24]

Rent seeking is undoubtedly one objective of most "special interests." Such organized groups want government to solve a problem in their favor and often at the expense of a great many others. Interest groups, however, do not leave a problem at government's doorstep. They knock, enter, cajole, bargain, threaten, make campaign contributions, cut a deal, reward, and punish. Some organized groups think of themselves as working for the "public interest," which suggests they represent a broader interest. But all groups with interests, narrow or broad, compete for government's attention. Organized lobbying endures as an important political convention.

Many people are appalled at the proliferation of special-interest groups. In fact, such groups have always been around. But their numbers and the competition were previously not so great. Some powers-that-be deplore this development because they no longer have the field to themselves. Business interests have to compete with environmental lobbyists, and "reform" groups who like to think of themselves as above the fray have to go head to head with more narrowly defined interests. Some political conservatives started using the term "special interests" to attack labor unions, and it has recently become a code word for any group whose agenda we oppose.[25]

The major objection to special interests has always been that they have more influence than those who are not organized, and this is seen to skew policy, tax, and regulatory outcomes, and not be fair to the unorganized. Special interests are able to leverage their political acumen and members' resources to deliver results that have to be paid for by either the general tax-paying public or targeted segments. For example, the total budget of nonprofit environmental groups lobbying for pollution abatement was $10 million in 1978. Legislation mandating pollution abatement in that same year levied a cost of $23 billion on various polluters. One dollar spent on lobbying bought $2,000 spent on pollution abatement.[26] Some think of special interests as producing pork barrel legislation and log rolling in state and federal legislatures. These are political conventions, which call upon legislators to favor each other's districts, often at the expense of the general public. Such political coordination assumes that one good deed deserves another, so a legislator whose district is favored by a particular project or subsidy is expected to reciprocate at some later time with a vote for other legislators' districts who seek to be similarly favored. It is the same tacit agreement of a quid pro quo that makes patronage a convention. When the unorganized let government do the problem solving for them, they find that public servants seem preoccupied with special interest problems, not to the exclusion of more general concerns, but certainly limiting the attention and government resources available to address them.

The convention of delegation assumes that we can change our minds and take back whatever authority we have loaned out. We let Sarah choose the restaurant, but next time someone else will, or we will settle on a place by some other means. And if Sarah does not choose a restaurant that we like after eating there, it may be some time before we ask her to choose another one. But it rarely happens when we delegate a problem for solution to government that we get to take it back. Of course in the deregulation of certain industries, we have done just that, but this is an exception rather than the rule. What is remarkable now is the almost total absence of debate as to whether government, especially the federal government, has any business getting involved in certain problem areas. It was not so long ago that "jurisdiction" was a major point of difference between conservative and liberal legislators. Jurisdiction was debated in the case of civil rights, Medicare, and aid to education, among others. Now we criticize government performance and cost, but the question of jurisdiction is rarely raised. It is as if some of us are convinced that our options for solving public problems are so limited without government help that we stand little chance of solving them otherwise.

Certainly those matters that concern special interests are hard to wrestle from government's grasp. Special interests that obtain sizable subsidies will do whatever they can to keep such benefits in place. Interest groups know that an individual taxpayer bears a tiny fraction of the cost and thus lacks a reason to protest or, at least, is rarely organized to do so.

Furthermore, government officials, who legislate or administer the wide array of supposedly problem-solving policies and programs, are self-interested parties. I do not share the view of those who think that public servants lack any motivation other than self-interest in what they do. That is too simplistic. Obviously one motivation among many is the desire to perpetuate oneself in elected or appointed office. What could be more human, although it troubles us to see others behave as we do when they represent us in public affairs. As representatives, they're supposed to be like us, but not too much like us.

Another expectation of government officials is that those who ask them to solve a problem may bring them to account if they don't. That may be reason enough for them to try new policies and programs although they have little idea whether such measures will work. The creation of a solution to a problem usually means finding people, money, and time in the hope of making the solution work. If the initial solution proves not to work, then public officials want to try something else. All this usually takes more people, money, and time to try to get the solution right. The work of government is rarely ideological; rather it is based on a shallow optimism that with the right people and enough time and money most problems can be solved. Americans believe in solutions, but as Daniel Boorstin points out, democratic government is a "process," not a "product."[27] What we usually get is a "process" posing as an answer. Government officials do not so much solve problems as produce outcomes.[28]

The absence of external competition often dulls the performance of government, although there is plenty of competition among public agencies and in the intergovernmental squabbling of local, state, and federal officials to see who gets the chance or resources to attack a particular problem. Even judges, traditionally rather passive instruments for social problem solving, have become far more aggressive in asserting their role in the implementation of their decisions, whether on school desegregation, living standards in mental hospitals and prisons, or pollution abatement.

In the last thirty years, both federal judges and legislators have often settled matters in the federal government's favor by preempting the field of potential problem solvers. For many problems, no one else except the federal government gets to propose solutions, although everyone else except the federal government gets to pay for them. We pass the buck to government in more ways than one. A while ago I read in a weekly newspaper that local taxpayers may soon be asked to pay more than $9 million for sewage treatment improvements mandated by the federal government. "We told them we had no money to bring the treatment plant up to par [federal standard], that we needed more time," said the mayor. "They told us, 'No, you go back to the people . . . and you tell them you need $9 million.'" The town has already been assessed a $120,000 penalty. Unfunded mandates are perhaps the most egregious examples of how, through the tutelage of government officials at the federal level, local governments are forced to pay for solutions that they often can't afford or don't agree need to be implemented.[29]

Like our preference for exit that for a time postpones having to confront certain social problems, so our preference for delegation frees us up to do other things while very little problem solving gets done by government. We do vote the rascals out of office, set term limits, and make mischief for public officials through referenda or the defeat of bond issues. Still, the shortcuts to government continue almost unabated. "The older a democratic society, the more centralized will its government be."[30]

OUR PREFERENCE FOR PRIVATE GAIN

One must therefore expect that private interest will more than ever become the chief if not the only driving force behind all behavior. But we have yet to see how each man will interpret his private interest. [Tocqueville][31]

The preference for private gain usually puts individual interest ahead of social interest. It is cousin to our preferences for exit and delegation in a society where liberty and personal advancement have always held sway. That is why we came here, and that is why others follow.

To put self-interest ahead of social interest, however, does not mean that we exclude entirely the consideration of social interest. That of course is what this book is about. When do strangers cooperate? How does that come about? And what is likely to get in their way? Under certain circumstances, when there is uncertainty and enough others to overcome uncertainty, we do coordinate and regulate our behavior with others in ways that often serve both our individual interests and the social interest.

The preference for private gain, however, can get in the way of developing new conventions.[32] Private gain is usually so much more self-evident than public gain. We often fail to cooperate because the desired outcome is just too far off in time to engage our present attention. Some call this "discounting future gains." Like the citizen from Hoxton, we abandon the stag-hunting party to catch our own rabbit, or like his heirs, we overgraze the New England commons until it is rendered worthless. Today, for example, we take short-term profits instead of reinvesting in research and development; we permit a physical infrastructure to deteriorate; and we ignore the care and development of children.[33]

"Discount rates" vary among individuals. Some of us live with shorter time horizons due to age or economic circumstance. Some of us have children, some do not. Some of us are of a religious faith that discounts the present for the future. For others, their faith or lack of it keeps them resolutely fixed on the present. Some of us do whatever is necessary to prolong our lives by proper exercise, diet, and right living.

Still others of us have so little information or so few projections about what the future is likely to hold that we do not so much ignore the future as remain oblivious to it. For the short term, at least, being oblivious to the longer term has its advantages. When I watch the Weather Channel on cable TV, I worry all week about what weather is coming, plan my activities accordingly, and warn others about our common weather fate. When I don't watch the Weather Channel, I go about my business quite happily, often with no greater inconvenience than if I had worried and planned my way through a week of weather reports.

Most of us remain preoccupied with our immediate lives—the everyday effort to make a living, raise a family, pay the bills, and get a little time to relax. The social interest often extends to people we do not know or to future generations we will for sure not have a chance to know, although the posterity of our children and grandchildren gives us an inkling. We spend most of our time worrying about getting what we want or, more important, not losing what we have. We feel the loss of something we already have more acutely than gains we have not yet experienced.

Social gains are slow in coming. When we conserve energy, the social gain of reduced reliance on foreign oil or the reduced emission of pollutants is not immediately apparent, whereas we know immediately that we live in a colder house or have fewer appliances working or drive less just for the fun of it. It is no wonder that when others try to get us to focus on the future, they talk about the coming "crisis"—environmental, financial, racial—to get our attention and, for a moment, ask us to imagine the loss of something in the future that we have not yet experienced—global warming, foreign lenders refusing to finance our national debt, or racial conflagration in our major cities. Even then we don't take on faith the future crises that others portray. We often have to actually experience a crisis to imagine what the future might hold. It took the oil shock of rising prices and shortages in the mid-1970s when we experienced long lines at gas pumps to finally get us to buy smaller cars, reduce our speed on the highways, and insulate our homes.

A number of variables affect our preference to put individual interest ahead of social interest. Sometimes we may think our self-interest coincides with the social interest, and we cooperate agreeably, as was the case of energy conservation in the late-1970s. Sometimes we may think we have more to gain by not cooperating. Sometimes we may change our minds when it appears that enough others are cooperating, so we have less to gain by not cooperating. When a line first forms, I may have something to gain by ignoring it and rushing to the front. If the line has already been established, I will probably wait my turn like everyone else. On occasion, I may still choose to ignore the convention, which is the case when I don't wait for my row to be called at an airline gate because I want to get on a crowded plane and stow my baggage before all the overhead space is taken. It all depends.

To achieve satisfactory outcomes we often find ourselves arriving together at a different place from where each of us started. Our preference for private gain has changed. In a classroom game that I conducted several times over a period of three years with more than 350 students, I came to understand the reasoning of individual students for promoting the social interest of their section. (There were about sixty students in a section.) The game was set up to explore how individual interest can be affected by expectations of what others will do.

In the game, each student was offered a choice to "cooperate" or to "defect," that is, whether to put individual interest ahead of the section's interest. If the student chose to cooperate, she or he would get $3 for every other student who also chose to cooperate. (If all sixty students chose to cooperate, each student would get $180.) If a student chose to defect, he or she would get $5 for every student who preferred to cooperate, but only $1 for each of those who also chose to defect. (If all but the one student chose to cooperate, the defector would get $275. But if all students chose to defect, each student would only get $60.) A student profited most if everyone cooperated but him, but there was no guarantee of a higher payoff for defection. Putting individual interest ahead of social interest did not necessarily mean a student would gain more; it depended on how many others chose to defect or cooperate. The game did not permit any communication among the students, and they registered their choices on a ballot which I collected.

The interesting part of the exercise for me was to have the students share with one another why they made the choices that they did:

1. For some students the absence of communication severely limited the possibility of maximizing the outcome for everybody, i.e., $180 per student. Without communication, they chose to pursue their self-interest and defect, which offered the prospect of a larger individual payoff.
2. Many students worried about their reputations and chose to cooperate. In communities where we are known, individual interest is more likely to coincide with social interest, if only because being known as a cooperator, rather than a defector, is to our advantage over the long run.[34]
3. Most students were fascinated by how an individual's interest in gaining a sizable payoff depended on what others chose to do. Let me paraphrase one response as somewhat typical of the quandary that the game presented.

To what extent does my preference inform me about others' preferences? For example, if I choose to cooperate, will most everyone also choose to do so? But then, if they do so, isn't it in my interest to defect? Of course if I can reason that way, so can they, and all of us will get far less by choosing to defect than choosing to cooperate. My ultimate preference inescapably is bound up in trying to figure out what others will do, and their preferences, in turn, are affected by what they think I will do.

It was interesting to see how few students treated the game as an economic one, maximizing individual gain, and how many thought of themselves instead as part of a group engaged in a social or political game, despite the prohibition of any communication among the players. They did not use game theory as their analytical framework, but relied instead on their social experience, however limited, with their fellow students in the section over the course of a semester.[35]

My classroom game suffered for not allowing communication. I wanted a purely cognitive play, but in real-world situations far more is going on. What was missing in the classroom game was the influence of early choices made by some students and communicated to others, tacit or explicit agreements arising out of their conversations, and conditional cooperation that could be tested among the students. The classroom game experience was, in many respects, improved when students, despite the communication ban, nonetheless took into account their ongoing social relationships and the norms arising from their relationships that ultimately informed their choices whether to cooperate or defect. Many students obviously concluded that the point of the game for them was to develop the social skill of discerning when self-interest should yield to and profit from opportunities for cooperation.

Many of us, however, do not go to the trouble of trying to figure out what others will do, especially if their numbers are large; and certainly in our everyday life among strangers, they far outnumber the sixty students who formed a section in my classroom. Even if our preference to put individual interest ahead of social interest is not fixed or predictable, without some kind of feedback of what others prefer or are doing, it is more than likely that each of us will go our own way. As a consequence we remain unorganized and full of complaints about the failure of governments or markets to advance the social interest.

OUR PREFERENCE FOR PARITY

> It is the inequality of a burden, not its weight, which usually provokes resistance. [Tocqueville][36]

Our preference for parity is the simple desire not to be put at some personal disadvantage. Although Tocqueville was talking about military service in a democratic society, his observation applies more broadly to how we respond in other situations. Whatever our liberty secures, many of us find it important to compare our possessions, status, and rights with what others have. Such comparisons help to put a value on what we have or seek to gain. Some of us become distressed with the inequality of circumstance when we compare our life chances with those of others—our education level, our employment opportunities, and general prospects. It is not just our personal limitations or bad fortune that concern us; it is the comparisons we make that worry and wound us.

It is understandable then that we make comparisons when confronted with a situation that requires coordination. In Litterville some homeowners protested that the litter on their lots came from somewhere else; landlords blamed tenants; storeowners blamed customers; and some homeowners became discouraged after clearing their lots and seeing that their neighbors did not. Our preference for parity, a rough equality, and our disgruntlement when it is not possible may very well undermine and frustrate the development of new conventions. We don't think we should bear a disproportionate burden in producing a desired outcome. Not only do we become easily discouraged by the futility of our individual efforts, but we also resent that others are not doing their fair share.

In Des Moines, Iowa, during the serious flooding in the summer of 1993 that disrupted water services, it was reported that Des Moines residents were "horrified" that some of their neighbors were the cause of a delay in the resumption of service because they had been using water at a time when all residents had been asked to turn off their taps so the municipal system could be refilled. This breakdown in coordination led to a Des Moines Waterworks hotline, which residents used to report on alleged violations by their neighbors, and water crews were dispatched to shut off the offending valve at the curb.[37] If the flood and water shortage had not been so severe, this would be an amusing story; but the point is that people deeply resent when their sacrifices are not equally shared, in this case by their next-door neighbors.

Even though we know that coordination is desirable in addressing a social problem, there are many different degrees of interest among us in making streets safe, cleaning up the environment, caring for children, conserving energy, and so forth. Imagine the complications in changing the work hours in a particular business. Let's say 9:00 to 5:00 becomes 8:00 to 4:00. The reason for the change might be to develop a staggered work hours' convention with other businesses in order to improve commuting times for all employees by stretching out the rush hours. But there will surely be those in any organization who find the new start hour to be inconvenient for a host of valid reasons. One employee drives two hours and must get up at 5:00 A.M. and leave home to drive in the dark. Another employee has no one to care for a child whose school hours don't correspond with the new business hours. Still another employee must find someone else to ride-share with since his car pool now has a different commuting time from his own. The change of a convention as to when people come to work and go home produces a new regularity and may serve the interests of the business and the staggered work hour project, but it would be quite a stretch to say that the individual interests of all employees are equally served.

When our interests vary, our insistence that everyone do their fair share may make it difficult to get the coordination needed to establish a convention. Some will excuse themselves while waiting for others to join in, or join in and get discouraged waiting for others to join in. When few of us want to be put at a personal disadvantage, our comparisons of what others are doing can be the undoing of a practice struggling to be accepted. By comparing our circumstances to those of others, we are also quick to detect when we have more to lose than they do. If you have a garden, water conservation measures fall more heavily on you than on someone who lives in an apartment with one window plant. If you are single and hold down two jobs, you may not see why you should find time to clean up outdoor spaces that I frequently use with my four children.[38]

Although paying taxes is ultimately coerced by government, the degree to which we willingly pay our taxes depends a great deal on our perception that others are also paying theirs. The perception of fairness is extremely important to the efficient collection of taxes. The costs of enforcement would be astronomical if we did not voluntarily pay our taxes when due. Tax reform is often not just a matter of generating more revenue or using tax policy to produce desirable economic and social incentives. Periodically, tax reform is necessary to reassure us that fairness is once more being reestablished, that loopholes are being closed, that those who have more will pay more, and so on.

The NIMBY phenomenon ("not in my backyard") makes clear how ready we are to resist solutions if we're asked to bear a greater burden than others, even though we know it is ludicrous to think that every neighborhood or no neighborhood should have a trash-burning incinerator or a homeless shelter. Although we sometimes organize and seek something from government at the expense of others, we don't like solutions that require something of us but not of the great majority of others.

I should note at this juncture that some commentators think that free riding—the citizen from Hoxton getting something for nothing—is a major obstacle to large-scale cooperation.[39] I don't think this squares with our preference for parity where we want everyone to do their fair share. Those who think that our natural disposition is to free-ride ignore social movements and nonprofit enterprises throughout our history that have originated and been sustained on moral grounds far removed from the rather simplistic notion that individual interest is always put ahead of social interest.

The Americans always cold in manner and often coarse, are hardly ever insensitive, and though they may be in no hurry to volunteer services, yet they do not refuse them. [Tocqueville][40]

For some people free riding is simply "morally wrong." No doubt others of us free-ride at one time or another, but more than likely, it is by fortuitous accident that others get a problem solved without us, not that we calculate in advance that we will take advantage of their efforts. We get the benefit of stricter environmental regulations that we had no hand in bringing about; we have a more just society as a consequence of the civil rights movement, in which most of us did not take part; we win wars that we didn't fight in, and so on. Our problem is not being free riders but being free agents who find it hard to get together. We have so many other things to do. Our preferences for exit, delegation, and private gain just take us off in all directions.

In other situations, we often sense that our contribution would not be of much value and fail to do anything about a problem, but I would not call this free riding. There I am, back on the sidewalk, trying to shovel all the snow on my block, or you are picking up litter in your neighborhood but no one joins you. We give up and go back to just minding our own business. A free rider is someone who tries to get away with something, but that is very different from failing to do something because there is so little organization or fairness that we choose not to be put at a personal disadvantage. What works in small group situations where there is an element of reciprocity—you don't drink tonight and drive us home, next time I don't drink and do the driving—doesn't work among a large number of people. Our individual efforts seem minuscule and futile and very few of us are interested "in doing minute favors for a multitude of individuals," most of whom we don't know.[41] This is an understandable myopia. Furthermore, many of us find it hard to believe that anyone cares what one individual does or doesn't do. Either way we see our own actions as insignificant to any social outcome involving large numbers of people.

Most commentators who examine the possibility of large-scale cooperation assume that you and I act independently of large groups because there is no rational way to ascertain what so many people are doing or what each prefers. We know that a problem we share with a few others is more easily confronted and solved than one we share with countless strangers. I may find it less rewarding to be self-seeking in my family or among a small group of friends or where I work. The possibility of small-scale cooperation depends on kin ties, friendships, and continued acquaintance where my preferences for exit or private gain will, in all likelihood, be met with disdain and reproach. As the size of any group gets larger, however, I may have more latitude to indulge my preferences and I may even think that there is good reason to do so. With nothing else to go on, I may assume that others think as I do, that organizing a solution is beyond any of us.

We regulate our conduct, in part, on whatever feedback there is. The visibility of the litter and what each homeowner was doing or not doing in Litterville was a form of feedback or communication, which helped others make up their mind about whether or not to cooperate. Unfortunately, in Litterville the feedback was not encouraging, so the campaign never got the litter off the ground, so to speak. Do we act differently in a crowd from the way we do in a small group? Not always. If a crowd is well behaved, we are likely to be so also. If a crowd is unruly, we may join in. Like the conventional speed on a highway, it all depends. What are most people doing? Undoubtedly it is more difficult to get such feedback when large numbers of unseen strangers are involved. In the next chapter I want to explore how feedback, using new telecommunication networks linking strangers, might affect what you and I do to help or hinder the development of new conventions.

Chapter Four

TALKING TO STRANGERS

New Telecommunication Networks

THE IMPORTANCE OF FEEDBACK

Talking to strangers is something our mothers told us never to do. The most formidable obstacle, however, to large-scale cooperation is the lack of communication among strangers. Without feedback a coordination problem is difficult to solve.[1] The purpose of this chapter is to explore the potential of new telecommunication networks that make feedback possible and large-scale cooperation among strangers less speculative. "[T]he revolutions in communication are ... changing the scale of human activities."[2] And that should encourage us despite a weakening of social ties, the proliferation of "special interests," and all the other signs that make us strangers to each other in everyday life. What is emerging is "group media," new ways of combining telephones, computers, and an abundance of cable channels, which permits communication among strangers where no single source necessarily originates the communication or dictates its content. The capacity and speed of such media will also give each of us the chance to seek out information that has not been previously available or has been too costly to deliver.

"If everyone had the same information as me, my life would be easier." What one British computer scientist understood is that we are infinitely more capable of solving problems if everyone has access to the same information at the same time.[3] We have not yet really tested the potential of a myriad of instantaneous sources of information, constantly provided and updated, that we will be able to share via telecommunication networks, and which go beyond the now meager menu of stock market quotations, weather forecasts, video-on-demand, and home shopping. There is the possibility that many other kinds of information will be accessible quickly and inexpensively—for example, keeping track of the status of any voluntary undertaking by members of the general public.

If we can readily learn from such network sources that we share a problem, perhaps you and I and others will be able to use such networks to share a solution by monitoring what others are doing and adjusting our individual conduct accordingly. By staying in touch, we may find ways to cooperate with strangers across town or long distance, and thereby develop new conventions.

Conditional cooperation is central to David Lewis's definition of a convention—"regularities of behavior that are sustained by . . . an expectation that others will do their part."[4] In the case of established conventions, at least those that are robust, there is little reason not to cooperate. We take for granted that almost everyone will do his or her part. Communication is less important because our expectations are satisfied time and again by a regularity of behavior that is no longer conditional. Cooperation is more conditional when developing new conventions. Sustaining our interest in coordination depends on whether we have ways of learning whether others are or are not doing their part. All of this adjustment among a large number of people, however, is inconceivable without communication.

In thinking about new interactive networks and the information that they have the potential to provide, my assumption is that a conditional framework for voluntary cooperation among strangers can arise if there is adequate feedback. Feedback facilitates strategic behavior—that is, behavior that arises not just from personal preferences, but is conditioned by what others are doing. Without feedback, it is presumed that you and I go our separate ways because it is impossible to know enough about so many others' preferences and behavior.

Much of the talk about possible telecommunication futures, linking strangers through new technologies, comes under the headline "information superhighways"—an apt analogy or metaphor for Americans, who like to travel fast even if we don't know exactly where we are going or why we should be in such a hurry to get there. But "networks," which have no fixed routes or destinations, are perhaps a better description than superhighways for what our telecommunication future is likely to provide. We should be encouraged but not euphoric about the possibilities.

There are a number of technological components that must be put in place before there is anything resembling interactive networks among countless strangers. It is like a new city to be built, whose infrastructure is still in development. It is difficult for planners and architects to know how such a metropolis will function when there is not yet agreement or even the economic rationale for what the water, sewage, electrical, and transportation systems will look like.

There is also the possibility that many people will not have access to the new superhighways or networks because such avenues will be like toll roads going places that don't serve everyone's interest. Some policy makers are pressing for "universal service," which means that those owning the fiberoptic lines and coaxial cables that reach our homes must provide such a service at reasonable cost just like in-state telephone companies now must do. Another unresolved issue is whether those who deliver a telecommunication line to our door will serve as a common carrier allowing "open access," like a phone service, to those wanting to use such a line to reach us, or limit the access of competing video and data services.[5]

Furthermore, although new telecommunication networks promise novelty and there are existing networks which help us understand some of their potential, there is no guarantee that we will use them to our mutual advantage. As Americans we are fond of using quantitative measures to describe what we own, but whether it is the horsepower of a car or the megabytes of a computer, it does not mean that we make good use of what we have. The buzz word is "interactive," but the convenience of ordering a movie or piece of merchandise via an electronic service from an easy chair seems no more "interactive" than getting cash by following the instructions on the screen of my bank's automatic teller machine.

And what will we do with the avalanche of information at our doorsteps? The capacity and speed of microchips, lasers, digital switches, and optical fibers are breathtaking, but like drinking from a firehose, it may be rather awkward when our thirst is quenched long before we know what to do with the excess.[6] We may not so much enter into a new age of enlightenment as stagger along trying to figure out what we have wrought.

One thing certain is that new telecommunication networks do not promise wired public forums where we will never have to leave our living rooms. On the contrary, such networks are more likely to indulge our individualized tastes and give us more options to create "our own little worlds." The suggestion that we are on the brink of a new age of teledemocracy where "community" is rebuilt on a scale that will revolutionize politics and representative government is romantic and bizarre.[7]

But if new telecommunication networks do not create new communities, they do offer millions of us the chance to coordinate our response to certain public problems, which require access to, and the exchange of, information. We may remain relatively distant from each other, but even as strangers we will nonetheless have good reason to promote new regularities of behavior. It is only if we believe that getting a majority to cooperate voluntarily is impossible without government direction that we are likely to grow accustomed to its coercion.

AN EXCURSUS ON TELECOMMUNICATION NETWORKS

The scale of each individual's public world is getting immeasurably larger as new technologies have the potential of delivering vast amounts of information to our workplaces and living rooms. Until recently, we thought of telephones, radio, and television as the major messengers bearing news of the outside world. Now they are being eclipsed by integrated service digital networks, satellites with global broadcasting capabilities, facsimile machines, fiberoptic computer-integrated telephone networks, video texts providing computer-based information services, and computer networks with conferencing capacities, electronic mail, and bulletin board systems.[8] We already use many of these technologies in currency and commodity markets, weather forecasting, scientific and economic data exchange, legal and bibliographic services, and in an array of business applications—electronic publishing, airline and hotel reservation systems, inventory systems, the financial and personnel record keeping of management information systems, real estate listings, and consumer credit.

Beyond what is up and running now, we are told that we will soon possess a "telecomputer" in our home that will be a computer and digital video processor connected by optical fibers to other telecomputers all over the world. The telecomputer will supposedly be superior to TV by being far more than a passive receiver of what others decide is our video fare. Instead we will use it like a telephone or a citizens' band radio initiating what we want to send and receive.[9] All such data will be in digital form, meaning that sound, brightness, and color are numerically encoded and can be stored and manipulated without deterioration. Moreover, optical fibers revolutionize the capacity to move data. Just as cable TV eventually emerged after the bandwidth capability of coaxial cable was developed in the late 1930s, now fiberoptics offers an even more efficient bandwidth. (Bandwidth is the transmission of data at an acceptable level of definition.) Comparing the capacity of fiberoptic threads to telephone wires is dramatized by the illustration of fiberoptics transmitting the entire contents of the Library of Congress in eight hours, while over a telephone line via a modem it would take 500 years.[10]

"Integrated broadband networks" already exist on a small scale among business firms, but with sufficient development that creates markets justifying the investment, it is expected that such networks will greatly expand. In recent years there has been a great deal of skirmishing as phone companies, software makers, broadcasters, and cable

TV firms circle each other trying to figure out how they can compete or collaborate and, more important, profit from the watershed in telecommunications that is seemingly so imminent.

Cable companies have the capacity to transmit large numbers of channels, but they don't have the two-way service that the phone companies provide.[11] The phone companies, on the other hand, have always provided two-way service but have quite limited capacity in their existing copper wire infrastructure. Some phone companies are already installing fiberoptic lines or integrated digital service networks that transform information into computer code that will permit the transmission of heavy loads of data over existing phone lines. Another possibility is the use of ATM, asynchronous transfer, an established technology in computer dialect that does not compress data, but through "packet switching" uses existing phone lines to transmit large amounts of data.

The competition between local phone companies and cable TV companies has not so much been settled as joined through their corporate maneuvering and their both seeking regulatory relief. Currently, state utility commissions limit the pass-along cost to customers when phone companies install new fiberoptic lines (the overall cost is estimated to be between $100 and $400 billion). It is possible, however, that much of the cost will be borne by those customers who want "advanced services" rather than by all rate payers.[12] In addition, the Federal Communications Commission (FCC) prohibits cross-ownership of phone and cable service in the same area, although such prohibitions are likely to be relaxed through new FCC rules.[13]

Although there is no agreed-upon electronic format that will be an industry standard or regulatory rationale in place that justifies the enormous investment needed to create such a standard, there already exists a working example of how we might become part of new telecommunication networks that will be the offspring. The existing network is "Internet," which probably links more than 20 million users and more than 1 million computers. It is estimated that this number will double annually for the remainder of the decade.[14] Internet is the world's largest data network, accessible in more than 100 countries.

The network includes digital libraries, commercial data bases, electronic mail, and access to software programs, weather information, interactive computer games, and data exchange. Most users are in government agencies, archives, universities, and large business firms. No one owns Internet; it is managed by volunteers, and its operating costs are paid by those who use it. There are more than 70,000 registered networks potentially interested in using data network lines in Internet. This "labyrinth has no overlord. It is an alliance of technical republics."[15]

Many states—Colorado, Iowa, New York, Ohio, Oregon, Pennsylvania, and New Mexico—have already developed telecommunication networks similar to Internet. In New Mexico, "Technet" links residents and school classrooms via a computer and a modem to state agencies, university libraries, businesses, and public interest groups. Seventy percent of the users, teachers and students, use Technet for free. The rest pay modest subscription and user charges to finance the network. In addition, "Free-Nets" are becoming more common in various cities. Starting in Cleveland in 1986 and now operating in almost 100 other jurisdictions, many of these community networks offer Internet access and serve as electronic forums for local discussions.[16]

Another critical mass of potential networkers are the devoted viewers of C-Span. C-Span is a creature of the cable industry that televises House (C-Span) and Senate (C-Span 2) proceedings and all manner of political events and public affairs programming. No tax dollars are used to finance C-Span's operation. C-Span reaches almost 60 million households and C-Span 2 is available to approximately 34 million households through over 400 CATV systems.[17] This small Washington-based enterprise has discovered that people are hungry for information and conversation, via "call-ins," about public problems whether it is 24-hour cable news, the large audience for the Perot "infomercials," or C-Span itself. It has had an 80 percent increase in viewers since 1988 and, remarkably, 98 percent of them voted in the 1992 presidential election. Otherwise the profile of C-Span viewers is not exceptional. They are almost evenly divided between men and women, Republicans and Democrats, and high- and low-wage earners.[18]

C-Span is used extensively in classrooms, especially in grades 7 to 12. There are no copyright restrictions and its service ranks third behind the Discovery Channel and CNN in the nation's schools.[19]

Each event C-Span televises "is aired without commentary, analysis, or interruption,"[20] what those at C-Span call "video verité."[21] It is a measure of TV's hyperactive pace that such a low-key presentation stands out as exceptional. Robert MacNeil of PBS says that political reporters "don't watch for all the sociology. . . ." C-Span lets people see "all the irrelevant and inconsequential stuff we edit out."[22] Of course, what is "irrelevant" or "inconsequential" is a judgment that broadcasters make on our behalf, and sometimes their judgments err.

I told Brian Lamb, its CEO and founder, that I thought C-Span's great appeal is its human pace, not edited or hyped but instead allowing the viewer to see how events and conversations actually develop. In new telecommunication networks, there will probably still be plenty of hoopla programming that resembles the visual and audio assault of commercial TV. But the ways in which Internet and C-Span have already evolved tell us that there will also be room for less managed content that develops from what those who use the new networks want from them.

A COORDINATION PROBLEM

To illustrate the potential of telecommunication networks to promote cooperation among strangers, it helps to have a particular coordination problem in mind and to imagine a plausible scenario of how a new everyday practice might gain widespread acceptance. There are many practices, or what I have called discrete conventions, such as "designating a driver" or having "safe sex," that work just fine whether or not a lot of people also observe the same convention. And there are organization and community conventions that can succeed as long as almost everyone in a particular workplace or neighborhood coordinates his or her behavior, such as work hours in the office or a block watch on the street. Some practices, however, are of little consequence unless there is society-wide coordination, such as observing the rules of the road, or going on daylight saving time, or getting immunized.

So any scenario should be centered on a new everyday practice that would only make sense if there were enough others, millions of us, who eventually coordinated our behavior in order to change things: such as taking three days off, instead of two, to enlarge "the weekend" and reduce automobile pollution in our major cities; or keeping schools open all year and eliminating the three-month summer vacation; or voluntarily surrendering all handguns; or no longer sending each other Christmas cards.

I want to imagine a scenario where consumers decide to alter their shopping routine by refusing to buy store products with excessive packaging.[23] The object of such a campaign would be to put the old convention of a boycott to a new purpose—reducing the amount of waste we generate, which goes by other names such as "source reduction" and "precycling."

The origin of a "precycling" campaign would not necessarily start with an ambitious agenda that called for a nationwide boycott of merchandise that had excessive packaging. But in constructing a scenario, I have assumed that precycling, which some Americans already practice, would be amplified via telecommunication networks so that it became a serious rather than just a symbolic protest. The term *precycling* was used by the city government of Berkeley, California, which in 1989 encouraged residents to "Reduce waste before you buy." "We recycle items after we've bought them . . . we can precycle while we shop."[24] Likewise, in the late 1980s the Citizens Clearinghouse for Hazardous Waste protested McDonald's use of Styrofoam. Members picketed the chain's fast food outlets and returned used packaging to its corporate headquarters. In November 1990, McDonald's decided to stop using the "clamshell" take-out hamburger container. Switching to paper, McDonald's predicted that its packaging volume would be reduced by 70 to 90 percent.

Precycling is a relatively new practice, but a boycott to get attention paid to such a practice is an established convention. It is not, however, an everyday routine. If successful, a boycott ends. I would assume that precycling would continue, in one form or another, as an everyday shopping routine.[25]

In 1960 Americans discarded an average of 2.7 pounds of trash per day for each person. Now we throw out four pounds daily for each man, woman, and child. This is twice the amount generated per person in Japan or Germany. Landfills fill up quickly; new landfills are difficult to site due to the quite natural resistance of those who would have to live nearby; some communities export their garbage across state lines to other communities, which, in turn, complain; and some garbage even goes abroad. Packaging represents about one-third of all this waste, much of it plastic. "In 1989, U.S. corporations used more than 12 billion pounds of plastic for packaging designed to be thrown away as soon as the package was opened." There are estimates that the amount of plastic packaging may double in the next ten years.[26]

There are many reasons why there is so much packaging to throw out. We like convenience in the products that we buy such as one-serving containers of juice or a single meal to be cooked in a microwave. We consume such portions quickly and dispose of their wrappings just as fast. We also want our products wrapped and sealed to preserve freshness or to resist tampering. And supermarket and discount store managers know that gaudy and oversize packaging, which shouts for our attention, is cheaper than hiring more employees to hype the merchandise or answer questions on how to use it. Moreover, a part of such savings is passed on to us in the form of lower prices. However, as taxpayers we ultimately bear the cost of disposing of product packaging. In some communities the average household may soon pay $1,000 or more a year, in the form of taxes or fees, just for trash removal.[27]

When I visited a large discount store in South Carolina, I was struck by how many products were sold in the aisles where the packaging was large enough to get attention from customers wheeling their shopping carts in what seemed a store with endless merchandise. And yet space in such a store is used as efficiently as possible. Merchandise was often sealed under plastic on cardboard backing that was attached to hooks that permitted the display of many products in a relatively small space. For example, five such packages, each containing one flashlight and two batteries, protruded from a display stand at a checkout counter. The flashlight and batteries were mounted under plastic on large, colorful cardboard that served as an advertisement for the product. The mounting of such merchandise allowed the store to hang it in a conspicuous place alongside similar racks of other products, all within easy reach as consumers brought their carts to one of thirteen checkout counters.

On my visit to this particular store, I saw several examples of excessive packaging on one main avenue that ran parallel to the checkout counters. It was like a boulevard for browsing and also one that everyone had to cross from the streets of merchandise that were perpendicular to it. Much of the packaging of products on the boulevard served the same purpose as the green, leafy kale that restaurants and food caterers use to garnish our plates. The kale is intended to make whatever portions that are served look more attractive. The kale also allows the portions to be smaller when surrounded by such cheap finery. On one avenue, I found—

- A rack of compact disks, each of which was packaged in a marquee-like box twice the size of the disk itself.
- Dozens of battery-powered toothbrushes, each placed in a plastic-wrapped box the size of a new bestselling book. The effect was to make the toothbrush look like it was in a diorama, as if a story were being told. Batteries were not included.
- A doll of a popular children's character, approximately six inches high and three inches wide, encased in plastic on a cardboard backing that measured eight and a half by ten and a half inches.
- A silk flower arrangement that was being sold in a box as big as a nineteen-inch TV set. The flower arrangement stood only ten inches high.
- Dozens of a glowing ball, the size of a large orange, under plastic and mounted on seven by ten inch poster board advertising its "amazing" properties.

When I looked for a ruler to measure the merchandise, even the ruler was packaged in a disposable container that was at least a third larger than the ruler itself.

After leaving the store, I noticed a sign in the parking lot. "Help keep your costs down. Return carts here for your safety and convenience." I thought to myself, if they really want to keep my costs down

. . . But then if the packaging inside the store were more modest, probably fewer of us would buy the products. Their "presentation," like the kale that decorates a dinner plate, may be the only way some products look attractive enough to whet our appetites when we cruise down the boulevard in such a store. After all, one reason we go there is to see the sights.

GETTING ORGANIZED

There is no way of knowing whether a "precycling" campaign will actually arise and, if it does, how it will come about. Although I do not discount the possibility of unplanned coordination, my scenario here assumes a more deliberate course of action, whether or not anyone knows, at the outset, that it will lead to the establishment of a new convention.[28]

I do not begin the scenario with what some "community" might do. That's putting the cart before the horse. Communities don't solve problems; individuals who live in communities do that. The local origins of "precycling" might be traced to the places where we find each other, as acquaintances or strangers, in coffee shops, health clubs, malls, bars, plazas, school auditoriums, church basements, community college classrooms. In those places, we tell stories, compare experiences, and offer opinions. In the case of waste disposal, we complain about how much trash has to be disposed of after Christmas and how much of it comes from the giant discount store that anchors the mall at the edge of town. We talk about the imminent closing of a local landfill and the higher cost of trucking garbage to out-of-state sites. We ask each other how we can avoid paying higher property taxes. Someone remembers reading that "if the packaging is designed to be thrown away immediately, all you're getting for your money is cleverly designed garbage."[29] Someone else suggests that if enough of us refuse to buy goods with excessive packaging, we might get the attention of retailers, wholesalers, or the people who make the products.

Such talk may lead to a "community" meeting or an article in the local newspaper that further organizes people's thinking about what we might do. Most everyone agrees that waste disposal is certainly a fundamental problem. After talking it over and after naming the problem, in all likelihood, we will disassemble it and look for manageable parts.[30] Lots of questions are asked. Can we agree on a new practice? Is it simple and unambiguous? Is it congenial to our everyday lives? Is there a precept of behavior that will sustain it? Will some people bear an unequal burden? Will some people find it difficult to participate? Will the new practice make sense in one place but not another, at one time but not another? Are there enough of us? What happpens if everyone precycles?

Assuming that an interest in coordination persists, a core group would probably emerge to take the lead. Even when there is unplanned coordination, leaders are important. They have a disproportionate influence. Their early actions lead others to join in: the first pedestrian off the curb whom we follow and stop traffic; the motorist who, for a time, sets the conventional speed on a stretch of highway; or the group in the front mezzanine that gets the standing ovation going at the opera house. Like a host at a cocktail party, someone has to provide the "action," make introductions, and keep things moving along.

Unlike the rest of us, the members of a core group are not tentative or conditioned by what others do. They simply believe that someone has to be the first off the curb to mobilize others, to follow and create the safety in numbers to get to the other side. Leaders often get where they are going with the help of others; what marks such people is an intensity about resolving a problem. For whatever reason, their motivations are better formed on certain issues, conditions, or desirable changes than those of a great majority of us who have "better things to do."[31]

In the case of precycling, someone has to take the lead in getting attention paid to the consequences of producer packaging and individual consumer behavior when few of us have the imagination to comprehend how much of a societal problem such packaging and behavior is. Even when we go to the local landfill, we can't see the accumulation. It is buried or in the process of being buried. The small piece of it that we dump hardly seems worth getting excited about. The work of leadership is to persuade you and me and others that each of us makes a difference for better or for worse and that large-scale cooperation is essential.[32]

In any community, a core group, which leads, is more than likely composed of people who know each other from the PTA, a neighborhood cleanup, block watch, car pool, or day-care site. As activists in one way or another, they have good reason to sustain such relationships or reciprocate past favors. Each member of a core group undoubtedly has links with other people at a workplace or church or other association, all of whom provide the beginning of a local network. Such a network is not electronic but can grow in the same random fashion as one that develops among computer users.

Members of a core group are likely to know how to use existing conventions to recruit strangers with "petitions" that enroll, "covenants" that commit, and boycotts that persuade. Like most conventions, except for discrete ones, boycotts don't develop with just a few committed souls even if such persons have a substantial interest and resources. Those few who are willing and able may get certain practices started, but they won't succeed unless enough others join them, join in. The nature of a boycott is to build a following that leads.

The core group might ask us to do the following:

- Refuse to buy products that are packaged under plastic and have excessive cardboard backing.
- Buy products that are in "recycled" packaging.
- Tell store managers what packaging we will buy or not buy.
- Call 1-800 toll-free telephone numbers, shown on the packaging of many products, and tell product manufacturers what packaging we will or will not buy.
- Start a phone tree by calling six of our friends, explaining the purpose of the boycott and seeking their cooperation. When we find six friends who are willing to go along, ask each of them to call six of their friends, and so on.[33]
- Urge town, city, or county officials to consider levying "pay-as-you-throw" charges on residents (paying for disposal per garabage can) to encourage them to reduce their expenses by shopping for products with less packaging.[34]

Each of us would be expected to precycle at those places where we normally shop—the supermarket, large discount stores, and wherever else we look for and buy products. We would be left to police our respective part of the line, so to speak, even though there would be little point in doing so unless the larger campaign took hold. Although any person's part would necessarily be local, the impact of a boycott would have to be felt in chain stores across the country.

Many problems these days are really beyond local remedy. A general store a century ago or a local downtown department store a generation ago could have been held to account to customers for the way it presented its produce and merchandise. But many "local businesses" now are actually franchises or outlets for national or international chains. They have far less control over what they sell and how they sell it. They are part of a system in which the pricing and trade practices are set by someone else. In most cases those practices also include how things are packaged for sale. When McDonald's decided to change the way its take-out food was packaged, that was a very big deal, affecting staff and customers throughout the country.

Precycling, as a new practice, launched by a boycott, would have to be nationwide in scope to be effective as a "source reduction" strategy. Local efforts would be necessary but not sufficient. Boycotts have no chance of succeeding without the force of numbers. Where the "numbers" might come from would depend on a core group using existing organizations and telecommunication networks to get across the terms of cooperation and the prospects of success. First I want to explore what those terms might be and then look at how the dynamics of a successful boycott might work.

THE TERMS OF COOPERATION

Our preferences for exit, delegation, private gain, and parity would be obstacles to coordinating a boycott and developing the convention of precycling. Most people see no problem with product packaging, at least not until their taxes go up to pay for waste disposal or their living expenses get so stretched that a campaign about unnecessary packaging starts to make sense. The great majority of us have yet to see that precycling is a pocketbook issue, not just a cause for "environmentalists."

Our preference for exit in this case would not involve moving away. It would be hard to avoid the "problem" of waste disposal anywhere we go. Instead, we would probably just be indifferent to precycling campaigns when we shopped at local supermarkets and discount stores.

Our preference for delegation might be tempting to anyone who thought government specifications for the packaging of goods in interstate commerce would achieve the same result with less personal effort. Environmental groups might seek laws and regulations mandating the limit and content of packaging, but such laws and regulations would not likely be passed or promulgated until a boycott or similar activities made clear there was substantial public support for "source reduction" measures. It is a mistake to think that government initiates action without some input from someone outside of government. Government officials rarely have time to think about, much less think up, what needs to be done about a certain problem until some pressure is brought to bear from some quarter.

Our preference for private gain would simply mean that many people would not forgo purchases of desirable merchandise until its packaging was changed. Any boycott means that those involved have to give up something in order to get something, and those who did not join such a campaign would probably discount any future gain of lower taxes and instead just go on buying and throwing away the packaging without much thought to the consequences.

The preference for parity, of course, is another way of talking about the conditions we put on our cooperation, and in a precycling campaign each person's attitude about "fair share" would depend, in part, on what others were doing or not doing at any given stage. Furthermore, there would be any number of disparities in circumstance and condition which people might use to justify their reluctance to cooperate. Doing our fair share is often a very subjective matter, and each of us prefers being the judge of what that fair share is.

Although leaders are not conditional cooperators themselves, they may recognize that conditional cooperation is ground enough for developing a new practice. Paradoxically, the conditional nature of cooperation is a strength, not a weakness, when enlisting others' cooperation. After all, if everyone else is going to do something, why do they need me? But if my cooperation is important for enlisting or maintaining others' cooperation, then I become important, not just marginal. Of course, if feedback tells us that other people are not joining together to solve a particular coordination problem, then you and I will probably adjust our conduct accordingly and go our separate ways. One commentator names two kinds of conditional cooperation. He calls one "brave reciprocity"—you cooperate until too many others don't. The other is "cautious reciprocity"—I cooperate only after enough others cooperate.[35] In both cases, however, our behavior is conditional until a successful outcome is no longer in doubt.

In a precycling campaign, many of us would not necessarily act as a group, but our membership in existing organizations or the idea of being a new "member" of a growing movement might very well account for why we would be willing to do our part. No doubt many national environmental and consumer groups would encourage their members to participate. In addition, local groups affiliated with national organizations or operating on their own would likely be found in a developing federated structure. A government agency, of course, might serve as a catalyst, but a federated structure of nongovernment groups would still be important in reaching, persuading, and sustaining participation. For example, the city of Seattle credited part of its successful recycling program to "voluntary block captains who helped their neighbors figure out how to make curbside recycling work."[36]

I noted in chapter three how group identity in a classroom game was very important in producing a cooperative outcome. Those who are responsible for managing organizations or leading movements know that being part of a group is something that most of us welcome and many of us need, especially at a time of weakening social ties when we have fewer chances to experience a sense of belonging. Belonging also assumes a reciprocity between the individual and the group as a whole or among other members individually. Feeling that we are part of a group helps to clarify what is expected of us. Clarifying expectations arises both in everyday conventions where no membership is involved and in activities where membership, a convention itself, explains why we regulate our behavior with other fellow members. When requests are made of us as "members" of a group, you and I find it hard to say "no."[37]

THE PROSPECTS OF SUCCESS

I was always struck by the concern of students with whom I worked at Yale's School of Management that the prospect of success was almost a necessary condition to engage and retain their interest in problem-solving cases and exercises. The idea that I might have presented them with "no-win" situations discouraged some students and made it more likely that they would give up too easily. They had been educated to compete and win, to savour their talents and what those talents could attain for them. They had not confronted many instances of individual failure. Collective failure seemed even more improbable. I found a re-luctance on the part of students to confront the sad fact that we can rarely exercise control over problems—to know how to plan their elim-ination and to execute a plan in such a way as to bring it off. So success was elusive for those students who measured their performance against impossibly high standards. More often than not, success in a class case and exercise was a flawed and compromised outcome, where some-thing was achieved, but certainly not what they had planned or worked for together. The real world rarely has happy endings, just new chapters that prolong the story.[38]

For example, a former student of mine with the New York City De-partment of Environmental Conservation wrote me telling of their quandary. Because of the need to curb water consumption, the city de-cided to meter homes and apartment buildings. (The old water-billing system averaged water use citywide so that large users were subsidized by small users.) According to my former student, there was no "fair" way, however, for allocating water use with multifamily buildings where 70 percent of the city's residents live. He noted that metering individ-ual apartments was "prohibitively expensive and almost impossible lo-gistically." Without a way to meter each apartment, a building has to pay for its total use. But who pays? If a building has a lot of large or doubled-up families, or if some tenants are home all day using water, some people pay a disproportionate amount for others' use. And my friend warns that if the landlord cannot pass on the cost, building abandonment is possible. This reminded me of the "no-win" situations that I used to construct for my students. My former student saw few prospects for success.

In some ways the attitude of my students is the prevalent and wholly understandable reflex of many Americans, of whatever age, who prefer exiting the scene rather than getting engaged with problems that seem to have no easy, much less ideal, solution. If precycling, as an everyday practice, were to be established, there would have to be enough others to make it work, and enough others might be hard to find unless there was a prospect of success. If your car is stuck in a snowbank, you have to persuade those of us who are passersby that our cooperation in rock-ing or pushing the car is absolutely necessary. You might even have to exaggerate the prospects of success. This would not be deliberate de-ception, but only a kind of unexamined optimism that draws others into an organized effort. If you are convinced that your car is hopelessly stuck, it does little good to recruit the help of passersby. We won't suc-ceed. If, however, you really don't know how many it will take, but you are sure that enough of us can manage to free the car from the snow-bank, then it is to your advantage and probably those of us who stopped to help that we assume each of us can make a difference. What any campaign must do is get the car rocking with the gift of opti-mism. In another context, William James said, ". . . faith in a fact can help create the fact."[39]

Whether our optimism is warranted is another matter. We often de-pend on the assurances of others who we think are competent, or more competent than we are, to make such judgments and predictions. For example, millions of us believe that less cholesterol is good for our health, without any investigation of our own that such claims are true.[40] We may very well be disposed to think that precycling makes sense and will eventually change things even though we also know that we are often mistaken in our assumptions. The error of those who find it hard to conceive of cooperation among strangers is that they think we somehow know or calculate the odds of success or failure. On the contrary, we often get involved because we don't. "[M]istake-making is one of the most characteristic of human actions, so that a good portion of the social world becomes unintelligible once it is assumed away."[41]

Moreover, the contemplation of what will succeed is very different from the experience of trying to make it happen. The exact course taken or eventual outcome can't be predicted, but only attended to. Like riding the back of a wild animal, it is hard to know precisely where it will take us, but those astride know that they are going somewhere. They are not standing still. Once we have become part of an undertaking, the experience itself may produce its own staying power. "Striving" becomes "the compensation for uncertainty."[42] When your car is stuck in a snowbank, those of us who stop to assist usually look for more help from others passing by to make the task easier and less time-consuming. Your expectations of us, as well as our own expectations, develop on the scene and keep us there. If there is such a thing as an "effort convention," it comes into play as we go through the experience together—each of us measuring our individual contribution against what others already involved are doing.[43] Few of us, having offered assistance, will walk away leaving you to fend for yourself because some passersby fail to stop and lend a hand. Any group of strangers once involved in trying to solve a coordination problem will, for the time being, probably pay more attention to finding allies than worrying about those who don't join them.

It doesn't matter what specific outcome we strive for; cooperation, seen as an "effort convention," has its own metaconvention: once engaged, do your fair share. Some armchair analysts think just the opposite—"if enough others help, they don't need me." But in their armchairs, each is like a passerby, not a participant. Once engaged, most of us don't look for excuses. We have invested time and energy, and we want to succeed. The problem with those who do a lot of thinking about cooperation is that they sometimes neglect in their reasoning to include a specific social context, which often shapes our choices and accounts for our persistence.[44]

Another way to look at the effort we are likely to make once engaged is to think of it as a sunk cost. Once we do something and endure whatever cost it exacts—waiting in line, trying to push a car out of a snowbank—it is not likely that we will abandon the project. The payoff is to get served at the head of the line or see the car up on the road again. Short of that, our time and energy have been wasted. We are not likely to exercise our preference for exit because we have too much invested.

In the case of precycling, once we have rearranged our buying habits to exclude overpackaged products, we would probably stick with the boycott if there were feedback that the campaign was gaining momentum, giving us reason to believe that there would eventually be some benefit to compensate us for our sunk costs. What a boycott like precycling would require is getting enough others to believe that a threshhold could be reached where the cost of cooperation—not buying overpackaged merchandise, which they otherwise find desirable—is exceeded by the benefit of paying fewer tax dollars for waste disposal. Once enough others regulated their behavior and produced a beneficial outcome, cooperation would be less speculative, and the "payoff" would increase as more people cooperated.[45]

FEEDBACK AND SUCCESS

When we aren't together in the same snowbank, we need some way of communicating with each other for mutual support. Obviously, there is a wide array of messages that people send and receive in their everyday contacts. But a large number of strangers don't have such opportunities. How do they get in touch and keep in touch? It would depend, in great part, on whether we could share information quickly and inexpensively through telecommunication networks linking us to other participants and sources of information about the status of the boycott.

Any scenario is only a very crude sketch of what might happen, since any campaign would have its own unpredictable dynamics which would encourage or discourage participation. In any event, much would depend on the perception of whether progress was being made. Scorecards, bulletins, and giant thermometers, like the ones used in fund-raising campaigns on TV and billboards, with updated reports on "how we're doing," would certainly encourage those already making the practice part of their everyday shopping routine and tell others that something was going on that they might want to be part of. Our crosstown or long-distance networks could help to explain what was at stake, what each individual could do, and pass on reports from those of us who chose to do something in support of the campaign. If this ongoing circulation of information showed that progress was being made, that more of us were precycling, then in all likelihood even more people would imitate our example, confident that coordination was already proving to be workable.

In developing both a local following for "precycling" as well as a national campaign, we would want to see that the numbers were building to publicize the practice of precycling and to make any boycott effective. The feedback would let us know that friends and acquaintances were joining in and that strangers elsewhere were also involved. Of course, if the campaign became "news," then the amplification would be even greater. In addition to status reports, the general public would be getting background stories and the reactions of spokespersons of retail, wholesale, and manufacturing sources. If progress were reported frequently, it would encourage us that success was possible and that it depended on each person's continued cooperation. Both sources of information, interactive networks and media news, would promote the development of a loose coalition trying to stick together and to achieve a stated purpose.[46]

A boycott depends in part on making visible other people's cooperation or defection. That is why picket lines seek to influence workers or customers to support their cause, if not physically join their ranks. You and I can be swayed by others telling us to do this or not to do that. Telecommunication networks, reporting on the progress of a precycling campaign, might in effect do the same thing. Each person's participation could be scrolled across a screen and particular individuals cited in stories, pictures, awards, and ceremonies. No matter how small a part we play in any undertaking, each of us likes to be acknowledged, publicly as well as privately. In fact, as we find ourselves more alone in a society of strangers, the more we may crave some recognition if only for a moment. What else explains sports fans waving to a TV camera as it pans the crowd? For a moment someone who knows us may see us projected on a TV screen that is being watched simultaneously by millions of people. The frantic wave and cheery grin are directed not just at possible friends and family who are watching, but at that great seeing public that for a moment watches a stranger waving to other strangers, who are unseen but constitute an audience nonetheless.[47]

Could one's failure to participate be highlighted as well? Whether or not such a tactic would be wise to pursue—civil libertarians would surely cry "foul"—no doubt it could be done. Every day the media indulges in negative stories about this person's peccadilloes or that person's acts that deviate from accepted norms. Most of such "news" is about well-known people who are easy targets. But anyone can get singled out. What would have happened in Des Moines if the names of homeowners who failed to observe the temporary convention of not using city water had been put on a computer/video network? Would the negative publicity of a few have persuaded others not to risk such unwelcome notoriety? Or consider videotapes showing men who come shopping for sex in neighborhoods that don't want such traffic. Imagine such tapes finding their way to home screens across a metropolitan area. For better or worse, when interactive networks are up and working, there will be a potential to communicate in a very public way what untold numbers of people are each individually doing or not doing about this problem or that project—landlords, local businesspersons, school principals, hospital board members, members of the clergy, or our next-door neighbor. Like it or not, we may all become more visible to one another. As a practice is firmly established, we may be less tolerant of those who fail to cooperate for whatever reason. The person who is "out of line" is often called to account when we are sure that a line is in place and working as it should.

The success of a boycott or precycling campaign would be entirely dependent on reaching the kind of numbers that persuaded those who had not joined that they really had very little to lose and perhaps much to gain. Most of us like the feeling of being a part of an effort that is proving to be successful. We have names for this: the "bandwagon" effect and something that "snowballs"; it is like reaching "critical mass" when enough others adopt a particular practice and it becomes a convention. Nothing succeeds like success, and it can create enough others cooperating to make a convention self-sustaining. There is an exhilaration that comes from being part of an undertaking that accomplishes more or less what it sets out to do. This is especially true among strangers when there are no other ties but those that develop, at least temporarily, because of their cooperation, as in military campaigns, political insurgencies, walk-a-thons, even the successful performance of the "wave" at Dodger Stadium.[48]

Any success, however, may be short-lived. When we seek to change and improve a situation, there is always the possibility that we won't— not because of a failure to get others' cooperation, but because that cooperation leads to problems that we did not foresee.[49] Feedback can produce its own mischief. For example, if we are told to avoid using a particular bridge during the morning rush hour because of construction, those who do not have such information may find the bridge relatively free of traffic, while those of us who acted on such information use different routes and produce pockets of congestion that delay our daily commute. The same may be true when we organize car pools in an attempt to relieve traffic congestion. Those who stopped driving and took mass transit because of such congestion may resume driving and thus create new congestion that car pooling temporarily relieved. If there is a successful water-conservation campaign, public authorities may be tempted to divert water to other areas that are more profligate, thus penalizing those who are more thrifty. If too many of us report suspicious activity to the police, we may overload the switchboard and prevent those requiring emergency help from getting through. There is no answer for fixing coordination problems once and for all. They have to be dealt with as they arise, and as they are resolved, new and unforeseen problems may very well intrude. Problems are hard to solve and "success" can create new problems.

Despite the surprises that may be in store for us after establishing any new convention, as strangers in need of each other we now have at our disposal networks of communication that make the prospects for successful cooperation much better than they have ever been.

Chapter Five

WHAT IF EVERYONE...?

The Possibility of New Conventions

In previous chapters I have examined a sample of our current repertoire of conventions and new practices, which counter the prevailing
assumption that only market incentives or government coercion can
get strangers to cooperate. In fact, many of our existing conventions
remain vital problem-solving mechanisms because markets and governments do not seem to have either the will or the capacity to solve
certain problems for us.

For example, despite our weak social ties and preference for putting
individual interest before social interest, we manage to establish land
trusts and thereby conserve open space when private developers and
tax hungry governments would have us do otherwise; we manage to
"adopt" and clean up large parts of our local highways choked by consumer trash and beyond the reach of government sanitation crews; we
manage to help ourselves and others in self-help groups, which go far
beyond what market remedies and government agencies alone can do
for us; we manage to feed the homeless by pooling and distributing excess foodstuffs that markets have no use for and government administration only makes more costly; we manage to serve on juries, to
recycle our household garbage, to designate drivers, to form hospice
teams, to donate blood, to maintain libraries, to provide wildlife sanc-

tuaries, and to boycott products and even entire states. There are literally hundreds of ways that we govern ourselves, or could govern ourselves, using conventions large and small.

The concluding chapter of a book that examines contemporary life
often fails the reader. Rather than just mercifully ending the critique,
the writer abandons analysis and resorts to hyperbole about what can
be done to make things better. I suspect one reason for such overreaching is that writer and reader alike prefer happy endings, even though
they know that the real world of problems does not so easily yield.

I don't believe anyone can write a happy ending to our contemporary problems. Instead, it depends on whether enough of us cooperate
in trying to solve them. With this in mind, my concluding chapter first
looks at new conventions that Americans are using to take back their
streets and then imagines how both old and new conventions can help
in the care and development of children.

TAKING BACK THE STREETS

Neighborhood street life is perhaps the most common everyday experience that we share with strangers. Certainly this is true in cities, large
or small, where the exigencies of commerce and the ethnic and racial
diversity of residents produce an uncertain but necessary mixing of
purposes and people. As the cityscape yields to suburbs and rural life,
such mixing is less likely to occur. Many people prefer it that way. Our
attitudes about cities have a great deal to do with how we regard life
among strangers. The alarm about crime in our cities, which has been
never-ending in our social history, has often reflected the apprehension
about the ceaseless flow of strangers who take up residence across the
street, down the block, even on the other side of town. At one time,
they were new immigrants from Europe, at another time they were
rural blacks from the South, and more recently, they are the polyglot of
races from Asia and the Caribbean.

The alarm about crime today is exacerbated by the perception that
family breakdown, structural unemployment, and more drugs, home-
lessness, prostitution, graffiti, and adolescent violence are shifting the
control of urban streets from residents and police to malcontents and

social misfits, strangers or not. This perception, and the fear that such a perception spawns of a breakdown in the social order at the block level where people actually live, makes public safety perhaps our most serious and seemingly intractable problem.

The street places that are safest, according to William Whyte's observations, are the attractive plazas and parks where there are many people. People like to go where other people like to go, whether alone or with a group. But fear of the streets makes us abandon these places, and their emptiness promotes crime and other undesirable behavior, reinforcing the fear that they now belong to dangerous strangers. Ironically, those public places that are designed not for comfort but for security—with walls, fences, and few benches—tend to drive people away, inviting others to take them over for drug dealing or for whatever purposes suit them.[1]

As people retreat from the streets, their front steps, or even their windows (as air conditioners replace open windows to lean out of, and TV draws people to private space inside), there is no longer a critical mass of eyes and movement, games and conversation, that mutually support each other in the public space outside. Such a retreat shrinks the perimeter that can be shared and defended. Buildings become stockades with razor wire and iron grating. Stores are vacated, churches are locked, and library windows are sealed, as urban neighborhoods surrender the streets to strangers.[2] In many places, the fear of the streets has discouraged the active street life that partly accounted for their safety. One commentator gets very specific when he says, "Powerless in the larger world of wealth and power, young black males rule the smaller world of street interactions and every day encounters."[3] Of course, it is not just young black males who frighten city residents, but any strangers of any age or color who seem hostile or indifferent to community conventions and norms.

Increasingly, even smaller cities and the enclave life of suburban developments seem affected by this same miasma. One example is Easton, Pennsylvania, a town of 25,000 people, but part of an urban triangle that includes Bethlehem and Allentown. Downtown Easton, where many of its residents still live, has been the site of crowded and prolonged "cruising" by young strangers from "out of town," who come to see and be seen on weekend nights. Cruising became a convention when enough young strangers converged in their cars on Easton's Central Square in the evening hours "to make the scene" and also to create a scene, according to downtown homeowners. They complained that cruising brought noise, drugs, and prostitutes to their neighborhood.

One Easton councilwoman proposed a cruise control ordinance, but residents thought it highly unlikely that an under staffed police force could enforce it. The proposed ordinance required police to monitor anyone suspected of cruising, i.e., passing the same point in a downtown "loop" three or more times in any two-hour period between 8:00 P.M. and 5:00 A.M. Those in violation of the ordinance would be subject to $100 fines. The same councilwoman offered another option, which would have residents record license plates, report violators of the ordinance to the police, and then testify against the cruisers in court. The attitude of most residents was that, one way or another, they wanted to undo the convention of cruising with their own convention of working with the police to take back their streets. No doubt the downtown homeowners in Easton would have loved to snap their fingers and have a new law enacted or an old law enforced that would sweep up the problems of cruising or homelessness or drug dealing or prostitution, but they knew that there was not enough money or manpower that could do that.[4]

Jane Jacobs understood that there was always the possibility of "new improvisations" on what she called the "ballet of the good city sidewalk."[5] But Jacobs's observations fit an era and a part of the city where there were more or less viable neighborhoods. Now we know there are many places in any city or town where residents no longer have a social life on the streets that coordinates public safety with or without police assistance. They confront new realities—weaker social ties, the erosion of family stability, and the decline of small neighborhood businesses.[6]

Nonetheless, when you look at what is happening throughout the country, bleak as the prospects of many city neighborhoods now seem, there are new improvisations to take back the streets, albeit less spontaneous and subtle than what Jacobs observed. You see people trying to fashion new conventions even if such coordination proves to be only fitful and temporary. They are not street activities for their own sake, the kind of unchoreographed dance that Jacobs described. They are meant to be a show of strength to command attention. Public safety, however, is a relative term and such improvisations run the risk of being defeated by those who initially retreat and then often reassert themselves to menace street life again.

It is not just crime that bothers city residents; it is the disorder of the streets where they feel outnumbered. Public drunkenness, aggressive panhandling, gangs loitering in parks, rowdy bars, gambling on the street corner, abandoned cars and buildings, all contribute to the fear that the streets are out of control. Whatever is done to reduce this anxiety by upgrading appearances and driving out the unwelcome will shift the advantage back to those who live there or to those strangers who use the same streets for more productive reasons.

Street problems cannot be solved by government agencies alone. They have neither the time nor the money to do it. More important, they do not know how to do it. At the end of her insightful book, Jane Jacobs wrote about "cities as problems of organized complexity . . . organisms that are replete with unexamined, but obviously intricately interconnected and surely understandable relationships."[7] What Jacobs thought essential in dealing with such complexity were the intuitions and participation of neighborhood residents, rather than the strategies of remote city planners.

Some neighborhoods try to clean up their environments with the expectation that the look of a place or a street will affect where a criminal element hangs out. Abandoned cars are removed, graffiti painted over, streetlights fixed, vacant lots beautified, broken windows repaired, sidewalks and curbs are cleaned by storeowners, and so forth. If this does not deter criminals, it does encourage residents to get out more and to use or safeguard the physical improvements that they have made. It follows that the troublemakers may go elsewhere given the increasing circulation of residents on their streets.

Camcorders in the hands of any citizen have become a weapon to record and publicize street incidents that disrupt a neighborhood. We know the power of the hand-held video camera from the endless playback on TV news of the Rodney King beating by Los Angeles police officers. Residents in Bayside and Glendale, two neighborhoods in the borough of Queens in New York City, used video cameras to record young people putting graffiti on neighborhood walls, fences, and buildings. Graffiti is seen as a virus which, if not checked, spreads throughout a neighborhood. This visibility makes both shoppers and shopowners nervous about the area. Business is curbed and shopowners may ultimately decide to relocate. As business moves out, stores are emptied and the street life deteriorates so that not just graffiti but drugs and prostitution often gain the upper hand. The Glendale effort produced twelve guilty pleas, and the Bayside effort was used as an "organizing tool" with parents to get their children to clean up the vandalism or face criminal charges or suspension from school.[8] Residents in Methuen, Massachusetts, also used video cameras but in this case to film prostitutes and their customers. The Methuen residents also noted license plates and car descriptions, to help the police.[9]

Other neighborhoods plagued by prostitution have not only recorded but publicized the identities of those men who come shopping for sex on their streets. In Wyandanch, Long Island, a civic association sent letters to the homes of men arrested for patronizing prostitutes.[10] In New Haven, Connecticut, residents put up posters, "John of the Week," warning others that their name might be on telephone poles and trees if they patronized prostitutes in the Edgewood Avenue neighborhood.[11]

In Chicago some neighborhoods worked with City Hall to have concrete barriers constructed that supposedly make streets less accessible to the drive-by drug dealers and prostitutes who plague them.[12] In one ward in Chicago where the "cul-de-sac" measure took hold, residents also installed front lawn lamps, which promoted more social exchange and circulation among neighbors.[13] Some neighborhoods, however, feared being isolated and opposed the street barriers, contending that with less traffic there are less eyes on the street. In the Five Oaks section of Dayton, Ohio, the neighborhood erected thirty-five iron gates on certain streets and twenty-six alley barricades to discourage prostitution and drug dealing. According to one report, violent crime fell by 50 percent.[14]

One convention that is thriving is the "blockwatch" where residents take turns being the eyes and ears of their neighborhoods. The blockwatch is very much like what Jacobs saw happening spontaneously on Hudson Street. A blockwatch resembles the convention of a search party to find lost children, hikers, confused older persons, or those stranded in storms or in accident sites. Each person covers a different portion of the street and public space so that no spot is overlooked. Many signs saying "Block Watch" or "Citizens' Crime Watch" or "Home Alert" or "Neighborhood Watch" are posted in neighborhoods, whether or not anyone is actually watching. Such measures do put residents in touch with each other, which no longer can be taken for granted, and the warning signs do seem to deter those who might make trouble otherwise. According to one source, residential crime has been reduced by 45 percent where there are such groups.[15]

In Chicago, an anticrime patrol called the Pink Angels worked with the police to prevent assaults against gays and lesbians in that city's North Side. Similar patrols were started in New York City, San Francisco, and Houston.[16] The patrols resemble auxiliary police, which have been used for many years in different cities to augment police coverage. Like the old-fashioned posse, citizens organize to help protect public space, just as in many smaller jurisdictions there are volunteer fire and ambulance crews.

Often the police are the essential partner in residents' efforts to take back the streets using a measure that is now called "community policing." Community policing is a form of coordination where a great many everyday activities of residents are put to the service of public safety. The coordination involves block association meetings, where patrol officers and residents discuss priorities, and daily exchanges of information on the streets between residents and police, who walk a beat instead of cruising in patrol cars. The practice of community policing seeks to foster or improve relationships among police and residents and to rely more on the opinions and the experience of those who live in neighborhoods to know what is going wrong and how to fix it.

Community policing seeks out the experience and understanding of residents, however inarticulate, as opposed to the directives of downtown brass who have little direct knowledge of how street life functions from one precinct to another. For the local precinct, deterrence becomes the priority, instead of investigations after the fact. Police officers are called upon to deal with general street problems, not just specific incidents.[17] For residents, helping with deterrence is a less onerous or dangerous task than getting involved with the local precinct as a witness or victim after a crime has been committed.[18]

"LEAVE NO CHILD BEHIND"

Looking out for children, as any parent knows, has no ending, happy or otherwise, but all of us, not just parents, can do more for children than we are presently doing. The evidence of too many children losing their way as they seek to become adults is everywhere—across the country or across town, down the street, next door, and perhaps even in our own homes.

I prefer calling them children, rather than youths, teenagers, or adolescents. Despite their "rights," elevated consumer status, and shadow life of sex, drugs, and violence, they are still children, and it is one measure of their distress when we ignore that obvious fact. Every adult generation laments what is happening to their children, but currently in America there is real cause for alarm. Something is quite wrong.

- A child dies every three hours from gunshot wounds.[19]
- 14.6 million children live in poverty.[20]
- Every year more than 500,000 children bear children out of wedlock.[21]
- A child is reported abused or neglected every thirteen seconds.[22]
- Every day 13,500 children bring a gun to school.[23]
- In the last thirty years, the rate of teenage suicide has tripled. "Suicide is now the second leading cause of death among adolescents."[24]

A study of children aged seven to sixteen years, for the period 1976 to 1989, showed an increase of withdrawal and social problems, attention and thinking problems at school, delinquency and aggression, anxiety and depression. Asked to comment on these findings, the director of the study cited "high levels of violence" in the streets and media, "less parental monitoring," and "less time with parents."[25]

The question of what has happened to America's children is bound up in the larger question of what has happened to us. Marian Wright

Edelman, Director of the Children's Defense Fund, challenges us "to leave no child behind," but we have and we continue to do so. It is hard not to leave children behind when so many of us are trying to get ahead. Despite the shock of statistics and scenes of violence and degradation on TV news and on the streets of our towns and cities, we pursue lives that often don't leave much room for children. Our sentiments for children are qualified by ambition for ourselves—making it at the workplace and pursuing a hectic life-style. For those of us who are going nowhere and see that as a grim prospect, children can be a consolation but a terrible burden too.

Political liberals want to use government policies and programs to address the problems of children. And it is true that our behavior and the institutional structures of American society are "inseparable."[26] Certainly there is no more important "structure," outside of the family itself, than the influence of government—its tax policies, divorce laws, public schools, welfare programs, public health measures, and juvenile justice system. What better example do we need of the inseparability of structure and behavior than existing government welfare programs which create dependence and discourage family formation and stability?

Political conservatives, on the other hand, believe that parental behavior is the crux of the matter and resist government "solutions." Even a policy-driven President like Clinton has said that governments don't raise children, parents do. If governments try to raise children, they only become clients of the state. Political conservatives, however, sometimes forget that children left to market forces, which ply them with advertising, programming, and products, become little else than consumers. Neither upbringing prepares them to be adults in a free society.

Most of the time, political liberals and conservatives act like two befuddled doctors in the practice of social medicine. The conservative prefers home remedies, but won't make house calls. The liberal is ready to operate, but doesn't know what organ should be removed or replaced.

In this day and age it will take more than parents or government to raise children. It will take all of us to help children find their way. Can we do anything for them? Of course. Will we do anything? I really don't

know. It is possible that enough children will have to become so dysfunctional or such a menace that we can no longer ignore their presence or tolerate their plight.[27] Then, perhaps enough of us, for their
sake as well as our own, will make room for new regularities of behavior
as part of our everyday lives—and theirs.

The "structure" of conventions rests on our invisible consent; we
hold no elections and pass no legislation. Our conventions, however,
are only coordination solutions. They do not necessarily solve the underlying problem of parents themselves not doing a better job of raising
their children. Children need both love and instruction. Love is being
there when children need us, not just giving of ourselves when it suits
our schedule. Instruction cannot be totally handed over to others—
schools, grandparents, older brothers and sisters. Instruction also includes the example parents or guardians set, whether they intend it or
not, about how they handle their own lives. Nonetheless, the way to
measure whether conventions could make a difference in the care and
development of children is to ask the question "What if everyone . . . ?"
Imagine the possibilities.[28]

Perhaps the best way to determine which conventions are needed is
to first think about what we want for children. Two priorities come to
my mind. First, we want children to be educated for productive lives
that contribute to their personal welfare as well as the general welfare.
But education should not just mean schooling. To educate also means
creating more occasions, more enterprises for children where they are
valued as important participants; it means giving dignity to their
work—all work—which they engage in with others. Too many children
only experience being consumers. A childhood that is consumed with
getting and spending cuts off too many other possibilities in children's
development. They are being cheated.

Second, we want children to find happiness of their own making,
but within moral and legal boundaries that cannot be of their own
making. What so frightens people now is seeing children who, for want
of a better word, have not been "socialized." They don't know how to
behave in relation to others because of being abused, neglected, or indulged by parents who have not established reasonable expectations
for their children's behavior. It doesn't matter whether children grow

up in poverty or wealth or somewhere in between, they all will eventually have to get along in a world of strangers who will not excuse their behavior because of where they come from. Conventions and boundaries are usually one and the same. They represent what enough others think is appropriate conduct in relation to others—especially strangers.

While I was preparing to write this book on conventions, I received a letter from a friend who advised me: "Let's not move on to new conventions, but reinforce the old ones that make sense."[29] Existing conventions are regularities of behavior that we are already familiar with; they have been field-tested and have proven workable. Building on what we know is always easier than breaking new ground. We take the well-worn path because we don't have to clear a way, and well-worn paths, more often than not, get us where we want to go.

Existing conventions, which are by definition already successful coordination solutions, provide us with prominent analogies useful for dealing with unsolved coordination problems, such as how to improve the care and development of children.[30] In game theory, "prominence" is a concept used to explain how some "pure" coordination problems are solved. For example, imagine that you and I had no way of knowing where to find each other in an unfamiliar town called Gardens Crossing. I could only guess what place in Gardens Crossing you might choose or think I might choose. I suspect we would probably both choose the only prominent intersection in Gardens Crossing, which logically enough is Main and First streets. In any such circumstance, we think of places that people generally choose when they want to meet each other—a landmark, a railway station, a crossroads—and by analogy these same places serve as likely candidates for where you and I think we will find each other.[31]

In imagining, therefore, the possibilities of doing more for the care and development of children, we should pick and choose from those conventions already part of our everyday experience. Some of them might make sense in new and different contexts. I think of them as conventions writ large, and I can imagine any number of starting points—by unplanned coordination, by explicit agreement, or by central authority—on these well-worn paths.

Discrete Conventions

There are a number of discrete conventions that center on looking after children. Some are well established—foster homes, adoption, godparents, chaperones—and others are relatively new. Perhaps the most notorious is the employment of "illegal nannies," which became so widely publicized in 1993 at the time of Zoe Baird's nomination for Attorney General. A vast number of working mothers and fathers hire undocumented aliens to care for their children and pay them in cash at below-market wages. Like political patronage, the arrangement is "off the books" and usually satisfies both parties for different reasons.[32] Less well known is the existence of "contract" families recently tried in Dallas.

> They have put together a model that invents families. For instance, an older person is housed in the same apartment with a younger single parent and infant child. Contractually, the older person agrees to care for the child on specified occasions. In return, the parent has responsibility for cooking needs and doing light housekeeping.[33]

Discrete conventions are those regularities of behavior that don't require a large number of people to make them work. "Enough others" may require only a few of us.

Consider:

1. HOMEMAKING. An important function of any family is the division of labor between fathers and mothers. The discrete convention of a man leaving home each day to earn a living while the woman stays at home to raise the children is dying of natural causes. Only one in five families in America still fits the description of the "traditional" family, in which the husband works and the wife is a "homemaker."[34] This sea change, however, does not preclude a man from doing more of the housework or caring for the children if his wife works. Such a practice is observed in some marriages, but it is far from becoming a widespread convention. As mothers spend more time outside of the home, obviously it would be helpful if fathers spent more time in the home. Such a convention cannot be legislated, but only negotiated between husbands and wives or undertaken unilaterally by husband-fathers who see that they are needed.[35]

It is amusing, as well as distressing, to hear well-meaning male friends talk about what "we the people" should be doing about their children's generation, but hardly ever considering what each of them might start doing in their own homes. If one of the problems in raising children is that mothers have less time for the care of children, then my friends should stop blaming women in general and start doing more themselves to care for their home and children. A new convention where both husbands and wives are "homemakers" does not guarantee that children would be the immediate beneficiaries, but at least boys would learn from the example of their parents what is expected of them when they marry and both parents are working.

2. MENTORING. Many children need mentors, other than parents or in the absence of one or more parents, who can help them learn to lead productive lives and learn to live within socially acceptable boundaries. Mentoring is a discrete convention in which the coordination usually involves one experienced person looking out for another person, younger and less experienced. Mentors give advice, critique performance, open doors of opportunity, and coordinate the kind of help that a novice needs. The value of mentoring is obvious, but it usually arises accidentally. If we were to coordinate mentoring more intentionally, so that more children were given that advantage, even though some relationships would fail, many would probably work well. I am struck by how often someone who succeeds in a chosen field finds it easy to remember and name a person who helped along the way. It may be a relative or a teacher or anyone who, for whatever reason, took an interest in that someone's development or career.[36]

Just as every child has some gift that can be developed, every person willing to be a mentor has some gift that children need. If parents cannot be all things to their own children, certainly mentors can't be all things to children they choose to look out for. One person acting as a source of support is usually not enough. Some of us are good at listening, others at offering remedial help, some feel most comfortable in using their contacts. With coordination, there is the possibility of developing a child's gifts by using each mentor's specific talents to meet the child halfway.

Halfway is important. Whether or not we think children are victims and whether or not they think of themselves that way, the inescapable fact is that "when you try to pick somebody up, they have to help."[37] Most conventions develop from implicit bargains of two or more people that if you do your part, I'll do mine. Mentoring is sometimes offered unconditionally, but more often than not, a mentor acts like an "educator," who expects that the person being helped has to do certain things if the relationship is to be sustained.

Furthermore, helping somebody doesn't mean that mentors have to put up with behavior that is self-destructive or threatening. For example, both blacks and whites are increasingly alarmed by the conduct of young disadvantaged blacks with a chip on their shoulder and with little regard for anyone else.[38] To understand another person's plight does not require that we also excuse their conduct. Mentoring can set its own terms, ignoring the ideology of those who want to help, no questions asked, and of those who don't want to help, claiming the problem is all the victim's fault. All children need to experience "tough love" that does not put conditions on love, but does express love's expectations; this includes learning to get along with strangers who of necessity create and recreate a public world of conventional expectations for each person's social behavior. When parents do not prepare their children for such a public world, then someone else has to introduce them to its well-worn paths.

3. "I HAVE A DREAM." "I Have a Dream" is a relatively new practice of helping an entire class of schoolchildren to get to college and then providing them with the necessary financial help to graduate from college.[39] Such a discrete practice is usually coordinated by a wealthy benefactor, but there are many others who can do the same thing. Any business firm, civic association, or group of people can pool available talents and resources to help one or more children. Such collective mentoring could give children role models, work with their parents, tutor their academic work, and provide them with job opportunities along the way. I discovered in talking with those who have already used the "I Have a Dream" model that all the members of a family often get involved in helping a child whom they collectively adopt.

The "I Have a Dream" model includes the expectation that young people who want to go to college will stay in school and get their diploma, not an unreasonable condition. For those offered the opportunity to get a college education, or training and employment beyond their individual reach, mentors can have a range of expectations of what children can do for themselves. It is not unreasonable to ask that a girl not become pregnant, or that a boy not get his girlfriend pregnant. Where once we had moral objections to children being born out of wedlock, now we are more likely to object on the practical grounds that children bearing or fathering children is a serious obstacle to becoming educated and employed.[40]

Mentors are entitled to make bargains with children whom they want to help. When such help is extended with conditions, it is not a question of children's "rights." It is a question of whether they are willing to regulate their behavior and learn that sometimes you have to give up something to get something. Parents often discount future gains—the proper development of their children—for the sake of immediate pleasure. Should we expect their children to be any different? It will be a hard sell. We haven't given them much of an example to follow. But mentors should at least try to help children learn.

4. REFERENCES. We all need references at one time or another, and this is especially true of children who approach college age or full-time employment and do not have others to vouch for them except young friends or parents, who often have no references of their own. When so many young people are treated with suspicion because of their race or background, they need proper introductions and knowledgeable support, which helps to reassure those who admit or hire them.

References, a discrete convention among strangers, works in several ways. We call it patronage in politics, where someone is favored for a job because he has a sponsor to whom something is owed. We call it the "old boy" network in professional and business circles, and more recently women have established comparable networks for themselves. Such conventions are often an intricate coordination of interests and expectations shared by those with something in common—school ties, gender, and so forth. Those who choose to mentor children can also develop and maintain similar networks with the means to finance, to employ, to promote—whatever it takes to help someone get started and keep going.

Organization Conventions

Most organizations do not have children in mind as they pursue their daily business. Nonetheless, the way they arrange organizational life has a substantial bearing on how children are raised. Consider the possibility of their promoting new organization conventions that try to accommodate the home as well as the workplace.

There are already a number of organization conventions that relate to child care. Although these practices usually benefit only those with children, they are accepted throughout an organization: examples include "flex-time" (permitting employees to alter their work schedules around family obligations); job sharing (two professionals, usually women, working part time and sharing one job at a firm); and day-care centers on site.[41]

There are other conventions to consider:

1. TELECOMMUTING. Perhaps the most significant new practice to accommodate parents is telecommuting, in which employees of an organization do not commute at all, but work nine to five at home. Office workers who have to commute to our large cities "do not have eight-hour days; they have twelve-hour days."[42] Telecommuting helps mothers and fathers coordinate their work hours with the needs of their children.

Before the Industrial Revolution, people by and large worked in or near their homes. Now, with the revolutions in telecommunication where information is moved cheaply and instantaneously from offices to outlying homes, data from the workplace can be delivered to home workers as easily as it is made available to office workers. Some organizations require a telecommuting employee to come into the office on a certain day or days each week depending on the work routine, but the rest of the time employees work at home using computers, modems, facsimile machines, and telephones. Some predict that at least forty million Americans will soon be working full time or part time from their homes.[43]

Telecommuting offers advantages to employers, separate and apart from what it does for families. Telecommuting reduces the need for office space, and studies show it promotes employee morale and productivity, with absenteeism and tardiness less likely to occur. The organizations most likely to use telecommuting are those whose line of business allows them to measure the output of their employees without having to monitor them directly. One spokesman for a health maintenance organization said, "When technology allows you to parcel out work to employees across the city and the customer doesn't know the difference, it's a no-brainer."[44]

Telecommuting is likely to have a remarkable impact on where people choose to live, the cost of that living, and, of course, the time they have for their family. Many will still find it necessary to arrange for child care during home "office hours." Children can be disruptive to any work routine. But not having to commute to and from work and being available when children have special problems or create unexpected emergencies can make an enormous difference in the time and energies parents have to meet such demands. They are there for their children, even though they are necessarily preoccupied with their "office" work. After school, having a mother or father at home is usually very reassuring to both children and their parents.

2. CORPORATE PARENTING. We are living through a time of transition not only for families but for almost all community institutions—schools, churches, private social agencies—as they struggle to reform themselves, keep members, or reconcile their missions with government services that often overshadow or preempt them. During such a transition I can imagine "corporate parenting" in the form of new workplace conventions, familiar in other community contexts, but equally applicable to large employers who cannot pick up and go somewhere else: utilities, banks, real estate interests, universities, hospitals, and public authorities. Such organizations are the ones most likely to defend and advance their corporate interests by getting more involved with how local children are raised.

Although many major employers already show an interest in "community relations" through corporate gifts, financial and in-kind, sponsoring of sports teams, or blood drives, they could become far more influential in helping children. The morale and productivity of their employees, their corporate "image," and their resistance to higher taxes to pay for more government services argue in favor of such a strategy.[45]

Some children might in effect become the wards of such organizations in the absence of community institutions with the resources to help them grow up. If that seems at first blush to be overreaching, consider that some of these children may one day be their employees and of what kind and how qualified will be of some consequence. Without help from some quarter in their growing up, others may be unemployable or on welfare or in prison—wards of the state and a charge against everyone's earnings.

The suggested conventions that follow are not indigenous to organizations. They are transplants from other social contexts which only need a core group in the workplace to put them in place. The organization itself can then provide the continuity for such practices over a sufficient period of time. Like discrete conventions entertained by only a few people but effective for their purposes, workplace conventions that emerge do not need nationwide or even community-wide acceptance if corporations have adequate resources—time, money, and manpower—to get them started and to see them through. Here are a few well-worn paths that I can imagine.

- Sanctuaries for children after school who do not feel safe on the streets or at home alone. Children would have a place to play or learn new skills in secure buildings or in fenced areas on company property. It would be nice if schools could serve this purpose, but until we find the money to keep them open and make some of them safer havens than they are now, the prospect is unlikely. Many corporations already have the spaces and deep pockets to provide such a refuge.
- Sweat equity projects in which children get to own what they make with their own labor. Sweat equity is usually associated with

low-income housing units, where tenants become owners by reno-
vating and improving a rundown property themselves. Sweat equity could also apply to a range of projects in which children took
symbolic "title" to youth centers, skating rinks, improved lots,
skateboarding plazas, whatever they built themselves or reworked
for the purpose of serving their recreation. Such places would belong to those who cleaned them, repaired them, painted them,
maintained and patrolled them. The sites would come from the
property inventories of organizations that had no present use for
them or considered the better use was for children to make them
temporarily their own.

- Sports leagues for every imaginable team sport that engages a child.
  Organizations already sponsor a broad range of athletic activities for
  children, but a great deal more could be done to provide team sports
  for girls and for those boys who are not normally included in the
  usual pickup games on playgrounds, basketball courts, and baseball
  lots. From a child's early years, games themselves are conventions,
  and organized sports are an extension and development of that experience. All children should have a chance to engage in activities
  that pose a common challenge and ask for everyone's participation.

- Cooperatives for children where they learn to pool their own resources and together create a market for themselves and perhaps for
  others. Imagine children learning to run their own landscaping
  nursery or petting zoo or bookmobile or bicycle recycling shed or
  used clothing outlet and conducting their own auctions, lotteries,
  and garage sales.[46]

- Children's juries that help children experience what it means to really listen, to reach a judgment for themselves, and then to share
  that judgment with others and to come up with a collective decision. Give them grievances to be heard, disputes to settle, and local
  or national problems that need their input.

- Self-help groups that bring together children who are experiencing
  similar problems at home or at school or on the streets. Give each of
  them a chance to tell her own story as well as listen to others' stories. In such a "peer" group the problem will not go away, but it may
  become more bearable when a child knows he doesn't have to go it

alone. Together children, with the help of adults, might even find a way to overcome the problem.

• Collateral that comes from corporate resources that help children get their joint undertakings started—cooperatives, sweat equity projects, credit unions—and teaches them to appreciate the importance of developing their own collateral. Collateral, like references, is a form of security between strangers, and children need such validation from those who help them coordinate their activities.

Community Conventions

The problems of working parents or those who struggle on welfare also become, unfairly, problems for their children. As a result, a child's welfare often depends on the care of professionals, which is a safe bet but not a sure one. We know that many of our schools are failing where professional educators thrive; we know that our juvenile justice "system," administered by professionals, is deeply flawed; we know there has been horrendous abuse in day-care centers run by so-called professionals.

Professionals are organized; those of us in "communities" with weak social ties are not. Nonetheless, the argument that only professionals should intervene is quite lame. Whatever the strengths and weaknesses of professionals, there simply are not enough of them, nor can we afford to pay the bill to hire enough of them no matter how much we prefer to remain uninvolved and delegate the problems of children to public agencies.

1. SEARCH PARTIES. Imagine that enough of us organized a search party to account for every child in our immediate vicinity. The convention of a search party to find lost children is employed only in an exceptional circumstance, but the point of the convention is that with enough people covering enough territory, no place is overlooked. In this case, no child would be overlooked.

So often we already know which children are in trouble without having to look for them. They are everywhere—latchkey kids next door, those who hang out on the corner, or those who may be our children's friends. They may even be our own children, who we know may need help beyond what we can give them or are willing to.

When only one child is lost, members of a search party have their work cut out for them. When there are many "lost" children, finding them may be easier, but what happens next will be harder. In some areas of our inner cities, just finding enough people for a search party may be a problem, knowing their numbers are unequal to the discoveries that they are likely to make.

When coordination is feasible, imagine what might happen if our search parties discovered neglect or a struggle to care for a child. Instead of just reporting our findings to a social welfare department, suppose we took it upon ourselves to get involved and help. Most parents resent meddling that reflects on their care. Here again, their liberty-centered instincts and ours make us wary. But if as neighbors, or even strangers, we pay attention to how others maintain their property or pets, we certainly can choose to express an interest in how they care for their children.

2. PATROL TEAMS. Jane Jacobs observed that surveillance and oversight of children can occur in a neighborhood through unplanned coordination, but fewer of us are at home these days and our routines usually don't include watching out for what children are doing. As concern grows for the safety of children, I can imagine a new convention of patrol teams deputized to look out for children. Crossing guards, park custodians, shopkeepers, private security guards, bus drivers, or police in patrol cars are hardly an adequate presence to do it for us. What would help is enough adults organized to take turns walking or driving a "beat" on the streets, in the parks, wherever children use public spaces. For those willing, joining a patrol would become a routine just like walking the dog or going out for a drive. But children would know, and their parents would know, that someone was out there keeping an eye out.[47]

The patrol teams would not be concerned with any and all threats to public safety. Very few of us have the time or inclination to serve as police officers. Their work is demanding and sometimes dangerous. The primary focus of the patrol teams would be on children—their safety and those neighborhood conditions that threaten them. Teams patrolling on a coordinated schedule would be a predictable presence. The teams would learn where children hang out, who is causing problems, and why. Hanging out is a convention, which children use to find each other, but adults need to know more about where it takes place and what goes on.

When citizens as "auxiliary police" work with local precincts and police departments, they are usually warned not to get directly involved in incidents or to create incidents themselves. Instead, they are asked to report what they find to law enforcement officials. With sufficient instruction and experience, each patrol team would learn what observations and incidents should be reported to the police, or other public agencies, and in what circumstances direct intervention was appropriate. In any event, such patrol teams would be available to children who sought them out, responding just as any group of strangers, in mutual support of each other, might do in response to an auto accident, a purse snatching, or a car stuck in a snowbank.

3. CURFEWS. Curfews are often temporarily imposed on an entire populace for the sake of public safety during a "blackout" or after an urban riot, a hurricane, or an earthquake. The convention of a curfew is also available to establish a limit on those hours when children can be out on their own in areas where they are endangered or endanger others. What ages and hours would be off-limits has to be determined by those who are willing to support a curfew with the assistance of police who would ultimately have to enforce it.[48]

Ah, but children don't like curfews. Of course they don't. And many children don't like to go to school, or do homework, or save their money, or get dressed up, or visit relatives, or do anything they don't feel like doing. It is a measure of our indulgence, usually not for their sake but for our own, that so many of us find it hard to cross even our own children, much less other people's children. The generation of children that presently troubles us has acquired, at a very early age, our adult insistence on liberty but without first learning how to manage it. If we give them license without boundaries, is it any wonder that they step out beyond where they should be and hurt themselves or others?

I think the convention of a children's curfew would have a better chance to work if it were part of a larger effort to look out for children—search parties, patrol teams, sanctuaries, mentoring, and such. Then it might not be seen as a punitive measure, and more children than we think might welcome it. Most of them desperately want to be accepted by their "peers" and sometimes do outrageous things to secure that acceptance. If some conditions were changed, children might be spared from getting into trouble. A curfew, at least, might make it more difficult for them to go haywire together.

Using the Media
and Telecommunication Networks

Discrete conventions work well enough for two or more people who choose to use them. Organization and community conventions require only enough others in a workplace or neighborhood to coordinate their behavior successfully. But some conventions associated with the care and development of children need more widespread acceptance in order to be effective. This will certainly be true if we are to curb the daily violence that assaults children in the media, not just on the streets. Children, who watch television an average of three hours a day, see a violent act committed every six minutes.[49]

Our inclination is to invoke liberty, not limit it, as movie makers and broadcasters constantly remind us. They are likely to succeed in the courts with such an argument, but their bottom line is making a profit, not winning First Amendment cases. It will probably require a nationwide boycott of advertisers who sponsor such prime-time effluent or the movie studios who finance and produce it to stem the tide. One family, or workplace, or community can do very little.

The same media, however, can also be used as a positive force. For example, the Center for Health Communication at Harvard's School of Public Health is trying to organize a media campaign "to convince kids that it is both smart and cool to withdraw from a confrontation." The media campaign will center on promoting a new convention, "squash it," a variant of the "time out" sign which we use with our hands. The "squash it" gesture would consist of the vertical part of the

"T" in the shape of a clenched fist and the horizontal part in the shape of a flat hand coming down to restrain the fist.[50]

Like sign language for the deaf, the nods of "yes" and "no," handshakes, or other body language that we use as conventions to communicate, the "squash it" media campaign would seek to persuade young people to use the new sign before there is physical violence. But to use it, the sign would first have to become a convention—the preferred way of avoiding violence. The gesture would have to be practiced by enough children to be accepted by the great majority. Unlike the designated driver practice, which the Center for Health Communication also helped to promote through the media, the "squash it" sign won't work if only a few use it. Like language it has to be in widespread use to be understood and serve its purpose.

As parents find less time for children or disrupt their lives by divorce, children resort to their friends as sources of support and direction. If we are to do more for their care and development, we will probably have to think of how we can get them to influence each other in the absence of a parent's guidance. For example, Jesse Jackson has told students that when they decline to report drug dealing and weapon carrying in schools, a "code of silence" makes those places more dangerous and destructive. Jackson asks them to abandon their convention of silence and use the power they already have to stop the killing.[51] National media campaigns, which influence children's tastes in athletic shoes or soft drinks or potato chips, can also urge them to "Do it for each other" or that "Together you can all make a difference." Imagine that children are educated through such campaigns to think of violence as offensive as smoking, to use their own "juries" to resolve the turf disputes of local gangs before they get out of hand, or to form their own patrols to help keep the streets safe for their younger brothers and sisters.

With or without the commercial media's help, all the conventions imagined here might develop and be immeasurably strengthened through unplanned coordination made possible by new telecommunication networks. I can imagine strangers in "cyberspace" sharing their opinions and experience about old conventions and new practices, reporting back and forth about how they work, the problems being encountered, and their "success" stories. There is no way to know which local practices will get sufficiently amplified to capture national attention and imitation. Some will make sense in one place and not another. Some will be used at one time and not another. Just like children, most practices take time to develop.

Even the failure to establish a particular practice may not be conclusive. When some people, although not enough of them, try to improve a situation, there is no telling what their efforts will lead to. It may be difficult to trace their influence, except to know that they helped some children, stopped some crime, saved some lives. Those who make the effort may not create a well-worn path that everyone will follow, but someday enough of us may discover their footprints and find they lead us where we want to go.

Metaconventions

Metaconventions help make other conventions work. I introduced the concept in chapter one to explain what expectation underlies the convention of a line. The metaconvention that promotes coordination and sustains a line is "first come, first served." This same metaconvention is also used in determining the rights of seniority in employee relations, setting up waiting lists for public housing, and allotting seats to opera season subscribers or spaces in overenrolled university courses.

In chapter four I mentioned the metaconvention of "effort" when each of us in the snowbank measures our individual contribution against what others already involved are doing to get your car back on the road. It doesn't matter what specific outcome our joint effort is trying to produce; such a metaconvention means that there is an expectation that each of us will do our fair share. I also referred to "reciprocity," a metaconvention that accounts for our expectations when, for example, we use the conventions of membership or patronage.

The metaconvention of "promise keeping" is implicit in some conventions such as making contracts or sharing secrets. The metaconvention of "truth telling" is indispensable to our conventions of checking references, making oaths, or waving a white flag of truce. Like norms, metaconventions reinforce fragile conventions and help some become robust. Here I want to focus on what some would call "the mother of all conventions"—the metaconvention of collaboration and how we might teach our children more about it.

COLLABORATIVE LEARNING. We need to correct the misconception, perpetuated by schools, that a child can and should solve problems all by him or herself. The world that is at our children's doorstep is interdependent. No matter how well trained each of them is to perform specific skills, each child will be relatively powerless to solve problems unless they have also been educated to work together. They might do a better job of solving future coordination problems if we did a better job now of educating them for cooperation: not just for "winning the competition" or "being #1." For want of a better term, I would call this mode of learning "collaborative," that is, two or more persons working jointly on an endeavor—a metaconvention of the first order.

So many young women and men that I know feel the ache of powerlessness despite their individual accomplishments of getting ahead. Treating students as "consumers" of education makes each of them feel important but also makes them ill-equipped for influencing events or solving collective problems. Children need to learn that real empowerment arises through organized forms of membership, enterprise, and social coordination.

Furthermore, these young people often have had no compensatory experience, outside of their schools, to practice the arts of cooperation. Increasingly, they are from families that have broken up; they no longer have contact with church membership; some of them have no idea of what it means to be part of any association. And the general neglect of children, which lets them pursue whatever takes their fancy—television, drugs, or being ardent consumers—as consolations for such neglect, leaves many of them unresponsive or unprepared for social collaboration.

Educators rarely offer children any learning structures in the classroom that resemble the complex organizations and diverse communities which await them. We know that two heads are better than one, and yet our penchant for encouraging personal advancement through individual competition has left out the equally important achievement of engaging in successful teamwork. That is why the conduct of sports teams in the schoolyard is often a better approximation of what happens in problem solving than what goes on in the classroom.[52]

The traditional learning model in an American classroom assumes that a student should supposedly succeed on his or her own. It reflects the long-prevailing American ethos that celebrates liberty and self-reliance but ignores the long-prevailing American experience that we rarely accomplish anything of social significance by ourselves. Texas farmers learned to form cooperative alliances to gain access to better markets; black church members advanced the cause of civil rights when they were willing to boycott the city buses in Montgomery, Alabama; and many diseases were tamed or conquered by public health measures when enough people cooperated in getting immunized.

We have been and will remain a society steeped in the ethos of competition. Collaborative learning compensates for the excesses of that ethos without making it a question of either/or. The convention of cheating in the classroom when students help each other is anathema to us, but we have let it dominate our thinking that everyone has to do his or her own work. Students will always compete for popularity, grades, and in a hundred other ways, yet they still should learn that competition is not very helpful for solving certain kinds of problems. Competition has little to do with solving traffic congestion or environmental degradation or reducing crime or promoting race relations. There is such a thing as "our" problems and "our" work to solve them.

In an era of assessment, "evaluators"—accrediting agencies, school boards, state legislators, and education administrators—need to know that individual performance in the classroom, which is easier to measure and hold others accountable for, should not be the only measure of whether we are getting children ready for the world they will inherit. I suspect that the more children learn to collaborate with one another in the classroom, the more likely evaluators, who usually follow rather than lead, will be able to find measures to track what is going on.

There are many ways to learn and practice the metaconvention of collaboration. I have worked with students at two very different schools to promote such learning. For ten years I taught at a graduate school of management and organization and for two years served as president of an undergraduate "work college," where all students served on various work teams to maintain the campus. These examples in higher education do not directly address what elementary and secondary schools can do to promote team problem solving, but my experience did teach me that whenever collaboration is practiced it provides valuable lessons.[53]

At the "work college," student-managed departments gave everyone an opportunity to experience what it means to organize into crews for all the jobs that need doing—food service; maintenance of the grounds, classrooms, and dormitories; servicing athletic teams; tutoring; assisting with laboratory work; operating the library and even building a new wing for it. Together students learned to recognize their interdependence on the campus they shared and had to maintain. Every problem in the organizing and the doing became an opportunity to learn. Students moved, even if tentatively and often with great conflict, from talking about "community" to being one.

Flawed and confused as any such undertaking is, I preferred it as a learning model to the prevailing consumer model in higher education which treats students like they are in a resort hotel, serviced by staff and left alone to do what they please when not performing in a classroom for their professors. In a "work college" you try to promote a social context that approximates the conditions that students will confront in organizations and communities when they leave. You know for sure they are not headed for a life in a resort hotel.

At the graduate school where I taught, collaborative learning entered the classroom by way of teaching cases and role-playing exercises. Finding the right answer in a classroom is a form of consolation, and it is often available to a student who works hard enough to find it. But it is much harder to know what the right answers are when we have to solve messy problems with other people. I wanted to simulate real-world conditions in the classroom, which allowed students to share in the difficult social enterprise of resolving problems.

The scaffolding that I used for collaborative learning was a series of experiential cases which students first analyzed and then entered into—a process I called "going through the looking glass."[54] My teaching cases tried to incorporate three experiences:

1. First there was the "analytical" experience, constrained by inadequate time and information, during which students, often in study groups of three or four, sorted and examined an array of unfamiliar facts and options.

2. Next there was the "interactive experience" of role playing, when they actually tried to solve the problem by producing outcomes with the other role players in a case exercise. Such exercises gave students a chance to compare their analytical experience of what they had anticipated they would do with the interactive experience of what they actually did in the exercise.

3. Finally, there was the "consequential experience" of reflecting on and living with the outcomes that they produced in the role-playing exercise. This did not just mean a debriefing in class, where they reviewed why their prior analysis and subsequent interactions worked or did not work. More important, the teaching case offered subsequent episodes in which students could trace and react to the consequences of their earlier actions. Such a "layered case" was a continuous story, throughout the semester, that grew more complex, but also assumed that students could become more adept through their increasing familiarity with the social context they were asked to manage.

The "looking glass" experience of the teaching cases dramatized my observation that problem solving in public life is a shared enterprise. What I tried to do was invent a dynamic environment, albeit in a classroom, where students could experience their interdependence and the skills needed for successful collaboration.

The metaconvention of collaboration can arise spontaneously in the classroom, as it does when students are given some latitude on how to prepare a response to an assignment or to prepare for an exam. But collaborative learning works better when there is some engineering on the teacher's part.[55]

First, teachers should choose problems, or be on the alert for problems that students may choose for themselves, that require coordination if they are to be solved. It does no good to structure collaborative learning around how to type or ride a bicycle. The experience of doing both is usually not improved by doing it with someone else. Collaborative learning exercises should be reserved for those learning experiences where we do better if we work with others—moving a heavy load, solving a puzzle, or preparing for an exam.[56]

Second, a teacher should establish a framework for the collaborative experience using a story or case, a laboratory experiment, or a role-playing exercise. Such a framework usually has rules, which set some boundaries for what each team can or cannot do, and rewards, if competition among teams is useful. The teacher, however, uses his or her authority sparingly, primarily to guide and clarify. My teaching cases had no predetermined outcomes. Each class section was free to produce its own and live with the consequences. My role was very similar to the one I assumed when later as a college president I put the faculty members' mail and coffee together in one place. What such an intersection produced in new joint undertakings was their doing; the intersection was mine.

Third, it is important that a teacher treat any problem that arises from such collaboration as a further opportunity for learning. If some students rely on others to do the work for them; if one or two students take over the problem solving by default; if some students claim to know more and ask the others to defer to them; if some students complain that others "goofed off" and ruined the outcome—all these "problems" are grist for useful discussions about what you do when they happen. Students should not see these as "glitches" in an otherwise flawless learning laboratory, but rather as the kind of problems that arise in any real-world collaboration.

One might argue that small-group work in classrooms hardly prepares children for the world of strangers that awaits them, where large-scale cooperation is problematic. No doubt it is problematic and will continue to be, but that is a world in which conventions become established nonetheless. It is usually in the intimate circle of family and friends that we learn about metaconventions—doing one's fair share, reciprocity, promise keeping—before we practice them with strangers. That is the order of our development, and there's no reason to think that classroom lessons in collaborative learning would not work the same way.

Robert Slavin says the peer group is the "one remaining free resource for improving schools," and he thinks we should use it more often than we do now.[57] And I have argued throughout this book that what others do shapes our behavior in everyday life, even when our "peer group" is composed of strangers. If children in their classrooms can experience the metaconvention of collaboration, which makes most conventions possible, it seems more likely that they will know how to develop them when new conventions are needed. Perhaps they will learn, better than we have, how to use social conventions to govern themselves. It's worth a try at least to help them get started.

NOTES

Introduction. "Sweet Land of Liberty"

1. David Rieff, *Los Angeles: Capital of the Third World* (New York: Touchstone/Simon & Schuster, 1991), p. 46. The exaggeration of independence may be a male construction. Separation versus connection is a common distinction in the literature that discusses gender differences. The male-dominated interpretation of America's development makes "rugged individualism" a shaping force even though it may not have seemed nearly as desirable to the women who shared in the nation's making.
2. Walter Lippmann, *An Inquiry into the Principles of the Good Society* (Boston: Little, Brown, 1943), p. 267. And for some Americans, few liberties existed until government administered some form of justice in their favor.
3. Daniel P. Moynihan, "The New Science of Politics and the Old Art of Government," *The Public Interest* (Winter 1987), pp. 22–35 at p. 27.
4. Jane Gross, "Collapse of Inner-City Families Creates America's New Orphans," *New York Times*, March 29, 1992.
5. Patricia A. Weiner, "New Crisis for Young: Being Alone," *New York Times*, June 30, 1985.
6. *CQ Researcher*, September 11, 1992.
7. Our confidence in government has been at an all-time low. Just weeks after the new Clinton administration was installed in Washington, D.C., only 23 percent of Americans polled thought that government does "the right thing most of the time." "Trust in Government," *USA Today*, March 26, 1993.
8. This reminds me, however, of Michael Walzer's admonition: "Individuals should be free, indeed, in all sorts of ways, but we don't set them free by separating them from their fellows." "Liberalism and The Art of Separation," *Political Theory* (August 1984), pp. 315–30 at p. 325. Walzer's point is that for liberty's sake institutions should be separate and autonomous, for that is where an individual thrives in relation to others, not separated from them.

9. In his time, Tocqueville used the "new idea" of "individualism," much as the communitarians do now, to mean the preference of each citizen to withdraw to his family circle and friends leaving "the greater society to look after itself." *Democracy in America*, ed. J. P. Mayer, trans. George Lawrence (New York: Anchor Books, 1969), p. 506.

10. "The Responsive Communitarian Platform: Rights and Responsibilities," *The Responsive Community* (Winter 1991/92), p. 7. For Etzioni "the community of communities," American society itself, is endangered. "Shared core values" are thus needed not only for "constituent communities—neighborhoods, ethnic groups, and so on," but to preserve "a firm sense of one supracommunity." Amitai Etzioni, *The Spirit of Community* (New York: Touchstone/Simon & Schuster, 1993), p. 155.

11. Communitarians rarely explore the possibilities of large-scale cooperation, preferring instead to encourage "the development of practices in various contexts among people who know and trust each other and have come to see themselves as responsible for each other." Robert Bellah, et al., *The Good Society* (New York: Knopf, 1991), p. 263. This is not much of a strategy for dealing with public problems. It appears to be more of a holding action, a counsel against despair that echos the end-game advice of Alasdair MacIntyre. "What matters at this stage is the construction of local forms of community within which civility and the intellectual and moral life can be sustained through the dark ages which are already upon us." Alasdair MacIntyre, *After Virtue*, 2nd ed. (South Bend, Indiana: University of Notre Dame Press, 1984), p. 263.

12. James M. Buchanan, *The Limits of Liberty* (Chicago: University of Chicago Press, 1975), p. 78.

13. Letter from John Callaway, February 24, 1992.

14. "In this new landscape, you wave good morning to your neighbor from the car. Driving alone to the office in that clump of glass buildings off Exit Whatever, you tune your radio to what passes for a community meeting: the call-in show. At work, your friendliest colleagues are the computer, database, phone and fax. You shop not in town (where's that?) but out on the strip, among strangers." Gerald Marzorati, "From Tocqueville to Perotville," *New York Times*, June 28, 1992.

15. Community Associations Institute, *Community Associations Factbook*, 1993. Forty-two percent of the associations are condominiums (residents own their units and jointly own the common property); 7 percent are housing cooperatives (residents own stock in the coop, which owns the units and common property and leases the units to its shareholders); and 51 percent are planned community units (residents own their own units and a corporation has title to the common areas. The Institute projects that by the year 2000, there will be 225,000 such associations. Diana Jean Schemo, "Rebuilding of Suburban Dreams," *New York Times*, May 4, 1994.

16. Stephen Macedo, *Liberal Virtues* (Cambridge, Mass.: Harvard University Press, 1991), p. 28.

17. Richard Sennett goes even further. "The challenge and the promise of Ameri-

can society lies in finding ways of acting together without invoking the evil of a shared national identity. To do so we need to draw on our capacity to cooperate rather than our desire to commune." "The Identity Myth," *New York Times*, January 30, 1994.

18. No doubt the idealism of Robert Bellah and his colleagues, who collaborated on *Habits of the Heart* (Berkeley: University of California Press, 1985) and *The Good Society*, has religious grounds.

19. Charles Lindblom remarks at Kettering/Etzioni conference in Washington, D.C., January 27, 1993. Lindblom thinks a better metaphor is a state of war, where there is much at stake.

20. Ben Barber, a political theorist and author of *Strong Democracy* (Berkeley: University of California Press, 1984), argues that it is imperative to strengthen "civil society"—churches, foundations, voluntary associations—so as to avoid what he calls the "two cell model" of government and the private for-profit sector. Barber is right, of course, but it is hard to see how this will happen. Barber's remarks were made at a meeting on "Reinventing Citizenship—Civic and Community Participation" in Washington, D.C., January 14–15, 1994.

21. Craig Calhoun, "The Radicalism of Tradition and the Question of Class Struggle" in *Rationality and Revolution*, ed. Michael Taylor (Cambridge: Cambridge University Press, 1988), p. 172. Daniel Kemmis, the Mayor of Missoula, Montana, tells of how Bitter Root Valley residents were barred from issuing stock to each other for investment in local businesses because they did not comply with federal securities laws, which seek "to protect unwary investors against exploitation." "[T]hey were not going to be allowed to treat each other like neighbors." Daniel Kemmis, *Community and the Politics of Place* (Norman: University of Oklahoma Press, 1990), p. 57. Robert Woodson, a community organizer, describes the difficulty for neighborhood self-help in Washington, D.C., where local day-care centers had a hard time contending with zoning, building codes, and the accreditation of workers. Robert Woodson, "The Importance of Neighborhood Organization in Meeting Human Needs, in *Meeting Human Needs*, eds. Daniel Thursz and Joseph L. Vigilante (Beverly Hills, Calif.: Sage Publications, 1975), pp. 132–49 at pp. 141–44.

22. You and I do not necessarily prefer being Aristotle's social animal. "Man is a social animal, indeed, a political animal, because he is not self-sufficient alone. . . ." Charles Taylor, *Philosophy and the Human Sciences* (Philosophical Papers 2) (Cambridge: Cambridge University Press, 1985), p. 189.

23. Mary Douglas, *How Institutions Think* (Syracuse, N.Y.: Syracuse University Press, 1986), p. 25.

24. L. Ivor Jennings, *The Law and the Constitution*, 3rd ed. (London: University of London Press, 1946). See Appendix III, "A Note on the Theory of Law," pp. 298–314.

25. David Hume, *A Treatise on Human Nature*, ed. L. A. Selby-Bigge, 2nd ed. (Oxford: Oxford University Press, 1978), p. 538.

26. Ibid.

27. Ibid., p. 539.

28. Mancur Olson, *The Logic of Collective Action* (Cambridge, Mass.: Harvard University Press, 1965). According to Olson, such organizations have difficulty getting members to contribute, by volunteering their time or paying dues, to the creation and maintenance of "collective goods"—things that are beneficial to the members but which the general public can be excluded from enjoying, e.g., good wages and seniority rights for labor union members, or inexpensive farm produce for members of a food cooperative.

29. Garrett Hardin, "The Tragedy of the Commons," *Science, 162* (1968), 1243–48. Hardin credited a British amateur mathematician, William Forster Lloyd, for the concept.

30. Jean Jacques Rousseau, *The Social Contract and Discourses*, trans. G. D. H. Cole (New York: E. P. Dutton, 1950), p. 238. At this point, a knowledgeable reader will probably dismiss out of hand the notion that the citizen from Hoxton could have inspired Rousseau's brief discussion of the stag hunt in his *Second Discourse (on the Origin and Foundation of Inequality among Men)*, since it was published in 1755 and Hume did not invite Rousseau to England until 1766. However, for my purposes here as a matter of speculation, it is possible that Rousseau raised the matter of a stag hunt with the citizen from Hoxton to compare the modern-day stag hunt with his own conjecture about stag hunts of a primitive era. Obviously the citizen from Hoxton's experience confirmed the universality of Rousseau's earlier observation that cooperation is a preferred course of action, but often difficult to achieve and maintain.

31. Thomas C. Schelling, *Micromotives and Macrobehavior* (New York: W. W. Norton, 1978), p. 218. The original dilemma involving the cooperation or defection of two prisoners is not important here. The dilemma was originally a two-party game of cooperation and defection invented by Merrill Flood and Melvin Dresher in 1950, and so named by A. W. Tucker, a game theorist at Princeton. Russell Hardin, *Collective Action* (Baltimore: Johns Hopkins University Press, 1982), p. 24.

32. Fred Hirsch, *Social Limits to Growth* (Cambridge, Mass.: Harvard University Press, 1976), p. 146.

33. David Lewis, *Convention* (Cambridge, Mass.: Harvard University Press, 1969), p. 208.

34. The *Oxford English Dictionary* offers two definitions: "(9) General agreement or consent, deliberate or implicit, as constituting the origin and foundation of any custom, institution, opinion, etc. or as embodied in any accepted usage, standard of behavior, method of artistic treatment, or the like; (10) A rule or practice based upon general consent, or accepted and upheld by society at large; an arbitrary rule or practice recognized as valid in any particular art or study." Volume IIC (Oxford: Oxford University Press, 1978), p. 938.

35. Fred Hirsch, *Social Limits of Growth*, p. 179.

36. I am indebted to Robert Edgerton for this insight common to almost everyone's experience. Robert B. Edgerton, *Rules, Exceptions, and Social Order* (Berkeley: University of California Press, 1985), p. 245.

37. Robert Axelrod, *The Evolution of Cooperation* (New York: Basic Books, 1984).

38. "When the waltz first came in, it was thought avant-garde and scandalous. After all, it caused men and women to hold on to each other and move rapidly, clinging wildly while their hair flew, their petticoats fluttered, and their hips rocked in unison." Diane Ackerman, *A Natural History of the Senses* (New York: Vintage Books, 1991), p. 210.

39. John Stuart Mill, *On Liberty* (New York: Appleton-Century-Crofts, 1947), p. 58.

40. Charles Lindblom, *Inquiry and Change* (New Haven, Conn.: Yale University Press; New York: Russell Sage Foundation, 1990), pp. 223–24.

41. "People who like crowds will be crowded with people who like crowds, without necessarily liking the people who like crowds." Thomas C. Schelling, *Micromotives and Macrobehavior*, p. 190.

42. Thomas C. Schelling, "On the Ecology of Micromotives," in *The Corporate Society*, ed. Robin Marris (London: Macmillan, 1974), pp. 19–64 at p. 27.

43. Using Jon Elster's term, conventions are one "mechanism" for "human action and interaction—plausible, frequently observed ways in which things happen." Jon Elster, *The Cement of Society* (Cambridge: Cambridge University Press, 1989), p. viii.

Chapter 1. When Strangers Cooperate

1. The line, however, is not a universal convention. It seems to work in western societies, like England and the United States, where there is a preoccupation with time. Lines are thought to be relatively efficient. My own preoccupation with time is so pronounced that even a line, which is meant to save me time by taming public disorder, makes me impatient. I order tickets in advance and let the line form by mail so I can be free to do other things while my order is being filled; I prefer automatic teller machines at odd hours; and I even join the "members club" of a hotel chain so checking out is done automatically without my having to endure a line at the front desk in the morning.

2. Leon Mann, "Queue Culture: The Waiting Line as a Social System," *American Journal of Sociology* (November 1969), pp. 340–54 at p. 345.

3. The handshake can signify some form of agreement or trust. It was used among the ancient Greeks and Hebrews in commercial trade, by strangers on frontiers who, perhaps by extending their hands, showed they had no weapon at the ready, and by members of fraternal societies as an act of recognition. Tad Tuleja, *Curious Customs* (New York: Harmony Books, 1987), p. 9.

4. Asking for a reference from an applicant's former employer is reliable since the applicant is not able to exercise any discretion in choosing his references. The convention of references does not work as well for a prospective employer when the applicant chooses references with an eye to their friendship and partiality. In early Sung China (A.D. 1020), a recommender "was held responsible for the person recommended." Jon Elster, *Local Justice* (New York: Russell Sage Foundation, 1992), p. 163. Elster quotes Robert Klitgaard's study *Elitism*

and Meritocracy in Developing Countries (Baltimore: Johns Hopkins University Press, 1986), p. 164.

5. About 6.25 million Americans belong to self-help groups. Marion K. Jacobs and Gerald Goodman, "Psychology and Self-help Groups," *American Psychologist* (March 1989), pp. 536–45 at p. 536. In a recent study, Robert Wuthnow estimates that 40 percent of Americans "belong to a small group that meets regularly and provides caring support for its members." That is 100 million people using Wuthnow's criterion that includes "support" and "discussion" groups, not just self-help. Robert Wuthnow, *Sharing the Journey* (New York: Free Press, 1994), p. 4. Wuthnow, however, concludes that the "social contract binding [these] members together asserts only the weakest of obligations" (p. 6). Still he sees such groups as a significant development that mitigates "the breakdown of traditional support structures" (p. 5).

6. Charles W. Smith, *Auctions: The Social Construction of Value* (Berkeley: University of California Press), 1990, pp. 17–18.

7. Relying on David Lewis's work on conventions, Thomas Pavel distinguishes between "conventions proper" and "'social games of coordination' which require cooperative solutions but do not necessarily lead to their entrenchment as conventions." For Pavel, crossing the street in sufficient numbers would not be a temporary convention but a social game of coordination. "Literary Conventions," *Rules and Conventions*, ed. Mette Hjort (Baltimore: Johns Hopkins University Press, 1992), p. 55. I am indebted to Thomas Schelling for the street corner example, which we all have experienced in a big city. Thomas C. Schelling, *Micromotives and Macrobehavior* (New York: W. W. Norton, 1978), pp. 92–93. William Whyte offers much the same observation about pedestrians in New York City when he writes, "Pedestrians form up in platoons at the light and they will move in platoons for a block or more." William H. Whyte, *City* (New York: Anchor Books Doubleday, 1988), p. 57. I like the term "platoons" since it suggests the kind of combat formation needed in order to cross some busy downtown avenues.

8. "An atomic pile 'goes critical' when a chain reaction of nuclear fission becomes self-sustaining." Schelling, *Micromotives and Macrobehavior*, p. 89. David Lewis talks about the threshold for a convention in terms of combustion. "Conventions are like fires: under favorable conditions, a sufficient concentration of heat spreads and perpetuates itself. The nature of the fire does not depend on the original source of heat." David Lewis, *Convention* (Cambridge, Mass.: Harvard University Press, 1969), p. 88.

9. Charles Lave, citing an earlier study of David Solomon, argues that "it is safest to drive at the median speed, and increasingly dangerous to deviate from the speed in either direction." "Speeding, Coordination and the 55 mph Limit," *American Economic Review* (December 1985), pp. 1159–64 at p. 1163.

10. Diane Ketcham, "About Long Island," *New York Times*, April 12, 1992.

11. MADD was founded in California in 1980. In 1993 MADD had 400 chapters with approximately 3 million members. The organization notes that since

1980 driving deaths have decreased by 20 percent—saving more than 39,000 lives. "We are MADD" New York brochure. The *New York Times* reports that a "majority of people who drink socially now say they have at some point been a designated driver or have been taken home from a party by a designated driver." B. Drummond Ayres, Jr., "Big Gains Are Seen in Battle to Stem Drunken Driving," *New York Times*, May 22, 1994.

12. Suzanne Goldsmith, "Saving Lives in Seattle: A Model for Civic Responsibility," *The Responsive Community* (Winter 1993/94), pp. 81–90.

13. David Lewis argues that most practices are a product of some prior agreement and cannot become conventions until the "influence" of such an agreement is forgotten or only dimly remembered. Lewis, *Convention*, p. 84. Terence Deal and Allen Kennedy point out that informal rules of behavior, "how to act in a given situation," save time and eliminate uncertainty in an organization. Terence Deal and Allen Kennedy, *Corporate Cultures* (Reading, Mass.: Addison-Wesley, 1982), p. 15.

14. Thomas J. Peters and Robert H. Waterman, Jr., *In Search of Excellence* (New York: Warner Books, 1982), p. 126 ("chunking"), pp. 193–94 ("town meetings"), p. 252 ("open lab stock"), and p. 245 ("800 number"). Both Peters and Waterman harvested many of these practices during their time together at the management consulting firm of McKinsey & Co.

15. City Harvest, a nonprofit organization in New York City, has been in business since 1982 and has distributed more than thirty million pounds of food. As of July 1993 there were seventy-four such programs in the United States. *City Harvest Newsletter* (Summer 1993). There is even a Community Garden in Houston, Texas, that stocks nine food pantries by producing more than 16,000 pounds of vegetables in both the spring and the fall. Earthworks Group, *The Next Step: Fifty More Things You Can Do to Save the Earth* (Kansas City, Mo.: Andrews and McMeel, 1991), p. 21.

16. John Larrabee, "Helping Boston's Homeless with Coupons," *USA Today*, May 31, 1994. "In some cities, coupons can also be used in laundromats or for public transportation."

17. Consider this ominous twist to the adopt-a-highway convention. It was reported that a Ku Klux Klan group based in Waco, Texas, sought to adopt a two-mile stretch of Texas Highway 105 that "runs past a recently desegregated housing complex in the East Texas town of Vidor." Sam Howe Verhovek, "Klan Chapter in Texas Seeks to Collect Trash Near Blacks," *New York Times*, February 6, 1994.

18. *LVIS Newsletter*, January 3, 1993.

19. *Taos Land Trust Newsletter*, Spring 1992. A staffperson of the Nature Conservancy explained that community land trusts "see certain places they'd like to see protected, and realize that the federal and state system is not going to do it for them, neither is the town, so they should do it for themselves." Constance L. Hays, "Vanguard in the Battle for Dwindling Open Space," *New York Times*, April 23, 1992.

20. Charles Lindblom and David Cohen used this example in discussing "interactive problem solving" in *Usable Knowledge* (New Haven, Conn.: Yale University Press, 1979), p. 23.

21. Mark Stencel, "The Growing Influence of Boycotts," *Editorial Research Reports*, January 4, 1991. Replicated in *SIRS Researcher CD-ROM* (Boca Raton, Fla.: Social Issues Resources Series, Inc., 1994), 1156 lines at lines 201–28.

22. Edwin McDowell, "Boycotts by Travelers Set a Record," *New York Times*, January 4, 1993.

23. Anna Quindlen, "Please Don't Inhale," *New York Times*, February 3, 1993.

24. Lynda Richardson, "Last Bastion for Foreign Smokers," *New York Times*, April 23, 1993. By 1992, 56 percent of America's workplaces were smokefree. Julia Lawlor, "Offices Kick Cigarettes to Sidewalks," *USA Today*, November 29, 1993. By 1994, fast food chains like McDonald's, Jack in the Box, and Taco Bell had banned smoking by their customers and employees, and the Defense Department banned smoking at work on military bases and ships anywhere in the world. Thomas J. Lueck, "Cracking Down on Smokers," *New York Times*, March 17, 1994.

25. By 1992, 40 percent of the municipal recycling programs were mandatory. In some communities, recycling has had the effect of reducing the number of garbage collection days, thereby saving tax dollars. Rodman D. Griffin, "Garbage Crisis," *CQ Researcher*, March 20, 1992. Replicated in *SIRS Researcher CD-ROM* (Boca Raton, Fla.: Social Issues Resources Series, Inc., 1994), 1312 lines at lines 198–201. Many experts believe that recycling, no matter how successful as a voluntary or mandatory program, will never be able to account for more than 25 percent of the waste produced. Frank Kreith, "Garbage, Garbage, Garbage," *State Legislatures* (October 1992), pp. 24–26.

26. Here I rely on the interesting summary of Ian R. Bartsky and Elizabeth Harrison, "Standard and Daylight Time," *Scientific American* (May 1979), pp. 46–53.

27. "In a Daylight-Saving Fight, an Hour of Defeat," *New York Times*, February 28, 1993.

28. Calvin Sims, "Motorists Are Still Shunning Car Pools: They Want to Be Alone," *New York Times*, November 4, 1991.

29. Sue Ellen Christian and Sarah Talalay, "Car-Pool Lanes Proves to Be Way to Go," *Chicago Tribune*, May 1, 1994. Still some of those who drive alone object. One New York area motorist was quoted: "We're all taxpayers and if they're making it [the Long Island Expressway] wider we should all get to use it. People shouldn't have special rights just because they are in a car pool." *New York Times*, May 28, 1994.

30. Again I am indebted to Thomas Schelling for a vivid example of a complicated social phenomenon. *Micromotives and Macrobehavior*, p. 141. The phenomenon of "tipping" is one reason why Oak Park, Illinois, bans "for sale" signs and "the town offers insurance that guarantees homeowners that they will not lose the value of their house and property because of a change in racial mix."

Avinash Dixit and Barry Nalebuff, *Thinking Strategically* (New York: W. W. Norton, 1991), p. 214.

31. Andrew Hacker, *Two Nations* (New York: Ballantine Books, 1993), p. 88.

32. It is curious that Robert Axelrod, who has done such valuable work on cooperation in game theoretic terms, seems confused about conventions. He cites the example of wearing a tie as a convention that has no direct payoff. But wearing a tie is not a convention; it is a fashion. There is a payoff for any convention, because it coordinates behavior and serves the interests of those who regulate their behavior accordingly. "An Evolutionary Approach to Norms," *American Political Science Review* (December 1986), pp. 1095–1111 at pp. 1107–8.

33. Here I rely on David Lewis's common sense distinction at p. 120 in *Convention*.

34. Jon Elster provides an unappealing but graphic example of a norm. "I don't pick my nose when I can be observed by people on a train passing by, even if I am confident that they are all perfect strangers whom I shall never see again and who have no power to impose sanctions on me." *Nuts and Bolts for the Social Sciences* (Cambridge: Cambridge University Press, 1989), p. 119. I have already noted that the existence of a metaconvention provides a rationale for a particular coordination solution such as "first come, first served," which makes sense of a line. A norm may have no obvious rationale.

35. David Lewis thinks of conventions as "a species of norms." "Any convention is, by definition, a norm which there is some presumption that one ought to conform to." *Convention*, pp. 98–99. Edna Ullmann-Margalit makes almost no distinction between norms and conventions. She defines conventions as "accepted and established solutions to past recurrent coordination problems which—with time—assume the status of norms." *The Emergence of Norms* (Oxford: Oxford University Press, 1977), p. 76.

36. I use the term *robust* somewhat differently from the way it has been employed in game theory literature. There it connotes a strategy that has successfully maintained itself in competition with several other strategies. James S. Coleman, "Norm-Generating Structures," in *The Limits of Rationality*, eds. Karen S. Cook and Margaret Levi (Chicago: University of Chicago Press, 1990), p. 252.

37. Tuleja, *Curious Customs*, p. 200. Tuleja's explanation relies on Albert Rose, *Public Roads of the Past* (American Association of State Highway Officials, 1952) and Richard H. Hopper, "Left-Right" *Transportation Quarterly*, 36, No. 4 (October 1982).

38. Lon Fuller, *The Morality of Law* (New Haven, Conn.: Yale University Press, 1969), p. 234. Philip Selznick says that the common law tradition shows "a preference for law that is more emergent than imposed." *The Moral Commonwealth* (Berkeley: University of California Press, 1992), p. 463.

39. Oliver Wendell Holmes, Jr., *The Common Law* (Boston: Little, Brown, 1881), p. 1. Holmes relates the rich history of British and American common law, a distinctive tradition of judicial decisions based on precedent and custom. The

story of the common law is the story of everyday practices of coordination, disputes arising from such practices, resolution of those disputes leading to revised practices of coordination, and so on.

Chapter 2. How Footpaths Get Started

1. Oliver Wendell Holmes, Jr., *The Common Law* (Boston: Little, Brown, 1881), p. 35. Conventions also resemble "taboos," which are not justified by knowing their origins but are respected for their settled prohibitions. Robert B. Edgerton, *Rules, Exceptions, and Social Order* (Berkeley: University of California Press, 1985), pp. 43–44.
2. Even when we think we know something about how a convention originated, we may disagree. Take the example of the first traffic light. In my own reading I came across two detailed but conflicting accounts. One writer credits Garrett A. Morgan, who in 1923 sold the rights to General Electric. Another writer credits Lester Farnsworth Wire, who in 1912 set up the first traffic light at Main and Second in Salt Lake City, Utah. Thomas Schelling footnotes this piece of arcane history about Morgan in *Micromotives and Macrobehavior* (New York: W. W. Norton, 1978), p. 120. Schelling relies on Russell L. Adams, *Great Negroes Past and Present* (Sacramento: California State Department of Education, 1973). Tad Tuleja uses the Wire version in *Curious Customs* (New York: Harmony Books, 1987), p. 189, citing Kevin Bechstrom, "A Salute to Lester Farnsworth Wire," *AASHTO Quarterly* (April 1986).
3. Robert Sugden, *The Economics of Rights, Co-operation, and Welfare* (Oxford: Basil Blackwell, 1986), p. 43.
4. David Lewis, *Convention* (Cambridge, Mass.: Harvard University Press, 1969), p. 208. Another commentator examined the Lewis definition and concluded that for Lewis a convention is "totally independent of its origin. It does not matter how R [a regularity of behavior] appeared within the population, whether it was a result of chance or of an explicit agreement, for it is the conditional preference for R that makes it a convention." Paul Dumouchel, "Hobbes on Literary Rules and Conventions," *Rules and Conventions*, ed. Mette Hjort (Baltimore: Johns Hopkins University Press, 1992), p. 323, footnote 9.
5. In her study of the emergence of norms, which she considers to be, in most respects, the same as conventions, Edna Ullmann-Margalit says that they result from "complex patterns of behaviour of a large number of people over a protracted period of time." *The Emergence of Norms* (Oxford: Oxford University Press, 1977), p. 8.
6. "Having become a norm, a convention *becomes* a standard of fairness; but . . . it does not become a norm *because* it is seen to be fair." Sugden, *The Economics of Rights*, p. 159. Russell Hardin discusses the QWERTY keyboard in *Morality within the Limits of Reason* (Chicago: University of Chicago Press, 1988), p. 51. Hardin relies on Steven Leveen, "Tangled Typing," *Science 81* (May 1981), pp.

84–86, and Paul A. David, "Cleo and the Economics of QWERTY," *American Economic Review Papers and Proceedings*, 75 (May 1985), pp. 332–37.

7. Michael de Montaigne, *The Complete Works of Montaigne*, trans. Donald M. Frame (Palo Alto, Calif.: Stanford University Press, 1957), Vol. 3, p. 730.

8. Montaigne is also the source for the sidewalk example. "He who walks in the crowd must step aside, keep his elbows in, step back or advance, even leave the straight way, according to what he encounters." Frame trans., p. 758. Charles Lindblom has written extensively on this phenomenon in social interaction, calling it "mutual adjustment." Most recently, Lindblom discussed mutual adjustment in *Inquiry and Change* (New Haven: Yale University Press; New York: Russell Sage Foundation, 1990), pp. 239–49.

9. The "invisible hand" quotation is Adam Ferguson's as it appears in Robert Grafstein, *Institutional Realism: Social and Political Constraints on Rational Actors* (New Haven: Yale University Press, 1992), p. 80. The philosopher Robert Nozick offers an interesting list of sources across many disciplines which use the "invisible hand" explanation to account for various phenomena. See Nozick's *Anarchy, State, and Utopia* (New York: Basic Books, 1974), pp. 20–21. Thomas Schelling singles out biology as "instructive." "Biological evolution involves the responses of billions of individuals each going about his own business, most of them—from the amoeba to the giraffe—without the slightest idea that they are engaged together in selective adaptation, separation of species, survival, and extinction. The results are statistical, collective and aggregate; the process is molecular and individual." "On the Ecology of Micromotives," *The Corporate Society*, ed. Robin Marris (London: Macmillan, 1974), pp. 19–64 at p. 54.

10. Frederick von Hayek, "Spontaneous ('Grown') Order and Organized ('Made') Order," in *Markets, Hierarchies, and Networks*, ed. Grahame Thompson, Jennifer Frances, Rosalind Levacic, and Jeremy Mitchell (New York: Sage Publications, 1991), p. 297.

11. I started to develop these observations after reading Thomas Schelling's own account of an auditorium filling to the back, leaving the first dozen rows empty. Thomas C. Schelling, *Micromotives and Macrobehavior*, pp. 11–12.

12. It is reported that sheer visibility launched the word *quiz*. According to one source, a Dubliner, in 1780, wagered that he could "invent a new word and that everyone would be using it" within a day. James Daly paid boys to chalk "quiz" on the walls, fences, and billboards of the city and the following day, the word *quiz* was being talked about throughout the city. M. T. Wyllyamz tells this Irish story in a calendar about the origins of certain words. (Price Stern Sloan, Inc., 1992, at March 23.)

13. Jane Jacobs, *The Death and Life of Great American Cities* (New York: Vintage Books, 1961), pp. 50–54.

14. Ibid., pp. 31–32. Jacobs's criteria for safe neighborhoods included (1) "a clear demarcation between what is public space and what is private space"; (2) "there must be eyes upon the streets"; and (3) "the sidewalk must have users on it fairly continuously" (p. 35).

15. William H. Whyte, *City* (New York: Anchor Books, 1988), p. 16 ("schmooz-ers"), p. 51 ("suspicious-looking people"), p. 160 ("a mayor"). Both Whyte's and Jacobs's observations have much in common with the more abstract no-tion of "focal points," whose "prominence," a particular intersection or busy place, promotes coordination. A city block has many of these focal points, in-cluding front stoops, street corners, an all-night delicatessen, a "mayor" at his usual station. For a discussion of focal points, see Thomas C. Schelling, *The Strategy of Conflict* (Cambridge, Mass.: Harvard University Press, 1960), pp. 57–58.

16. Russell Hardin cites the JFK example in *Collective Action* (Baltimore: Johns Hopkins University Press, 1982), p. 210.

17. Those who have studied the practice of "water witching" note that it is more likely to arise where the source of water is particularly uncertain. For example, settlers who lived in Cotton Center, Texas, and had access to known water sources made no use of water witching until they came to Fence Lake, New Mexico, where water sources were more elusive. Evon Z. Vogt and Ray Hyman, *Water Witching U.S.A.* (Chicago: University of Chicago Press, 1959), p. 210.

18. William De Buys and Alex Harris, *River of Traps* (Albuquerque: University of New Mexico Press, 1990), p. 107. The same *parciante* explained how a ditch develops, much like a footpath that becomes well-worn, simply because it works. "They dig a little, and they put a little water to see how it goes. Then they dig some more until it goes how they want. They don't worry where to put the ditch. They just let the water tell them" (p. 22).

19. Such criteria are called "design principles" by Elinor Ostrom in her study of enduring "common-pool resource" institutions. *Governing the Commons* (Cambridge: Cambridge University Press, 1990), p. 90.

20. Thomas Glick, *Irrigation and Society in Medieval Valencia* (Cambridge, Mass.: Harvard University Press, 1970), p. 5.

21. Ira G. Clark, *Water in New Mexico* (Albuquerque: University of New Mexico Press, 1988), p. 28. "[T]he thousand acequias of New Mexico form a cultural web of almost microscopic strands and filaments that have held the culture and the landscape in place for hundreds of years." Stanley Crawford, *Mayor-domo* (New York: Anchor Books Doubleday, 1988), p. 176.

22. In Stanley Crawford's excellent book *Mayordomo*, which chronicled his own term as a mayordomo, Crawford notes that there is a change through litiga-tion that is establishing "a fixed share" of water "measured in acre feet" rather than a variable share in the water "entering an acequia's headgate . . ." (p. 174). The effect of such a change permits the sale or retirement of water rights that favor industry, development, or recreation, which undermines the acequia convention as "more fields are lost to production; less water is re-leased into the acequias; fewer people contribute to maintenance." Camille Flores-Turney, "Will the Acequias Survive?" *New Mexico Magazine* (May 1994), pp. 52–62 at p. 56.

23. Lon Fuller, *The Morality of Law* (New Haven, Conn: Yale University Press, 1969), p. 234.

24. The "herd immunity" excuse is really fallacious. For example, although 75 percent of children were immunized against measles, a recent epidemic in New York State between 1989 and 1991 produced 4,000 cases and twenty-three deaths. Peter Marks, "Shots Are Often Free, but Many Children Miss Immunization," *New York Times*, February 14, 1993.

25. Barbara Tuchman tells of how Milan in the fourteenth century avoided the spread of the bubonic plague by walling up the healthy as well as the diseased occupants in an infected home like "a common tomb." *A Distant Mirror* (New York: Knopf, 1978), p. 108. The "Black Death" of that century swept through many parts of Europe. For example, the plague devastated Paris, taking the lives of 50 percent of the population within three years (p. 95).

26. Paul Starr, *The Social Transformation of American Medicine* (New York: Basic Books, 1982), pp. 184–85.

27. Jane Brody, "Personal Health," *New York Times*, August 11, 1993. By the age of two, a child could be vaccinated against diptheria-tetanus-pertussis, polio, measles, mumps, rubella, hepatitis B, and *Hemophilus influenzae* type B. By 1993, public health dollars paid for approximately one-half of the vaccines administered to children.

28. "Shots Are Often Free," *New York Times*, February 14, 1993.

29. Robin Marantz Henig, "The Immunity Myth," *New York Times*, March 3, 1993.

30. Jane Brody, *New York Times*, August 11, 1993.

31. Jason DeParle quoting Senator Judd Gregg, "Free-Vaccine Plan Creates Unusual Array of Skeptics," *New York Times*, April 22, 1993. In England, a free vaccine program in the 1970s failed to increase immunization rates until doctors were given financial bonuses to administer the shots. Jason DeParle, "With Shots, It's Not Only about Costs, but Stories," *New York Times*, May 16, 1993.

32. Robert Pear, "Clinton in Compromise, Will Cut Parts of Childhood Vaccine Plan," *New York Times*, May 5, 1993. Robert Pear, "Serious Troubles Are Found in Federal Vaccine Program," *New York Times*, July 17, 1994.

33. In 1993, the New York City Health Department adopted regulations that permit confinement for more than a year, if necessary, of a tuberculosis patient who fails to take his or her antibiotics. Boston and Denver already exercised such powers. Only those actively infected with TB can infect others. Many people may carry the TB germ but do not pose a public danger. Mireya Navarro, "New York City to Detain Patients Who Fail to Finish TB Treatment," *New York Times*, March 10, 1993.

34. Ronald Bayer, *Private Acts, Social Consequences* (New Brunswick, N.J.: Rutgers University Press, 1991), p. 11, citing Merritt, "The Constitution Basis," *Hastings Center Report*, 3.

35. AIDS is acquired immune deficiency syndrome, which at the present time "is

an incurable viral disease that destroys the body's immune system, leaving patients vulnerable to a host of diseases that eventually kill. It is primarily spread
through sexual contact, intravenous drug use involving shared needles, and
contact with infected blood." *New York Times*, January 12, 1993. By 1993,
242,000 cases had been reported in the United States and over 158,000
Americans had died. It is estimated that at least one million Americans are
infected with the virus. "Spread of AIDS Expected to Slow: 330,000 Deaths
Are Seen by '95," *New York Times*, January 15, 1993.

36. Bayer, *Private Acts*, p. 252.
37. Mireya Navarro, "In the Age of AIDS, Sex Clubs Proliferate Again," *New
    York Times*, March 5, 1993. The American Association of Physicians for
    Human Rights has also "urged the avoidance of one-time encounters with
    anonymous partners and group sex; oral-anal contact ('rimming'); the inser-
    tion of the fist into the rectum ('fisting'); active or passive rectal intercourse;
    fecal contamination ('scat'); and mucous membrane (mouth or rectum) con-
    tact with semen or urine." Bayer, *Private Acts*, p. 28.
38. During 1993, there were approximately 13,000 weekly needle exchanges in
    New York City alone. Mireya Navarro, "New York Needle Exchange Called
    Unusually Effective," *New York Times*, February 18, 1993. The exchanges
    reach approximately 12 percent of the city's intravenous drug users. Felicia R.
    Lee, "Data Show Needle Exchange Curbs H.I.V. among Addicts," *New York
    Times*, November 26, 1994.
39. Bayer (*Private Acts*, p. 40) quotes David Goodstein in the *Advocate*, May 15,
    1984, p. 7.

Chapter 3. *"It's a Free Country"*

1. One commentator simply states that a "coordination problem is an interaction
   situation in which the interests of the participants coincide. A P.D. [prisoner's
   dilemma] problem, in contrast, is an interaction situation of interdependent
   decision in which the interests of the participants both conflict and coincide;
   it is a 'mixed motive' problem." Edna Ullmann-Margalit, *The Emergence of
   Norms* (Oxford: Oxford University Press, 1977), p. 114.
2. When I looked into the history of sanctuary as a convention, I found that it
   was not uniformly accepted despite the religious authorities who supported it.
   One such account tells of the death of a Robert Haulay during high mass in
   the church of Westminster. Haulay had taken refuge there after escaping from
   the Tower of London. He was pursued by the Constable of the Tower and a
   large number of armed men, who discovered Haulay at a prior's stall in the
   church where both he and a sexton were slain. Robert B. Edgerton, *Rules, Exceptions, and Social Order* (Berkeley: University of California Press, 1985), pp.
   119–20. Edgerton relies on J. Bellamy, *Crime and Public Order in England in the
   Later Middle Ages* (London: Routledge and Kegan Paul, 1973), p. 109.
3. Anyone who uses the "exit" concept is indebted to the work of Albert O.

Hirschman, *Exit, Voice, and Loyalty* (Cambridge, Mass.: Harvard University Press, 1970), pp. 106–20.

4. Robert Axelrod asks the question: "Is there any reason for an individual to co-operate when non-cooperative behavior is rewarded?" Axelrod and Douglas Dion, "The Future Evolution of Cooperation," *Science* (December 9, 1988), pp. 1385–90 at p. 1385. Our preferences for exit, delegation, and private gain do reward us by putting space between us and social problems or give us more time and opportunity for whatever it is we desire. But there are many rewards for cooperation just as there is an expectation that noncooperation will be rewarded.

5. Alexis de Tocqueville, *Democracy in America*, ed. J. P. Mayer, trans. George Lawrence (New York: Anchor Books Doubleday, 1969), p. 536. Tocqueville's observations of an earlier period still have great explanatory power of how Americans prefer to live. Too much economic and political analysis about our limitations and possibilities is done in windowless rooms where models are constructed without attention paid to the evidence of our social history and everyday life.

6. Louis Hartz, *The Liberal Tradition* (New York: Harcourt Brace & World, 1955), pp. 64–65, as footnoted on p. 106 of Hirschman, *Exit, Voice, and Loyalty*.

7. Thomas Schelling observes, "Often the individual is not free to change the result, he can only change his own position within it, and that does him no good." But changing my position can do me some good; it just doesn't change the result, which I assume in Schelling's context means an undesirable social outcome. "[Some] severe problems result not from the evil of people but from their helplessness as individuals." "On the Ecology of Micromotives," in *The Corporate Society*, ed. Robin Marris (London: Macmillan, 1974), pp. 19–64 at pp. 55–56.

8. I'm reminded of Andrew Hacker's explanation of why a taxi driver might pass by a black pedestrian trying to hail a cab. "He may actually feel sorry for the person he left standing in the rain . . . sad to say, actions that are often unfair can also be reasonable, at least insofar as they are based on sufficient experience to give them a degree of validity." Andrew Hacker, *Two Nations* (New York: Ballantine Books, 1992), pp. 20–21.

9. One professor said, "The problem with going back home is that they're going back to where they were raised, where they got their attitudes to begin with." Isabel Wilkerson, "Racial Tension Erupts, Tearing a College Apart," *New York Times*, April 10, 1992.

10. "I picture a kind of underground railroad, delivering us in the dead of night from the inner city to the suburbs." Shelby Steele, *The Content of Our Character* (New York: Harper Perennial, 1990), p. 22. William Julius Wilson points out that with the exit of stronger black families from inner-city neighborhoods, such neighborhoods have become more socially isolated and dysfunctional. *The Truly Disadvantaged* (Chicago: University of Chicago Press, 1987), pp. 137–38.

11. Desegregation plans from 1969 to 1976 saw a drop in enrollment of white students from 39.3 percent to 18.6 percent in Detroit; from 68.5 percent to 44 percent in Boston; from 65.6 percent to 48.1 percent in Denver; from 41.2 percent to 27.6 percent in San Francisco; from 38.2 percent to 11.7 percent in Atlanta. Thomas Burns Edsall with Mary D. Edsall, *Chain Reaction* (New York: W. W. Norton, 1992), p. 129. In the Los Angeles Unified School District, the enrollment of white children dropped from 252,000 in 1966 to 88,000 in 1990. David Rieff, *Los Angeles: Capital of the Third World* (New York: Touchstone/Simon & Schuster, 1991), p. 231. According to the National School Boards Association, in 1989 83 percent of all black children attended segregated schools in Illinois, 81 percent in New York, 77 percent in Michigan and California, 73 percent in New Jersey, 68 percent in Ohio, 64 percent in Texas, 63 percent in Pennsylvania. Hacker, *Two Nations*, pp. 162–63. The Harvard Project on School Desegregation reported that in 1991–92 60 percent of all black students (and an even higher percentage of Hispanic students) in America's public schools attended "predominately minority schools." This was the highest level since 1968. William Celis III, "Study Finding Rising Concentration of Black and Hispanic Students," *New York Times*, December 14, 1993.

12. Hacker, *Two Nations*, p. 164.

13. Isabel Wilkerson, "Des Moines Act to Halt White Flight after State Allows Choice of Schools," *New York Times*, December 10, 1992. Jonathan Kozol in the same news story made the sardonic observation: "All these white parents once passionately opposed to busing for integration because it was unfair to keep children on a bus for an hour are now putting their children on two-hour bus rides to get away from black and Hispanic children. The bus ride was never the issue. The destination was the issue."

14. Hacker, *Two Nations*, pp. 35–36. Blacks may not want to live near whites for its own sake, but they surely do want better schools, safer streets, and other public amenities that white neighborhoods often offer.

15. Ian Fisher, "In a Striving Section of the Bronx, the Races Mix, but Don't Mingle," *New York Times*, January 2, 1993.

16. Nathan Glazer notes that when Jewish neighborhoods started being comfortable for Jews they started being uncomfortable for non-Jews. Nathan Glazer, *Affirmative Discrimination* (Cambridge, Mass.: Harvard University Press, 1987), p. 157. Glazer identifies three quite different factors that lead to residential concentrations of any ethnic group: (1) discrimination; (2) economic limitations where people can afford to live; and (3) cultural cohesion to support local institutions (p. 153). Glazer defends racial quotas in residential housing on the ground that quotas address the expectations of existing tenants or homeowners who want an integrated community to be maintained (p. xxiv).

17. Tocqueville, *Democracy in America*, p. 671.

18. Michael Walzer, *Obligations: Essays on Disobedience, War, and Citizenship* (Cambridge, Mass.: Harvard University Press, 1970), p. 230.

19. Alan Wolfe makes a case for government intervention: "One of the enormous advantages of allowing government to intervene in society is that once it establishes procedures, half of the difficulties of being modern are relieved: people can argue with each other over their share without having always to start from scratch." *Whose Keeper?* (Berkeley: University of California Press, 1989), p. 228. But it is also true that when we govern ourselves by using conventions, no one ever starts from scratch again. The regularities of behavior to which each of us subscribes settle most differences. Russell Hardin argues, however, that with so much already delegated to governments, they will increasingly make rules to resolve many new coordination problems, so that there will be less place for voluntary agreements which might generate new conventions. *Morality within the Limits of Reason* (Chicago: University of Chicago Press, 1988), p. 52.

20. Public goods are Hume's meadow-draining project, bridges, harbors, clean air, water, public space—beneficial things that you and I cannot be excluded from enjoying.

21. Of course it all depends on the gravity of the problem, our options, and whether a new convention sufficiently ameliorates the problem. If Litterville residents were to clean up their act, maintaining the appearance of the town would eventually require less effort on everyone's part than the initial effort to get a grip on the problem.

22. Tocqueville, *Democracy in America*, pp. 690–95.

23. Ibid., p. 672.

24. "Rent" is thought to be a form of profit seeking when groups are favored by government through regulation, licenses, legal monopolies, or special subsidies. The profit is that amount which exceeds what could be obtained in a competitive market. The assumption is that rent seeking produces "social waste." Social waste, however, is often in the eye of the beholder and is usually seen only in terms of economic efficiency. Margaret Levi, *Of Rule and Revenue* (Berkeley: University of California Press, 1988), p. 180. The efficiency argument is normally advanced by those who would have market competition deliver better services at lower cost. But most of the problems on the public agenda are tasks that private enterprise shuns. I am sympathetic toward those in government whose efficiency is often found wanting on problems that private firms have decided they can't make a profit on. For example, a private bus company will "cream" the better bus routes on which it can make a profit, leaving the rest to public transit. When public transit runs a deficit, the critics compare the performance on the "dog" routes that the privates didn't want in the first place with the performance of the privates on the better routes, whose revenues public transit can't use to offset its deficit. When I was in government, an investment banker friend readily conceded to me that "business does what is doable and government gets all the rest."

25. Irving Howe said it is healthy, though confusing, to have more special interests, rather than fewer. Howe called it "a triumph for democracy." Irving Howe, "Special Interest Cant," *New York Times*, March 8, 1984.

26. Russell Hardin, *Collective Action* (Baltimore: Johns Hopkins University Press, 1982), p. 135.

27. Daniel Boorstin, *Democracy and Its Discontents: Reflections on Everyday America* (New York: Random House, 1971), p. 121.

28. Here I owe a great debt to Charles Lindblom for his clarifying work on how public problems are addressed and ameliorated. See a useful summary in *Inquiry and Change* (New Haven, Conn.: Yale University; New York: Russell Sage Foundation, 1990), pp. 1–14.

29. Mike Stauffer, "Officials: Federal Mandates Choke Local Budgets," *Taos News*, November 11, 1993. The town has already had to pay for a new landfill, $3 million to build, $1 million to operate; new storm water regulations that cost $30 per year per resident; and $130,000 to bring a juvenile detention facility into state compliance.

30. Tocqueville, *Democracy in America*, p. 672.

31. Ibid., p. 527.

32. I was reminded of our propensities in comments that I received from those I asked to read a monograph out of which this book emerged. One friend wrote to me: "Cooperation is less likely to work well if the gains from noncooperation exceed the gains from cooperating." Another wrote: There are "many situations, in which it is in each individual's interest to defect. Without such recognition, you risk making 'coordination' seem too easy." Both correspondents wanted me to take into account the classic "prisoner's dilemma," which game theorists use as a framework to analyze the possibilities of cooperation between two or more people.

33. David Hume explained "discounting" as follows: "Contiguous objects must have an influence much superior to the distant and remote. Accordingly we find in common life, that men are principally concern'd about those objects, which are not much remov'd either in space or time, enjoying the present, and leaving what is afar off to the care of chance and fortune." *A Treatise on Human Nature*, 2nd ed., ed. L. A. Selby-Bigge (Oxford: Oxford University Press, 1978), p. 428. Tocqueville also took note of "discounting." "When everyone is constantly striving to change his position, when an immense field of competition is open to all . . . the present looms large and hides the future, so that men do not want to think beyond tomorrow" (p. 548).

34. Robyn Dawes and his colleagues found that the development of group identity in a game can be very important in producing a cooperative outcome, and that communication is important in fostering group identity. "Cooperation for the Benefit of Us—Not Me, or My Conscience," in *Beyond Self-Interest*, ed. Jane J. Mansbridge (Chicago: University of Chicago Press, 1990), pp. 97–110.

35. Game theory, the formal study of rational expectations, assumes goals of participants who are not individualized. It is deductive rather than empirical. Those who use game theory as a framework for analysis readily concede that it does not approximate real-world situations. It is "a limitation of any theory that tries to deal with the full multi-dimensional complexity of imperfect decision makers." Thomas C. Schelling, "What Is Game Theory?" in *Choice and*

Consequence: Perspectives of an Errant Economist (Cambridge, Mass.: Harvard University Press, 1984), p. 239. Amartya Sen criticizes game theory for its insistence on "social ignorance" that deprives players of a context in which they make their choices. Sen sees the assumption of social ignorance as contrary to how rationality works in the real world. "The point is not that rationality must take us to the communal principle, rejecting the individualistic one, but that there is a genuine ambiguity here about what rationality might require. . . ." "Goals, Commitment, and Identity," *Journal of Law, Economics, and Organization* (Fall 1985), pp. 341–355 at p. 346.
36. Tocqueville, *Democracy in America*, p. 672.
37. Mark Bradsher, "Mark Twain Would Understand the Water Crisis That's Corrupting Iowans," *New York Times*, July 22, 1993.
38. We may make exceptions for those who are ill or infirm, or where we know there is no avoiding differences in circumstance. For example, those who live upstream and refrain from polluting gain nothing, while those who live downstream do. Schelling, "On the Ecology of Micromotives," p. 32.
39. The most frequently cited work is Mancur Olson's *The Logic of Collective Action* (Cambridge, Mass.: Harvard University Press, 1965). Free riding, however, doesn't explain very much when regularities of behavior are involved. Before a convention is established, some people undoubtedly choose not to cooperate, but they have nothing to free-ride on because nothing yet has been gained until there is a measure of successful coordination. Once a convention has been established, free riders may be resented, but we are not likely to give up whatever we have gained from coordination just because a few invariably take advantage.
40. Tocqueville, *Democracy in America*, p. 571.
41. Schelling, "On the Ecology of Micromotives," p. 30.

Chapter 4. Talking to Strangers

1. "Beyond some limit—a limit that on the scale of a country (let alone humanity) is infinitesimally small—concrete knowledge of the others is flatly impossible. Beyond infinitesimally small limits, then, the 'community' is no longer a body of concrete human beings actually known to one another, much less an association of friends; it is an aggregate of distant persons called class, nation, country, humanity, or what not. How is a citizen to apprehend the interests of the people who comprise aggregates like these?" Robert Dahl, *Dilemmas of Pluralistic Democracy* (New Haven, Conn.: Yale University Press, 1982), p. 144.
2. Daniel Bell, "The Third Technological Revolution," *Dissent* (Spring 1989), pp. 164–76 at p. 175.
3. John Markoff, "A Free and Simple Computer Link," *New York Times*, December 8, 1993. Tim Berners-Lee developed a form of information retrieval called "hypertext" so that physics researchers could exchange information.

4. David Lewis, *Convention* (Cambridge, Mass.: Harvard University Press, 1969), p. 208. If people "need to know how others are choosing, to make their own choices, it will matter whether or not they can find out what everybody is doing." Thomas C. Schelling, *Micromotives and Macrobehavior* (New York: W. W. Norton, 1978), p. 215.

5. The Electronic Frontier Foundation argues, "The superhighway should be required to provide so-called open platform services." Mitchell Kapor and Jerry Berman, "A Superhighway through the Wasteland," *New York Times*, November 24, 1993. Others go even further. The Telecommunications Roundtable, composed of seventy-one nonprofit organizations, wants a network that provides "free access to information that is needed to participate fully in a democratic society . . . and [a] chance for the public to be involved fully in making policies related to the network." Thomas J. DeLoughrey, "Guaranteeing Access to the Data Highway," *Chronicle of Higher Education*, November 3, 1993.

6. For example, e-mail is fast becoming junk mail. With so many sources on a network, a networker can be overwhelmed by an uninvited volume of inquiries, gossip, and solicitations.

7. For example, the communitarian Amitai Etzioni speculated twenty years ago that the new media would allow "millions of people [to] enter into dialogue with each other and their representatives." Amitai Etzioni, Kenneth Lauden, and Sara Lipson, "Participatory Technology: The MINERVA Communication Tree," *Journal of Communication* (Spring 1975), pp. 64–74. But in a study of thirteen experimental electronic town meetings it was found that most citizens do not participate. Christopher Arterton, *Teledemocracy: Can Technology Protect Democracy?* (Newbury Park, Calif.: Sage, 1987), p. 197. Ithiel de Sola Pool warns that "a society in which it becomes easy for every small group to indulge its taste will have more difficulty mobilizing unity. A society where mass publishing has to compete with specialized information resources will have more trouble establishing coherence of intellectual debate." *Technology without Boundaries*, ed. Eli M. Noan (Cambridge, Mass.: Harvard University Press, 1990), p. 261. In the absence of other forms of community, however, electronic "virtual communities" no doubt are important to those who want to connect with others. See Howard Rheingold, *The Virtual Community* (Reading, Mass.: Addison-Wesley, 1993).

8. By technology I mean nothing more than a technical method of achieving a practical purpose. "Many of the great inventions of modern communications are devices to convert non-electronic signals to electronic ones or back again. Examples are the telegraph, telephone, microphone, loudspeaker, teletypewriter, facsimile machine, video camera, television receiver, tape recorder, cathode ray tube, video cassette recorder, and optical disc player. Each starts with an electronic signal and turns it into something humans know how to sense, or vice versa. It is increasingly feasible to convert any given signal to a form in which it can be moved by whatever transmission medium is most convenient and economical." Pool, *Technology without Boundaries*, p. 23.

9. George Gilder, *Life after Television* (Knoxville, Tenn.: Whittle Direct Books,

1990), pp. 14–17. There is already a potential system called Bidirectional Uni-cable Switching System ("BUSS"), which can allot two exclusive TV channels to each subscriber for whatever transmission and reception of high-speed data transmission he or she chooses. Julian M. Weiss, "Adding Vision to Telecommuting," *Futurist* (May/June 1992), pp. 16–18. Gilder sees the media changing from "a mass-produced and mass-consumed commodity to an endless feast of niches and specialties" (p. 35). He makes the interesting point that "[t]elevision is not vulgar because people are vulgar; it is vulgar because people are similar in their prurient interests and sharply differentiated in their civilized concerns" (pp. 19–20). Ithiel de Sola Pool said much the same thing in *Technology without Boundaries*. "The economics of broadcasting . . . depended upon reaching millions of people with a uniform message" (p. 60). For Pool, it was no wonder that TV is "a medium for passing time, for being amused, and for taking it easy" (p. 241).

10. Steven R. Rivkin and Jeremy D. Rosner, "Shortcut to the Information High-way," *Progressive Policy Institute* (July 1992), No. 15, p. 4, footnote 6.

11. In Orlando, Florida, Time Warner's cable system is installing new trunk lines of fiberoptics and adding video compression that puts information into existing residential lines. Time Warner is also installing video servers, which are storage devices for information that customers can access. Paul Farhi, "Time Warner Plans 2-Way Cable System," *Washington Post*, January 27, 1993. Tele-Communications, Inc., of Denver plans to use digital compression to upgrade its system in 150 cities by 1996, enlarging the range of channels from fifty to 500. Like Time Warner, it is also replacing its trunk lines with optical fibers. Edmund L. Andrews, "Cable Company Plans a Data 'Superhighway,'" *New York Times*, April 12, 1993.

12. Edmund L. Andrews, "Big Risk and Cost Seen in Creating Data Superhigh-way," *New York Times*, January 3, 1994.

13. The FCC also will have to decide whether to reallocate more of the electro-magnetic spectrum (broadcasting) to accommodate digitally compressed sig-nals.

14. John Markoff, "Building The Electronic Superhighway," *New York Times*, January 24, 1993.

15. William J. Broad, "A New Way of Doing Science: On the Network," *New York Times*, May 18, 1993. There's no telling what will happen to Internet. It is getting more commercial and its growth is phenomenal, creating all kinds of operating difficulties that may change how it is governed and to whom it is made available. For example, "flash crowds" are beginning to appear when a particular network receives publicity. One executive remarked that it is like "a traffic jam caused by rubber neckers on the nation's data highway." John Markoff, "Traffic Jams Already on the Information Highway," *New York Times*, November 3, 1993.

16. Beverly T. Watkins, "Putting New Mexico on Line," *Chronicle of Higher Education*, October 20, 1993. David L. Wilson, "Putting Citizens on Line," *Chronicle of Higher Education*, July 27, 1994. Ashley Dunn, "Local Groups Are

Attempting to Knock Down the Information Superhighway's Tollbooths," *New York Times*, August 4, 1994.

17. Elizabeth Kolbert, "Some Cable Systems Are Cutting C-Span for Other Channels," *New York Times*, June 20, 1994. C-Span also covers sessions of the Canadian Parliament, the Israeli Knesset, the Japanese Diet, the French Senate, and the German Bundestag. "C-SPAN, the Little Network that Could," *TV Guide*, July 18, 1992. According to C-Span, Presidents Reagan and Clinton have used C-Span to keep track of the Congress's daily machinations, and congressional staff members on Capitol Hill use C-Span to keep track of each other. *C-SPAN Digest*, April 12, 1993, and May 10, 1993.

18. "C-Span Audience Demographics" (C-Span Survey '92).

19. *C-SPAN Digest*, July 19, 1993.

20. "C-Span Facts" (undated).

21. Thomas J. Meyer, "No Sound Bites Here," *New York Times Magazine* (March 15, 1992), p. 46.

22. James Warren, "Taking the Long View," *Chicago Tribune*, March 15, 1992.

23. Excessive packaging, of course, is a subjective measure. Economists would argue that there is no such thing since the profit motive of a product maker does not permit "excessive" packaging but only the amount of packaging, and its associated cost, that is needed to sell his product. "[P]ackaging is designed to make a product stand out and compete. It's not as simple as saying excessive packaging isn't economical. In some cases it's very economical, because it's what sells." Jay Stuller quotes Gordon Hart of the Sierra Club in "The Politics of Packaging," *Across the Board* (a publication of the Conference Board), January/February 1990. Replicated in *SIRS Researcher CD-ROM* (Boca Raton, Fla.: Social Issues Resources Series, Inc., 1994), 469 lines at lines 152–55.

24. The EarthWorks Group, *50 Simple Things You Can Do to Save the Earth* (Berkeley, Calif.: Earthworks Press, 1989), p. 66.

25. Albert Hirschman thinks of a boycott as "on the borderline between voice and exit." Exit is of course leaving a problem behind. "Voice" in Hirschman's terms means doing something about a problem. Hirschman goes on to say that "boycott is often a weapon of customers who do not have, at least at the time of the boycott, an alternative source of supply. . . ." *Exit, Voice, and Loyalty* (Cambridge, Mass.: Harvard University Press, 1970), p. 86.

26. Rodman D. Griffin, "Garbage Crisis," *CQ Researcher*, March 20, 1992. Replicated in *SIRS Researcher CD-ROM* (Boca Raton, Fla.: Social Issues Resources Series, Inc., 1994), 1312 lines at lines 76–80. The estimate was reported by the EarthWorks Group, *The Next Step: 50 More Things You Can Do to Save the Earth* (Kansas City, Mo.: Andrews and McNeel, 1991), p. 35.

27. Griffin, "Garbage Crisis." Ibid. at lines 980–83.

28. David Lewis, who does not account for the origins of any particular convention, assumes that "[a] convention is produced when a big enough fluctuation meets strong enough amplifying forces. The source of the fluctuation is unimportant given its size. It does not matter whether it was created with the intention of starting a convention or whether it occurred in some or all of the

population." *Convention* (Cambridge, Mass.: Harvard University Press, 1969), p. 86.

29. The EarthWorks Group, *The Recycler's Handbook* (Berkeley, Calif.: Earthworks Press, 1990), p. 29.

30. Charles E. Lindblom, *Inquiry and Change* (New Haven, Conn.: Yale University Press; New York: Russell Sage Foundation, 1990), p. 37. Giving names to problems is something people do when they want attention paid. For example, sexual harassment has only recently been named although the objectionable conduct has long been a problem. The naming has established boundaries for what is appropriate behavior among employees in the workplace. Market products have names and so do government programs. The naming does not make them better products or more useful programs, but they are handles that we need to identify them. The same is true of new practices not yet widely known. The naming helps to clarify and promote them.

31. Dennis Chong says much the same thing in his study of collective action and the civil rights movement. *Collective Action and the Civil Rights Movement* (Chicago: University of Chicago Press, 1991). Chong notes "'unconditional cooperators,' whose actions are not contingent upon the actions of others, are usually needed to initiate collective action. Such individuals step into the breach and pay the heavy start-up costs, while everyone else waits for more favorable circumstances before contributing" (p. 235).

32. Chester Bernard was one of the first analysts of modern organizational life to acknowledge the importance of what he called "morale work." "We are all in this together and if you will cooperate, everyone else will respond in kind." Gerry J. Miller, "Managerial Dilemmas: Political Leadership in Hierarchies," in *The Limits of Rationality*, eds. Karen Schweers Cook and Margaret Levi (Chicago: University of Chicago Press, 1990), pp. 324–48 at p. 337.

33. This simple idea has been promoted by People for the American Way in mobilizing phone calls to legislators. EarthWorks Group, *You Can Change America* (Berkeley, Calif.: Earthworks Press, 1993), pp. 46–47.

34. Seattle has such a program and, along with other measures, the city has reduced its municipal waste by 40 percent. Griffin, "Garbage Crisis." Ibid. at lines 1017–21.

35. Robert Sugden, *The Economics of Rights, Co-operation and Welfare* (Oxford: Basil Blackwell, 1986), pp. 115–21. Jon Elster observes that "most individuals are subject to both of these psychic mechanisms, and it is hard to tell before the fact which will dominate. *Nuts and Bolts for the Social Sciences* (Cambridge: Cambridge University Press, 1989), p. 9.

36. David Osborne and Ted Gaebler, *Reinventing Government* (New York: Plume, 1993), p. 53. "Nested enterprises" is another term for a federated structure, sometimes used by those who examine how successful collective action works. Nested enterprises are "larger organizational units . . . built on previously organized smaller units." Elinor Ostrom, *Governing the Commons* (Cambridge: Cambridge University Press, 1990), p. 189. Russell Hardin sees the advantage of "overlapping small group and large group relationships" which may "enable

even very large groups to achieve cooperation. . . ." *Collective Action* (Baltimore: Johns Hopkins University Press, 1982), p. 229. When groups that already exist for other purposes enlist in a campaign, Hardin calls it "piggybacking" (p. 43).

37. Michael Taylor, "Rationality and Revolutionary Collective Action," in *Rationality and Revolution*, ed. Michael Taylor (Cambridge: Cambridge University Press, 1988), p. 84. "We all have many identities and being 'just me' is not the only way we see ourselves. Community, nationality, class, race, sex, union membership, the fellowship of oligopolists, revolutionary solidarity, and so on, all provide identities that can be, depending on the context, crucial to our view of ourselves, and thus to the way we view our welfare, goals, or behavioral obligations." Amartya Sen, "Goals, Commitment, and Identity," *Journal of Law, Economics, and Organization* (Fall 1985), pp. 341–55 at p. 348. For an interesting discussion of the importance of membership, see Robert Axelrod, "An Evolutionary Approach to Norms," *American Political Science Review* (December 1986), pp. 1095–1111 at pp. 1105–6.

38. Charles Lindblom created a useful term for this unpredictable and uneven process which he called "muddling through." "The Science of Muddling Through," *Public Administration Review*, 19, no. 2 (Spring 1959), pp. 78–88. Also see "Still Muddling, Not Yet Through," *Public Administration Review* (November/December 1979), pp. 517–26. Lindblom can be downright gloomy about "solutions." "In actual historical fact, the 'solution' to many social problems is simply continuing suffering. Or repression. Or a solution that itself creates new problems." Charles E. Lindblom and David K. Cohen, *Usable Knowledge* (New Haven, Conn.: Yale University Press, 1979), p. 91.

39. William James, *The Will to Believe* (New York: Dover, 1956), p. 25. Dennis Chong offers a marvelous example of "how a widespread expectation that an upcoming rally will attract a large number of supporters can amount to a self-fulfilling prophecy. An individual will attend because he wants to be a part of a memorable and successful historical event; but it is actually his participation and the participation of hundreds or thousands of other like-minded individuals which ensure that the rally is both successful and memorable." Chong, *Collective Action and the Civil Rights Movement*, p. 176. Chong also observes that in the civil rights movement young blacks who were optimistic about social change were more likely to take part (pp. 136–37). Chong goes on to point out that individual optimism is not so much based on what one person can do than "the prospect of collective success, i.e., the possibility of making a difference collectively" (pp. 148–49).

40. Herbert Simon offers the cholesterol example and names our "acceptance without full evaluation" as our "docility" mechanism. "A Mechanism for Social Selection and Successful Altruism," *Science* (December 21, 1990), pp. 1665–68 at p. 1666.

41. Albert O. Hirschman, *Shifting Involvements* (Princeton, N.J.: Princeton University Press, 1982), p. 81. Sometimes I think social scientists misunderstand how things happen—even in scientific undertakings. "[There is a] rockbound

difference between scientific work as it appears in print and the actual course of inquiry. . . . The difference is a little like that between textbooks of scientific method and the ways in which scientists actually think, feel, and go about their work. The books on methods present ideal patterns, but these tidy, normative patterns . . . do not reproduce the typically untidy, opportunistic adaptations that scientists really make. The scientific paper presents an immaculate appearance which reproduces little or nothing of the intuitive leaps, false starts, mistakes, loose ends, and happy accidents that actually cluttered up the inquiry." Robert K. Merton, *Social Theory and Social Structure*, enlarged ed. (New York: Free Press, 1968), p. 4.

42. Hirschman, *Shifting Involvements*, p. 89. Hirschman also points out that striving is not just for the sake of what I can do to solve a social problem, but what my work and activities do for me, "regardless of any real changes in the state of the world that I might achieve" (p. 90). Hirschman thinks the benefit for an individual "is not the difference between the hoped-for result and the effort furnished by him or her, but the sum of these two magnitudes" (p. 86). Hirschman chooses the term *striving* because it "precisely intimates the lack of a reliable relation between effort and result." Hirschman, "Against Parsimony," in *Rival Views of Market Society* (New York: Viking Press, 1986) pp. 142–60 at p. 149.

43. For a discussion of an "effort convention," see Harvey Leibenstein, *Inside the Firm: The Inefficiencies of Hierarchy* (Cambridge, Mass.: Harvard University Press, 1987), pp. 79–86.

44. During World War II, "most individual soldiers never fired their rifles—no matter how long a battle lasted, how brave they were, or what targets presented themselves—while weapons that required joint action by two or three soldiers, like feeding a belt of ammunition into a machine gun or loading and aiming an artillery piece were regularly fired as intended." Thomas C. Schelling citing S. L. A. Marshall's *Men Against Fire* in Schelling's "Against Backsliding," in *Development, Democracy, and the Art of Trespassing: Essays in Honor of Albert O. Hirschman*, eds. Alejandro Foxley, Michael S. McPherson, and Guillermo O'Donnell (South Bend, Ind.: Notre Dame University Press, 1986), pp. 233–38 at p. 235. Albert Hirschman thinks that a potential defector from a group is more hesitant to defect than someone who never chooses to join an effort. Having tried to improve a situation, those who cooperate believe that things will get worse if they leave. *Exit, Voice, and Loyalty*, pp. 98–99. Other commentators argue that those who choose to cooperate, by definition, are less likely to defect than those who never choose to cooperate in the first place. John M. Orbell, Peregrine Schwartz-Shea, and Randy T. Simmons, "Do Cooperators Exit More Readily than Defectors?" *American Political Science Review*, 78 (1984), pp. 147–60.

45. Michael Taylor, *The Possibility of Cooperation* (Cambridge: Cambridge University Press, 1987), p. 108.

46. It should be noted, however, that media coverage of a boycott is problematic. According to one activist, "It is very, very difficult to get the media very much

concerned [about a boycott, because] the people we are boycotting are huge advertisers." Mark Stencel quoting Donovan McClure, a public relations executive, in "The Growing Influence of Boycotts," *Editorial Research Reports*, January 4, 1991. Replicated in *SIRS Researcher CD-ROM* (Boca Raton, Fla.: Social Issues Resources Series, Inc., 1994), 1156 lines at lines 467–71.

47. Our need to see and be seen recalls Garrison Keillor's delightful story about Flag Day in Lake Wobegon where townspeople paraded as a "living flag" and each one participating wanted to step out of the line of march to see what had been created. *Lake Wobegon Days* (New York: Penguin Books, 1986), pp. 123–24.

48. The philosopher Charles Taylor is more ambitious. "[F]ragmentation grows to the extent that people no longer identify with their political community. . . . Successful common action can bring a sense of empowerment and also strengthen identification with the political community." *The Ethics of Authenticity* (Cambridge, Mass.: Harvard University Press, 1991), p. 118. Michael Sandel says it another way. "When politics goes well, we can know a good in common that we cannot know alone." *Liberalism and the Limits of Justice* (Cambridge: Cambridge University Press, 1982), p. 183.

49. Thomas Schelling points out that describing problems in statistical terms only means that other problems are bound to displace those we have solved or ameliorated. "[I]f tuberculosis diminishes as a cause of death, other causes together must increase, as long as we impute a cause to every death." *Micromotives and Macrobehavior*, p. 53. Even too many boycotts might reduce the chances of new such undertakings. "The public can only assimilate so many of these things before they throw up their hands and say, 'The hell with all of them.'" Mark Stencel quoting Richard Perry of the AFL-CIO in "The Growing Influence of Boycotts." Ibid. at lines 835–38.

Chapter 5. What If Everyone . . .?

1. William H. Whyte, *City* (New York: Anchor Books, 1988), p. 105 and p. 158.

2. Even the convention of the "stall" where we put a personal marker to preserve our public space—a hat on a theater seat, a beach towel on a plot of sand, a tote bag on an airport lounge chair—is in decline as we cannot be sure that someone might not take the hat or tote bag and we lose more than our stall. I was reminded of this convention in Erving Goffman's *Relations in Public* (New York: Harper Torchbooks, 1971), pp. 33–34.

3. Alan Wolfe, "The New American Dilemma," *New Republic*, April 13, 1992, pp. 30–37 at p. 32.

4. Matt Assad, "Residents Urge End to Cruising," *Morning Call*, April 28, 1993. Residents of Easton also knew that ordinances that seek to order public behavior are vulnerable to challenge by civil libertarians and that police presence and crackdowns to safeguard many streets are subject to challenge by those who see the police as "unrepresentative" or repressive. Easton has an

abundance of laws on the books that were once enacted to reassure residents but are virtually unenforceable—ordinances that prohibit public begging, swearing in public, spitting on the sidewalk, and on and on. It has been over twenty years now since the Supreme Court found a "vagrancy" statute in Jacksonville, Florida, unconstitutional. The decision forced jurisdictions, large and small, to be more tolerant of what goes on in the streets. Justice Douglas concluded the majority opinion by saying, "a presumption that people who might walk or loaf or loiter or stroll or frequent houses where liquor is sold, or who are supported by their wives, or who look suspicious to the police are to become future criminals is too precarious for a rule of law." *Papachristou v. City of Jacksonville*, 405 U.S. 156 at p. 171 (1971). However much neighborhoods want safe streets, the enactment of stricter public ordinances does not seem a likely solution.

5. Jane Jacobs, *The Death and Life of Great American Cities* (New York: Vintage Books, 1961), p. 50.

6. Ramon Daubon of the Ford Foundation/Andes, who had previously worked with Puerto Rican neighborhoods in New York City, told me that when the extended family no longer exists, mom and pop, children and grandparents, there are not enough hands to mind the store.

7. Jacobs, pp. 438–39.

8. Joseph P. Fried, "Watch Out Scrawlers, You're on Graffiti Camera," *New York Times*, April 6, 1992.

9. "Town Puts Prostitutes on Video Tape," *New York Times*, March 21, 1993.

10. "Prostitutes' Patrons Could Lose Their Cars," *New York Times*, December 21, 1991.

11. "Curbing Prostitution on Demand Side," *New York Times*, April 20, 1992. Civil libertarians object to "publicity" as a measure to deter crime, whether it is publishing the names of apprehended juveniles in local newspapers or the local measures described here. They argue that accused individuals and their families should not suffer from public calumny for what are only allegations.

12. Isabel Wilkerson, "Chicago Plans Barriers to Hinder Street Crime," *New York Times*, January 23, 1993.

13. Kevin Johnson, "Cities Try to Divert Traffic in Crime," *USA Today*, February 16, 1993.

14. Mitchell Owens, "Saving Neighborhoods One Gate at a Time," *New York Times*, August 25, 1994. Owens reports that street gates are also being used on some thoroughfares in Coconut Grove, Florida, Austin, Texas, and Bridgeport, Connecticut.

15. EarthWorks Group, *You Can Change America* (Berkeley, Calif.: Earthworks Press, 1993), p. 56. The EarthWorks Group also reports that there is a "National Night Out," a once-a-year effort to get neighbors out to meet neighbors, usually in early August (p. 34).

16. Don Terry, "'Pink Angels' Battle Anti-Gay Crime," *New York Times*, April 7, 1992.

17. James Q. Wilson and George L. Kelling, "Making Neighborhoods Safe," *Atlantic Monthly* (February 1989), pp. 46–52 at p. 52.
18. "The basic idea is to make public safety a community responsibility, rather than simply the responsibility of the professionals—the police." David Osborne and Ted Gaebler, *Reinventing Government* (New York: Plume, 1993), p. 50. In New York City neighborhoods where homeowners predominate, community policing is more accepted than in tenant neighborhoods, at least where there is a lack of strong tenant organizations. People in tenant neighborhoods, because of racial differences with the police or having little stake in property values, are more suspicious and less cooperative. Clifford J. Levy, "Walking the Beat, the Police Find Many Allies on the Street," *New York Times*, April 4, 1993. In a more recent story, Sam Roberts reports that community policing in New York City has been modified by the Giuliani administration, which has "granted more leeway to precinct commanders" allowing them "to create more mini-beats near schools, commercial blocks and other crime-prone locations." "Community Policing Leaves Some Promise Unfulfilled," *New York Times*, August 7, 1994.
19. "In 1990, handguns were used to kill 13 people in Sweden, 91 in Switzerland, 87 in Japan, 68 in Canada, 22 in Great Britain, 10 in all of Australia and 10,567 human beings in the United States." Marian Wright Edelman, "Leave No Child Behind," Cardozo Lecture at the Association of the Bar of the City of New York, December 17, 1992, as reprinted in the Association's *Record* (March 1993), pp. 159–76 at p. 167. In 1992, 13,220 people were killed by handguns in the United States. Bob Herbert, "Deadly Data on Handguns," *New York Times*, March 2, 1994. If Edelman's and Herbert's data are correct, they represent a 25 percent increase in just two years.
20. U.S. Department of Commerce, Bureau of the Census, *Statistical Abstract of the United States*, 1992. Edelman points out that the majority of these children are not black or on welfare, nor do they live in a city. They are in suburbs and rural America. Edelman, Cardozo Lecture, p. 164.
21. Marian Wright Edelman, *The Measure of Our Success* (New York: Harper Perennial, 1993), p. 85. "About 80% of the children born to unwed, teenage dropouts will live in poverty." Jason DeParle, "President to Campaign against Teen-Age Pregnancy," *New York Times*, June 10, 1994.
22. Edelman, Cardozo Lecture, p. 170.
23. Edelman, *The Measure of Our Success*, p. 87. "An estimated 1.2 million latchkey children of elementary school age have access to guns in their homes." Bob Herbert, "Deadly Data on Handguns." Senator Joe Biden was quoted as saying that people are especially fearful of "some fourteen-year-old with a gun but no social conscience acting in a random way." Neil A. Lewis, "Crime: Falling Rates but Rising Fears," *New York Times*, December 8, 1993.
24. William J. Bennett, *The Index of Leading Cultural Indicators* (New York: Touchstone/Simon & Schuster 1994), p. 78.
25. Neil A. Lewis, "Crime: Falling Rates but Rising Fears," *New York Times*, December 8, 1993. The divorce rate increased by 30 percent between 1970 and

1990. Unmarried women accounted for 25 percent of all births in 1990. More than 20 percent of all-white families, 33 percent of all Hispanic families, and 60 percent of all black families were headed by a single parent. Fifty percent of all children will probably spend part of their childhood and adolescence in a single-parent home. Dennis A. Ahlburg and Carol J. DeVita, "New Realities of the American Family," *Population Bulletin*, August 1992. Replicated in *SIRS Researcher CD-ROM* (Boca Raton, Fla.: Social Issues Resources Series, Inc., 1994), 1006 lines at lines 79–80. "Children from single-parent families are two to three times as likely as children in two-parent families to have emotional and behavioral problems. In addition, they are more likely to drop out of high school, become pregnant as teenagers, abuse drugs, and become entangled with the law." Bennett, *The Index of Leading Cultural Indicators*, p. 52, citing *Survey on Child Health*, National Center for Health Statistics, 1988.

26. Cornel West, *Race Matters* (Boston: Beacon Press, 1993), p. 12. "The undeniable fact is that our children's future is shaped both by the values of their parents and the policies of our nation." "Putting Children and Families First: A Challenge for Our Church, Nation, and World," National Conference of Catholic Bishops, Pastoral Letter, November 1991, cited by Marian Wright Edelman, *The Measure of Our Success*, 1993, p. 80.

27. Charles Lindblom notes that for certain problems, including juvenile delinquency, "solutions remain closed off unless and until people experience sufficient distress to induce them to reconsider the institutions, social processes, or behavioral patterns up to that moment regarded as parameters." *Inquiry and Change* (New Haven, Conn.: Yale University Press; New York: Russell Sage Foundation, 1990), p. 217.

28. My suggestions here are meant to provoke imagination, not to satisfy it. The experience of existing conventions is accessible to anyone, and thinking about the possibility of new ones does not require a degree in public policy. Thomas Spragens properly notes that the "liberal agenda is not the apotheosis of self-indulgence but the creation of a society where people can be self-governing." "The Limitations of Libertarianism," *The Responsive Community*, Vol. 2, Issue 1 (Winter 1991–92), p. 34.

29. Letter from David W. Lyon, Vice President, RAND, July 6, 1993. I agree with my friend, although old conventions don't preclude our being on the lookout for new practices that also make sense.

30. "When people face new problems of the kind that are resolved by convention, they tend to look for prominent solutions by drawing analogies with other situations in which conventions are well established. Thus conventions are spread from one context to another. The conventions that are best able to spread are those that are most general (i.e., that can be applied in the greatest range of uses) and most fertile (i.e., most susceptible to extension by analogy)." Robert Sugden, *The Economics of Rights, Co-operation, and Welfare* (Oxford: Basil Blackwell, 1986), p. 94.

31. Thomas C. Schelling, *The Strategy of Conflict* (Cambridge, Mass.: Harvard University Press, 1960), pp. 54–58 (I also noted this concept in footnote 15 of

chapter two). In chapter four I imagined the prominent convention of a boy-cott allied to a new practice of precycling. The "prominence" of a boycott as a coordination solution is its evident success in often getting enough others to forgo something to get something else. Boycotts are put to many uses, employed by whatever "cause" needs a proven way to reach its objective. The concept of "prominence" as a framework for thinking is used in certain artificial intelligence computer programs that employ "case-based reasoning." The protocol of such programs is to learn from the experience of others who have used the same program to solve operating problems as they arise. Each solution is incorporated in the program. Sabra Chartrand, "Compaq Printer Can Tell You What's Ailing It," *New York Times*, August 4, 1993. For a useful discussion of "precedent-based reasoning," see Stephen J. Majeski, "An Alternative Approach to the Generation and Maintenance of Norms," as a "Comment" to James S. Coleman's "Norm-Generating Structures," in *The Limits of Rationality*, eds. Karen Schweers Cook and Margaret Levi (Chicago: University of Chicago Press, 1990), pp. 273–281 at p. 278.

32. Lynda Richardson, "A Nannygate for the Poor," *New York Times*, May 2, 1993. Child care, being such a personal and unavoidable daily concern for parents, has also spawned an estimated 550,000 to 1.1 million unlicensed day-care facilities in the United States to supplement licensed facilities which serve only 20 percent of the 30 million children, age 12 or under, whose parents work. The majority of children, age 6 or under, are still cared for by relatives, baby-sitters, neighbors, older siblings, or working parents forced to stay at home or to take their children to work when other arrangements fail. Louis Uchitelle, "Lacking Child Care, Parents Take Their Children to Work," *New York Times*, December 23, 1994.

33. Letter from John G. Davies, President of the Baton Rouge Area Foundation, March 26, 1992. In the Chicago area there is a "Grandma Please" practice where children can call a group of volunteer senior citizens between 3:00 and 6:00 P.M. In a Minnesota school district there is a "Home Alone" hotline for latchkey children, where volunteer seniors do much the same thing as their Chicago counterparts. Earthworks Group, *You Can Change America* (Berkeley: Earthworks Press, 1993), p. 21.

34. Howard V. Hayghe, "Family Members in the Work Force," *Monthly Labor Review*, vol. 113, no. 3 (March 1990), pp. 14–19. Replicated in *SIRS Researcher CD-ROM* (Boca Raton, Fla.: Social Issues Resources Series, Inc., 1994), 385 lines at lines 187–89.

35. The Catholic Bishops of America have urged that men view "their traditional roles as 'provider' for a family in more than an economic sense. Physical care of children, discipline, training in religious values and practices, helping with school work, and other activities, all these and more can be provided by fathers as well as mothers." Peter Steinfels, "U.S. Bishops Urge Men to Share Work in Home," *New York Times*, November 18, 1993. Many mothers would settle for their husbands just doing more of the housework.

36. Several years ago, Professor John H. Stanfield, a professor of sociology and

Afro-American studies at Yale, reported on his study of twenty-one black physicians who moved out of poverty into successful professional careers. They attributed their success to both "expressive" mentors, those who offered hope and encouragement, and "instrumental" mentors, those in a position to provide resources and educational opportunities. *Yale Weekly Bulletin and Calendar* (May 11–18, 1987).

37. Thomas Byrnes Edsall with Mary D. Edsall, *Chain Reaction* (New York: W. W. Norton, 1992), p. 6.

38. Jesse Jackson is quoted as saying, "When a person is down in a hole, you don't scream down in there a sermon on good behavior. You drop them a bucket to pull up on." Jackson goes on, "The victims are not responsible for being down, but they must be responsible for getting up." "Jackson's Message Is Values," *Charleston Post and Courier*, January 4, 1994. Shelby Steele writes, "The price blacks pay . . . for placing too much of the blame for our problems on society is helplessness before those problems." *The Content of Our Character* (New York: Harper Perennial, 1990), p. 163. Ken Hamblin, a black Denver broadcaster, puts it more bluntly. "I want to know why 60% of black babies are being born out of wedlock. Is that the fault of white people?" Hamblin goes on, "I think it's time we started demanding, challenging, expecting." Dirk Johnson, "In Denver, the Surprising New Face of Right-Wing Talk Radio," *New York Times*, January 2, 1994. When blacks say these things, whites sit still. When whites say these things, some whites and blacks pull the fire alarm and cry, "Racist." It is not a reasoned response, but like a fire alarm it produces a panic for the exits so that there are few left who are willing to listen.

39. The practice was started by a New York industrialist, Eugene Lang, for a class of minority children in a junior high school in Harlem. Lang's example has been emulated throughout the country, in part, through further coordination by the I Have A Dream Foundation.

40. There is something of a movement to urge teenagers to practice chastity. For some, this effort does not rest on moral grounds, but merely tries to show one way for them to move out of poverty or to avoid falling into it. One million teenagers each year become pregnant. A news story reports that young women are joining "virgin clubs." One counselor says, "We tell them the opportunity to get an education can pass you by, but the opportunity to have sex ain't going nowhere." Jane Gross, "Sex Educators for Young See New Virtue in Chastity," *New York Times*, January 16, 1994. The promotion of condom use is also a new practice in schools, albeit controversial, to curb pregnancies as well as AIDS. Since 1991, school districts in New York City, Philadelphia, Washington, D.C., Los Angeles, San Francisco, Seattle, and many smaller cities have established "condom availability programs." Sam Dillon, "Controversy and Convenience in Condom-Giveaway Program," *New York Times*, January 11, 1994.

41. Continental Insurance gives its expectant-father employees beepers to keep in touch with developments at home. Eastman Kodak organized a Working Parents League, which allows employed parents to exchange ideas through elec-

tronic mail. Susan Chira, "Obstacles for Men Who Want Family Time," *New York Times*, October 24, 1993.

42. Peter Drucker as quoted by Robert S. Boyd, "Taking Job Home No Longer Just for Work-aholics," *Boca Raton News*, May 22, 1989.

43. By 1992 14 percent of America's large business organizations allowed some of their employees to work at home. Kathleen Murray, "Telecommuting: Another Way to Get the Work Done," *St. Paul Pioneer Press*, March 29, 1992. The state governments of Arizona, Minnesota, Florida, Washington, Virginia, and Colorado have already put telecommuting in place for some of their employees. Julian M. Weiss, "Adding Vision to Telecommuting," *Futurist* (May/June 1992), pp. 16–18.

44. Calvin Sims, "Earthquake Leaves a Glimpse of the Future of Commuting," *New York Times*, January 20, 1994. The same article told of how telecommuting received an unexpected boost in the aftermath of the Los Angeles earthquake in January 1994. With so many damaged highways and freeways, employers scrambled to put in place or enhance telecommuting for their employees. One government spokesman said, "If we can change people's behavior permanently, some good can come of this tragedy." Telecommuting may have several configurations, only one of which is allowing people to work in their homes. At the time of the earthquake there were already twelve telecommunication centers in the Los Angeles area. Such centers take working parents out of their homes, but keep them closer.

45. "The New American Revolution" is a recent initiative of founder James B. Hayes, publisher emeritus of *Fortune*. Hayes has called on business firms, large and small, to bring "the private sector together in a massive commitment to our children." The campaign wants businesses to change their culture so as "to accept responsibility for America's youth," to commit more of their resources to that end, and to foster new community youth programs. Undated letter and brochure sent to a mailing list in November 1994.

46. For example, there are "credit unions" for children in parts of New York City, Chicago, Seattle, and Philadelphia as well as small towns. "The general goals are to infuse low-income minority children with concepts of ownership and to equip them with skills for jobs in the financial services industry." Joe Sexton, "Children's Credit Union Aims to Teach Savings," *New York Times*, February 11, 1994.

47. So many of us go off to work each day that the weekday daylight hours would be difficult to cover with such patrols, which is all the more reason to establish "sanctuaries" and supervised activities for children who need them during after-school hours. The deployment of civilian patrol teams, however, could be at full strength during evenings and weekends. No doubt some neighborhoods have very mean streets. Developing ways to get adults to support each other for the sake of their safety and not just the children's would require imagination and great persistence.

48. Curfews for teenagers have been undertaken in Miami, Chicago, Dallas, Newark, Phoenix, and Tampa. Bruce Frankel, "Teen Crime Surge Sparks Crackdown," *USA Today*, March 17, 1994. In Dallas, "Children are barred

from public places after 11 on weeknights and midnight on weekends. The curfew lasts until 6 A.M." The U.S. Supreme Court let the Dallas curfew stand in part because it includes reasonable exceptions—for children running errands, commuting to and from jobs, or taking part in school and church activities. Mark Potok, "Cities Deciding That It's Time for Teen Curfews," *USA Today*, June 6, 1994.

49. Children's Defense Fund, "The State of America's Children," 1992, p. xii.

50. Bob Herbert, "The 'Squash It' Campaign," *New York Times*, December 8, 1993. In May 1994, the TV series "South Central" was the first prime-time program to use the "squash it" gesture. "Squash It!" *Harvard Magazine*, November-December 1994, pp. 12–13.

51. Bob Herbert, "Blacks Killing Blacks," *New York Times*, October 20, 1993. In his campaign to address the penchant for violence among children, especially black children, Jackson argues that, "What faces us today is preventable. . . . It is within our power to change our behavior."

52. A 1961 study by J. S. Coleman "documented the low value of academic success to the peer group and contrasted it to the high value of sports success. Coleman noted that in sports, success reflects well on others, where in academics, success is had only at the expense of others. . . ." Robert H. Slavin, *Cooperative Learning* (New York: Longman, 1983), p. 2. Individual competition for positions on sports teams does weed out those who might otherwise rely on the talents of others to win the game. In the classroom it is harder, but not impossible, to make sure that everyone contributes to team solutions. Slavin points out that group learning can be structured to reward teams in competition with each other. In some cases each member of the team is tested and individual scores contribute to the overall team score. This encourages the better students to help those who are not doing as well, and those in the latter position realize that their performance matters to the team (p. 32).

53. For example, I discovered a norm had developed when my students chose "cooperation" rather than "defection" in the MPD game, discussed in chapter three. They had already worked together in study groups and role-playing exercises. As a consequence, most of them relied on their social experience in those groups and exercises when they made their individual choices, even in what was ostensibly an "economic" game.

54. Most teaching cases that I had read before constructing my own put the student reader outside the case, analyzing but not participating in the outcome. They were case histories of other people's decisions in which the student was asked only to be a disinterested spectator and critic.

55. Slavin, *Cooperative Learning*, p. 23.

56. Ibid., pp. 8–9.

57. Ibid., p. 128. One form of collaborative learning is "peer tutoring" or "peer counseling," which has been in place in secondary and higher education for some time. Kenneth A. Bruffee tells the success story in higher education in *Collaborative Learning: Higher Education, Interdependence, and the Authority of Knowledge* (Baltimore: The Johns Hopkins University Press, 1993), pp. 80–97.

SELECTED BIBLIOGRAPHY

Anderson, Charles W. (1990). *Pragmatic Liberalism*. Chicago: University of Chicago Press.

Argyle, Michael (1991). *Cooperation: The Basis of Sociability*. London: Routledge.

Axelrod, Robert (1984). *The Evolution of Cooperation*. New York: Basic Books.

—— (1986). "An Evolutionary Approach to Norms." *American Political Science Review*, 80: 1095–111.

Axelrod, Robert and Douglas Dion (1988, Dec. 9). "The Further Evolution of Cooperation." *Science*, 1385–90.

Barber, Benjamin (1984). *Strong Democracy*. Berkeley: University of California Press.

Bartsky, Ira R. and Elizabeth Harrison (1979, May). "Standard and Daylight Time." *Scientific American*, 45–53.

Bayer, Ronald (1991). *Private Acts, Social Consequences*. New Brunswick, N.J.: Rutgers University Press.

Bell, Daniel (1989a, Spring). "The Third Technological Revolution." *Dissent*, 164–76.

—— (1989b, Spring). "'American Exceptionalism' Revisited: The Role of Civil Society." *Public Interest*, 38–56.

Bellah, Robert, Richard Madsen, William Sullivan, Ann Swidler, and Steven Tipton (1985). *Habits of the Heart*. Berkeley: University of California Press.

—— (1991). *The Good Society*. New York: Knopf.

Bennett, William J. (1994). *The Index of Leading Cultural Indicators*. New York: Touchstone/Simon & Schuster.

Boorstin, Daniel (1971). *Democracy and Its Discontents: Reflections on Everyday America*. New York: Random House.

Boyte, Harry C. (1989). *Commonwealth*. New York: Free Press.

Bruffee, Kenneth A. (1993). *Collaborative Learning: Higher Education, Interdependence, and the Authority of Knowledge*. Baltimore, Md.: Johns Hopkins University Press.

Buchanan, James M. (1975). *The Limits of Liberty: Between Anarchy and Leviathan*. Chicago: University of Chicago Press.

Chong, Dennis (1991). *Collective Action and the Civil Rights Movement*. Chicago: University of Chicago Press.

Clark, Ira G. (1988). *Water in New Mexico*. Albuquerque: University of New Mexico Press.

Community Associations Institute (1993). *Community Associations Factbook*. Alexandria, Va.

Cook, Karen Schweers and Margaret Levi, eds. (1990). *The Limits of Rationality*. Chicago: University of Chicago Press.

Crawford, Stanley (1988). *Mayordomo*. New York: Anchor Books Doubleday.

Crouch, Colin (1983). "Market Failure: Fred Hirsch and the Case of Social Democracy," in *Dilemmas of Liberal Democracies*, eds. Adrian Ellis and Krishnan Kumar. London: Tavistock.

Dahl, Robert A. (1982). *Dilemmas of Pluralist Democracy*. New Haven, Conn.: Yale University Press.

Dawes, Robyn M. (1988). *Rational Choice in an Uncertain World*. Orlando, Fla.: Harcourt Brace Jovanovich.

De Buys, William and Alex Harris (1990). *River of Traps*. Albuquerque: University of New Mexico Press.

Deal, Terence and Allen Kennedy (1982). *Corporate Cultures*. Reading, Mass.: Addison-Wesley.

Dionne, E. J., Jr. (1991). *Why Americans Hate Politics*. New York: Simon & Schuster.

Dixit, Avinash and Barry Nalebuff (1991). *Thinking Strategically*. New York: W. W. Norton.

Douglas, Mary (1986). *How Institutions Think*. Syracuse, N.Y.: Syracuse University Press.

EarthWorks Group (1989). *50 Simple Things You Can Do to Save the Earth*. Berkeley, Calif.: Earthworks Press.

——— (1990). *The Recycler's Handbook*. Berkeley, Calif.: Earthworks Press.

——— (1991). *The Next Step: 50 More Things You Can Do to Save the Earth*. Kansas City, Mo.: Andrews and McMeel.

——— (1993). *You Can Change America*. Berkeley, Calif.: The Earthworks Press.

Edelman, Marian Wright (1993, March). "Leave No Child Behind." *Record* of the Association of the Bar of the City of New York, 159–76.

——— (1993). *The Measure of Our Success*. New York: Harper Perennial.

Edgerton, Robert B. (1985). *Rules, Exceptions, and Social Order*. Berkeley: University of California Press.

Edsall, Thomas Burns with Mary D. Edsall (1992). *Chain Reaction*. New York: W. W. Norton.

Ehrenhalt, Alan (1991). *The United States of Ambition*. New York: Times Books.

Elster, Jon (1984). *Ulysses and the Sirens*, rev. ed. Cambridge: Cambridge University Press.

———— (1989a). *The Cement of Society: A Study of Social Order*. Cambridge: Cambridge University Press.

———— (1989b). *Nuts and Bolts for the Social Sciences*. Cambridge: Cambridge University Press.

———— (1992). *Local Justice*. New York: Russell Sage Foundation.

Etzioni, Amitai (1993). *The Spirit of Community*. New York: Touchstone/Simon & Schuster.

Fallows, James (1990). *More like Us*. Boston: Houghton Mifflin.

Fischer, Claude S. (1982). *To Dwell among Friends*. Chicago: University of Chicago Press.

Flacks, Richard (1988). *Making History: The American Left and the American Mind*. New York: Columbia University Press.

Flores-Turney, Camille (1994). "Will the Acequias Survive?" *New Mexico Magazine* May: 52–62.

Frank, Robert H. (1988). *Passions within Reason*. New York: W. W. Norton.

Fuller, Lon L. (1969a). "Law and Human Interaction," in *Social System and Legal Process*, ed. Harry Johnson, 1978. San Francisco: Jossey-Bass.

———— (1969b). *The Morality of Law*. New Haven, Conn.: Yale University Press.

Garreau, Joel (1991). *Edge City*. New York: Doubleday.

Geertz, Clifford (1973). *The Interpretation of Cultures*. New York: Basic Books.

———— (1983). *Local Knowledge*. New York: Basic Books.

Gilder, George (1990). *Life after Television*. Knoxville, Tenn.: Whittle Direct Books.

Glazer, Nathan (1987). *Affirmative Discrimination*. Cambridge, Mass.: Harvard University Press.

Glick, Thomas (1970). *Irrigation and Society in Medieval Valencia*. Cambridge, Mass.: Harvard University Press.

Goffman, Erving (1971). *Relations in Public*. New York: Harper Torchbooks.

Granovetter, Mark S. (1973). "The Strength of Weak Ties." *American Journal of Sociology* 78: 1360–79.

Griffin, Rodman (1992, March 20). "Garbage Crisis." *CQ Researcher*. Replicated in *SIRS Researcher CD-ROM*. Boca Raton, Fla.: Social Issues Resources Series, Inc., 1994. 1312 lines.

Hacker, Andrew (1993). *Two Nations*. New York: Ballantine Books.

Hampton, Jean (1987). "Free Rider Problems in the Production of Collective Goods." *Economics and Philosophy*, 3: 245–73.

Hardin, Garrett (1968). "The Tragedy of the Commons." *Science*, 162: 1243–48.

Hardin, Russell (1982). *Collective Action*. Baltimore, Md.: Johns Hopkins University Press.

———— (1988). *Morality within the Limits of Reason*. Chicago: University of Chicago Press.

Hart, H. L. A. (1961). *The Concept of Law*. Oxford: Clarendon Press.

Hayek, Frederick von (1991). "Spontaneous ('Grown') Order and Organized ('Made') Order," in *Markets, Hierarchies, and Networks*, eds. Grahame

Thompson, Jennifer Frances, Rosalind Levacic, and Jeremy Mitchell. New York: Sage Publications.

Hechter, Michael (1987). *Principles of Group Solidarity*. Berkeley: University of California Press.

Hirsch, Fred (1976). *Social Limits to Growth*. Cambridge, Mass.: Harvard University Press.

Hirschman, Albert O. (1970). *Exit, Voice, and Loyalty*. Cambridge, Mass.: Harvard University Press.

——— (1982). *Shifting Involvements*. Princeton, N.J.: Princeton University Press.

——— (1986). *Rival Views of Market Society*. New York: Viking Press.

Hjort, Mette, ed. (1992). *Rules and Conventions*. Baltimore, Md.: Johns Hopkins University Press.

Holmes, Oliver Wendell, Jr. (1881). *The Common Law*. Boston: Little, Brown.

Hume, David (1978). *A Treatise on Human Nature*, ed. L. A. Selby-Bigge, 2nd ed. Oxford: Clarendon Press.

Jacobs, Jane (1961). *The Death and Life of Great American Cities*. New York: Vintage.

Jacobs, Marion K. and Gerald Goodman (1989). "Psychology and Self-Help Groups." *American Psychologist*, 44: 536–45.

Jennings, L. Ivor (1946). *The Law and the Constitution*, 3rd ed. London: University of London Press.

Kemmis, Daniel (1990). *Community and the Politics of Place*. Norman: University of Oklahoma Press.

Lane, Robert E. (1983). "Market Thinking and Political Thinking," in *Dilemmas of Liberal Democracies*, eds. Adrian Ellis and Krishnan Kumar. London: Tavistock.

Lave, Charles (1985). "Speeding, Coordination and the 55 mph Limit." *American Economic Review*, 75: 1159–64.

Leibenstein, Harvey (1987). *Inside the Firm: The Inefficiencies of Hierarchy*. Cambridge, Mass.: Harvard University Press.

Levi, Margaret (1988). *Of Rule and Revenue*. Berkeley: University of California Press.

Lewis, David (1969). *Convention: A Philosophical Study*. Cambridge, Mass.: Harvard University Press.

Lindblom, Charles E. (1977). *Politics and Markets*. New York: Basic Books.

———. (1988). *Democracy and Market System*. Oslo: Norwegian University Press.

———. (1990). *Inquiry and Change*. New Haven, Conn.: Yale University Press.

Lindblom, Charles E. and David K. Cohen (1979). *Usable Knowledge*. New Haven, Conn.: Yale University Press.

Macedo, Stephen (1991). *Liberal Virtues*. Cambridge, Mass.: Harvard University Press.

MacIntyre, Alasdair (1984). *After Virtue*, 2nd ed. South Bend, Ind.: University of Notre Dame Press.

Mann, Leon (1969). "Queue Culture: The Waiting Line as a Social System." *American Journal of Sociology*, 75: 340–54.

Mansbridge, Jane J., ed. (1990). *Beyond Self-Interest*. Chicago: University of Chicago Press.

March, James G. (1978). "Bounded Rationality, Ambiguity and the Engineering of Choice," in *Rational Choice* (1986), ed. Jon Elster, at pp. 142–70. New York: New York University Press.

Marwell, Gerald and Ruth E. Ames (1979). "Experiments in the Provision of Public Goods. I. Resources, Interest, Group Size, and the Free-Rider Problem." *American Journal of Sociology*, 84: 1335–60.

Marwell, Gerald, Pamela Oliver, and Ralph Prahl (1988). "Social Networks and Collective Action: A Theory of the Critical Mass III." *American Journal of Sociology*, 94: 502–34.

Marwell, Gerald and Pamela Oliver (1993). *The Critical Mass in Collective Action*. Cambridge: Cambridge University Press.

Mathews, David (1984, March). "The Public in Practice and Theory." *Public Administration Review*, 120–25.

Merelman, Richard M. (1984). *Making Something of Ourselves*. Berkeley: University of California Press.

Montaigne, Michel de (1957). *The Complete Works of Montaigne*, trans. Donald M. Frame. Palo Alto, Calif.: Stanford University Press.

Moynihan, Daniel Patrick (1987, Winter). "The New Science of Politics and the Old Act of Government." *Public Interest*, 22–35.

Oliver, Pamela, Gerald Marwell and Ray Teixeria (1985). "A Theory of Critical Mass. I. Interdependence, Group Heterogeniety and the Production of Collective Action." *American Journal of Sociology*, 91: 522–56.

Olson, Mancur (1965). *The Logic of Collective Action*. Cambridge, Mass.: Harvard University Press.

———. (1982). *The Rise and Decline of Nations*. New Haven, Conn.: Yale University Press.

Orbell, John M., Peregrine Schwartz-Shea, and Randy T. Simmons (1984). "Do Cooperators Exit More Readily than Defectors?" *American Political Science Review*, 78: 147–60.

Osborne, David and Ted Gaebler (1993). *Reinventing Government*. New York: Plume.

Ostrom, Elinor (1990). *Governing the Commons: The Evolution of Institutions for Collective Action*. Cambridge: Cambridge University Press.

——— (1992). *Crafting Institutions for Self-Governing Irrigation Systems*. San Francisco: ICS Press, Institute for Contemporary Studies.

Palmer, Parker (1983). *The Company of Strangers*. New York: Crossroad.

Parfit, Derek (1986). *Reasons and Persons*. Oxford: Oxford University Press.

Peters, Thomas J. and Robert H. Waterman (1982). *In Search of Excellence*. New York: Warner Books.

Pool, Ithiel de Sola (1990). *Technology without Boundaries*, ed. Eli M. Noan. Cambridge, Mass.: Harvard University Press.

Rheingold, Howard (1993). *The Virtual Community*. Reading, Mass.: Addison-Wesley.

Rieff, David, (1991). *Los Angeles: Capital of the Third World*. New York: Touchstone/Simon & Schuster.

Rosenblum, Nancy L., ed. (1989). *Liberalism and the Moral Life*. Cambridge, Mass.: Harvard University Press.

Rousseau, Jean Jacques (1950). *The Social Contract and Discourses*, trans. G. D. H. Cole. New York: E. P. Dutton.

Sandel, Michael (1988). "Political Theory of the Procedural Republic," in *The Power of Public Ideas*, ed. Robert B. Reich. Cambridge, Mass.: Ballinger.

Schelling, Thomas C. (1960). *The Strategy of Conflict*. Cambridge, Mass.: Harvard University Press.

———— (1974). "On the Ecology of Micromotives," in *The Corporate Society*, ed. Robin Marris. London: Macmillan.

———— (1978). *Micromotives and Macrobehavior*. New York: W. W. Norton.

———— (1984). "What Is Game Theory?" in *Choice and Consequence: Perspectives of an Errant Economist*. Cambridge, Mass.: Harvard University Press.

Selznick, Philip (1992). *The Moral Commonwealth*. Berkeley: University of California Press.

Sen, Amartya K. (1967). "Isolation Assurance and the Social Rate of Discount." *Quarterly Journal of Economics*, 80: 112–24.

———— (1973). "Behaviour and the Concept of Preference," in *Rational Choice* (1986), ed. Jon Elster, at pp. 60–81. New York: New York University Press.

———— (1978). "Rational Fools: A Critique of the Behavioral Foundations of Economic Theory," in *Beyond Self-Interest* (1990), ed. Jane J. Mansbridge, at pp. 25–43. Chicago: University of Chicago Press.

———— (1985, Fall). "Goals, Commitment, and Identity." *Journal of Law, Economics, and Organization*: 341–55.

Simon, Herbert A. (1985). "Human Nature in Politics: The Dialogue of Psychology with Political Science." *American Political Science Review*, 79: 293–304.

———— (1990, Dec. 21). "A Mechanism for Social Selection and Successful Altruism." *Science*, 1665–68.

Slavin, Robert H. (1983). *Cooperative Learning*. New York: Longman.

Smith, Charles W. (1990). *Auctions: The Social Construction of Value*. Berkeley: University of California Press.

Spragens, Thomas A., Jr. (1991, Winter/1992, Spring). "The Limitations of Libertarianism." *The Responsive Community*, 27–37 and 43–53.

Starr, Paul (1982). *The Social Transformation of American Medicine*. New York: Basic Books.

Steele, Shelby (1991). *The Content of Our Character*. New York: Harper Perennial.

Stencel, Mark (1991, Jan. 4). "The Growing Influence of Boycotts." *Editorial Research Reports. Replicated in SIRS Researcher CD-ROM*. Boca Raton, Fla.: Social Issues Resources Series, Inc., 1994. 1156 lines.

Sugden, Robert (1984). "Reciprocity: The Supply of Public Goods through Voluntary Contributions." *Economic Journal*, 94: 772–87.

———— (1986). *The Economics of Rights, Co-operation and Welfare*. Oxford: Basil Blackwell.

Taylor, Charles (1989). *Sources of the Self: The Making of the Modern Identity*. Cambridge, Mass.: Harvard University Press.

Taylor, Michael (1982). *Community, Anarchy and Liberty*. Cambridge: Cambridge University Press.

———— (1987). *The Possibility of Cooperation*. Cambridge: Cambridge University Press.

———— (1988). "Rationality and Revolutionary Collective Action," in *Rationality and Revolution*, ed. Michael Taylor. Cambridge: Cambridge University Press.

Tocqueville, Alexis (1969). *Democracy in America*, ed. J. P. Mayer, trans. George Lawrence. New York: Anchor Books.

Tuleja, Tad (1987). *Curious Customs*. New York: Harmony Books.

Ullmann-Margalit, Edna (1977). *The Emergence of Norms*. Oxford: Clarendon Press.

Wade, L. L. (1985). "Tocqueville and Public Choice." *Public Choice*, 47: 491–508.

Walzer, Michael (1974). "Civility and Civic Virtue in Contemporary America," in *Radical Principles* (1980). New York: Basic Books.

———— (1984, Aug.). "Liberalism and the Art of Separation." *Poltical Theory*, 315–30.

West, Cornel (1993). *Race Matters*. Boston: Beacon Press.

Whyte, William H. (1988). *City*. New York: Anchor Books Doubleday.

Wildavsky, Aaron (1987). "Choosing Preferences by Constructing Institutions: A Cultural Theory of Preference Formation." *American Political Science Review*, 81: 3–21.

Wilson, James Q. and George L. Kelling (1989, Feb.). "Making Neighborhoods Safe." *Atlantic Monthly*, 46–52.

Wilson, William Julius (1987). *The Truly Disadvantaged*. Chicago: University of Chicago Press.

Wolfe, Alan (1989). *Whose Keeper?* Berkeley: University of California Press.

———— (1992, April 13). "The New American Dilemma." *New Republic*, 30–37.

Wuthnow, Robert (1994). *Sharing the Journey*. New York: Free Press.

INDEX